Olive trees around my table

Growing up Lebanese in the old South Africa

Cecile Yazbek

East Street Publications
www.eaststreet.com.au

Published by East Street Publications
11 Gibson Street. Bowden, Adelaide, SA 5007, Australia
www.eaststreet.com.au

The National Library of Australia
Cataloguing-in-Publication

Yazbek, Cecile (Cecile Isobel), 1953- .
Olive trees around my table : growing up Lebanese in the old South Africa.

ISBN 9781921037214 (pbk.).

1. Yazbek, Cecile (Cecile Isobel), 1953- . 2. Lebanese - South Africa - Biography. 3. Lebanese - New South Wales - Biography. 4. Immigrants - New South Wales - Biography. I. Title.

305.89275692068092

Cover design by Ellie Exarchos
Front cover picture: L to R: Michele, Anita, Mark, father Joe, mother Bertha, Paul, Cecile and dogs Askim and Justice. 1965
Designed and typeset by David Bradbury
Typeset in 11/15 Weiss BT
Printed and bound by Griffin Press, South Australia

In gratitude for the privilege
of my life among
my ancestors and my children,
the women who mothered me,
those who showed me the preciousness of all existence.

Your wife will be like a fruitful vine in your house
And your children will be like olive trees around your table

Psalm 128.3, Good News Bible

Foreword

Mother tongues: mine were as many as the women who mothered and cared for me. Motherland: the one I was born in was hostile to most of my mothers.

I began to wonder about my upbringing and origins and all the languages I had spoken as a child: Arabic with my grandmother, English with my parents, Afrikaans and Xhosa with my nursemaid and the other servants; I learnt German at school from the nuns. What sort of identity has that left me with? Where do I really belong?

Of all my siblings and the countless cousins in my extended Lebanese family, I am one of only a couple who have left South Africa. I went on a search to find out why.

Note:
To protect people's privacy, I have changed some of their names.
As far as possible, dates have been checked but there was virtually no agreement among my sources, so I have used approximates.
Italicised passages denote what I have imagined.

Prologue

But if in your thought you must measure time into seasons,
let each season encircle all the other seasons.
And let today embrace the past with remembrance and the future with longing.

The Prophet
Kahlil Gibran

Home – The sweet hills of Bangalow

Old Bangalow Road to Byron Bay snakes through voluptuous curves and landscape folds made sensuously green after rain. From the top of Hayter's Hill, the first glimpse of the sea hurries one to the coast. On a calm blue day, a palpable stillness fills one's ears. Stolid cows that own the hillside and its full seaview, flick flies with their tails in desultory fashion. But when the wind blows gales across the ridge, the forty-five degree lean of the trees is explained and one prays that the gigantic bamboo clump on the edge of the road stays upright long enough for a safe drive past.

Views across hill and dale that could be anywhere, but for me they are African–the Eastern Cape of South Africa, my birthplace. At any moment, I expect a line of women carrying firewood or buckets of water on their heads to round a bend and follow a worn track through long grass to a cluster of thatch-roof mud huts in the distance. But there are no huts and no burdened women. They dot the countryside of my inner eye, visions born of nostalgia perhaps vicariously enhanced by a dawn whiff of weed, wafting over the fence from my neighbour!

My husband and I and our son and daughter arrived in Australia more than twenty years ago and went to live and work in Sydney. During our first winter I suffered from a long and debilitating bout of flu. On the third visit to my doctor, he wrote yet another prescription for me. In the car on my way to the pharmacy I discovered he'd written, 'Byron Bay, swim, eat vegetarian food, walk on the beach', and a phone number for accommodation. It sounded wonderful and the spring school holidays found us on Belongil Beach at Byron Bay. At dawn, we walked the endless shore beyond the creek. On the way back, the sun gilded the lighthouse and brightened the dark water to glint off surfing dolphins. In the shallows, schools of tiny fish and silvery rays told of an ocean richer in wild life than even the forest that fringed the bay. With solitude and contemplation, I began to recover. In the evenings, we met all sorts of people whom we would probably never have come across in our urban daily life.

The Sunday market seemed to be the place to eat and meet. On a glorious day we joined the throng. Music, colours, delicious food aromas and incense lured us up and down the rows of stalls. Buddhist prayers flapped in the breeze in front of the flag lady's stall. I selected a set of mini-flags for my vegetable garden back in Sydney. We strolled on past numerous reflexologists, sacro-cranial balancers and *sannyasins* massaging instant relief and even enlightenment into tired city souls. Hippies from the hills wove rush baskets and hats. Among the Indian bedspreads and blouses, beautifully turned camphor laurel candelabra and sculpted coolabah burls entranced us. At the music tent, a few groovers still stoned from last night, last week or last month throbbed to the chill-out rhythm of the drums.

To get me back to Sydney was quite an effort. We postponed our return twice and in the end we had to rush home to be in time for work and school. Trips up and down the coast continued for years.

On one of those visits in the early nineties, our lust for avocados opened a door which was to change my life. I was waiting to be served at the avocado stall by the friendly looking couple and as the queue shortened, I heard their unmistakable South African accents. When my turn came, I whispered my order. I didn't want to be a South African, especially like some I had met in Australia. I wanted to be a local, an

Aussie or even better, a country lass, but my nose, hair, accent, all conspired to betray me.

The man leaned forward, 'What's that? What would you like?'

I spoke up slightly, 'Five dollars worth, please.'

'Where are you from?'

'Same as you,' I sort of obliged.

'No you're not. I'm from a small town,' he smiled.

'I mean South Africa,' I replied. 'East London, to be exact.'

'You're joking,' he laughed. 'So are we. My wife Kay's family farmed citrus in the district and my dad was a hairdresser, last name, Mould. I'm Michael Mould. What's your last name?'

'I was a Yazbek.'

'Well, I never. Your dad was a lawyer there and I was at de la Salle College with Mark. He is your brother, isn't he?'

'Yes. Are you the builder of Queensland-style houses?'

'That's us—me and my son, Richard.'

A few days before in Bangalow, I had picked up their brochure in the estate agency and stuffed it into the glove box in the car.

Michael giggled and pointed to my exposed shoulder, 'So what happened to you there?'

'My children said they are too old for face painting, so I stood in the line and that delightful boy from drama school painted this sunbird dipping into a full-blown rose. Don't you love it?'

SOME YEARS LATER, again at Byron market, I sat sipping dandelion tea in the Oasis tent, my reverie punctuated by visits from my German friend Karin. Ex-neighbours from Sydney, Karin and her husband Manfred had moved to Coorabell where they grew Russian garlic and chillis which they made into a bewitching relish to sell on the markets.

'Think about it,' she goaded me. 'You are so happy and well when you are here and you have so many friends in this area. Why not move here?'

'Yes, but how?' I mused, and with some relief at not having to make a decision, left the idea hanging in my mind.

'Have you bought your avos from Michael and Kay yet?' Karin reminded me.

'No, better get going.' I roused myself and ambled along to stand dreamily in front of the avocado stall. Suddenly Kay grabbed me from behind and said loudly in Xhosa, '*Molo Nkoskas Unjani na? Ufuna ntoni na?* (Hello Madam. How are you? What do you want?)'

My stomach lurched and my heart began to race. Suddenly I was thrown right back to my childhood. There, in a place that could not have been more distant from my early life.

'I want a house here. I want to live here,' I burbled as if underwater and then I surfaced. 'Ten dollar's worth to take back to Sydney, please Kay. Gosh, you shocked me, and now I don't know where I am.'

'What did you say?' she insisted. 'What do you want? You want to live here? Look, this place is heaven. We travelled all around Australia and when we got here, we stopped. No decisions to make. Leave it. You've put it out there. Now let us see what the angels deliver.'

Angels, past lives, portals to other dimensions–the soul and mythology of the New South Wales north coast percolates as near or as far as one chooses.

IN 2001, WHEN my husband returned to live in South Africa, I sold my house in Sydney. My children were settled in their own lives, working and studying. I wanted to live closer to nature in a warmer place. So, I took the cat and the dog and motored north. Michael Mould had built me a house in Bangalow on a block of land I'd never seen, but which he had recommended.

'The angels took over,' he said. 'No job was ever as hassle-free or easier to complete.'

At first, living alone in a large house and tending a big garden was quite demanding as I am not a physically robust person. But I soon found out what I could do and what I could reasonably ask others to help me with. After a year, the best neighbours in the world came to live next door to me. We talked food and gardens and so much more. Robert helped me not only with the heavy digging and lifting, but his desktop skills as a graphic designer got me publishing recipe booklets.

My wonderful Sydney friends visited frequently and I was welcomed into the local community. A Lebanese grocer opened in Byron Bay and I cooked in his shop, sharing recipes and my passion for good food with receptive palates. As a single middle-aged woman, I felt useful and accepted.

Far from my overseas family but swaddled in a landscape so approximate to the green hills of Xhosa country that roll gently down to the sea—white water, blue sky and red earth—I felt as though I was back in my home country.

BUT THIS BOOK is not only about being in Bangalow or Australia. It is about the scenes and pictures from my South African childhood that would not rest, or allow me to rest.

LEBANON
SOUTH AFRICA
RHODESIA
MOZAMBIQUE
Beira
River
Limpopo
Transvaal
BOTSWANA
Pretoria
Johannesburg
Soweto
SOUTH AFRICA
Lourenço Marques
SWAZILAND
SOUTH WEST AFRICA
Kroonstad
Welkom
Orange Free State
Natal
Orange
River
Bloemfontein
Maseru
LESOTHO
Pietermaritzburg
Durban
Cape Province
ATLANTIC OCEAN
Umtata
Transkei Coast
INDIAN OCEAN
Queenstown
Fort Beaufort
Butterworth
Mooiplaas
Laingsburg
Great Karoo
King William's Town
East London
Grahamstown
Port Elizabeth
Cape Town
South Africa 1970
Capital City
Other City
Country border
Province border
N
0
250
500 k
Scale

1

The kwela child

This childhood is that idyll familiar to us from parts of the world where white children ran wild with black servants as companions: an education of the heart, it could be called.

DORIS LESSING ON *MUKIWA* BY PETER GODWIN

Silence enveloped the child, stilling her face and hands, muting her dancing body. Her glassy stare was louder than any wailing. The bustle and chatter in the household continued around her. Only the big brown dog sometimes pushed her with his warm body and licked her face, which was at the same height as his. She put her hand on his ear when he did that, but didn't stroke him as she usually did.

From their bedroom windows, her sisters saw her lying on the back lawn looking straight up into the blue.

WHEN I WAS born, according to my mother, my older sister Michele, who was three, became unsettled and started wetting her bed. It was therefore decided that my Xhosa nursemaid, Rosie would take over and mother me so as to quell the problems with my sister. I had always spent my days with Rosie or her daughters, Gladys and Thandiwe. Since their departure the week before, I had stopped speaking,

Crossing the courtyard I went to sit on the top step, which led to the back lawn. I had always been carried on Rosie's back, and when we reached the lawn, the towel holding me would be untied and I'd be transferred into her accommodating lap. With me snuggled into the folds of Rosie's huge bosom, she would shuffle her bottom across the lawn, pulling weeds and talking non-stop to me while stroking my head gently. Our sweat matted my hair and my pale face became flushed with our heat.

After rain, earthworms sent up little wet mud piles that Rosie taught me to snatch off fast enough to see the grey-green worms shoot back into their holes. Then we'd pop the black mud into our mouths. It was a funny thing to do: facing each other, we'd open our muddied mouths wide, swirling the gritty blackness about. Then, smacking our tongues against our upper palates, we swallowed repeatedly till our teeth were white and mouths were pink again. No one, least of all housemaid Sara, knew of our secret food.

The view to the vegetable gardens was interrupted by the abelia and lemon verbena hedge. Every few days, we'd walk beyond the cultivated beds to the giant compost pits where the *imfinu* (wild spinach) grew. Rosie picked bunches to be cooked and eaten with cornmeal and (*amasi*) sour milk. Unaccompanied children never went there because of the snakes. Sitting on the step, I wondered if I'd ever see that part of the garden again.

To my left were the wash line and loquat tree under which Gladys and I had sat peeling and eating the golden fruit, spitting the slippery brown pips at each other. Catching us, Rosie would lift both sticky girls, drop us into the big bath in the children's bathroom, and, perched on the side, wash us all over, then sing to us while we splashed about. My last memory of Rosie was of such a bath: in the middle of the scrubbing, Rosie had accidentally slid in to the water, her bulk almost drowning us. Dripping and soggy, she'd sloshed her way through the house, up the long kitchen and as she entered the laundry, she'd slipped yet again. Sara the housemaid shrieked in fright and Mother had come running. 'You see, you are too fat, you can't work properly anymore.'

One minute Rosie was there, the next minute gone at the whim of the madam. My white mother had dispatched the woman I knew as one of my real mothers.

In those preschool weeks the usual characters—my mother, Sara, the shopkeepers, my grandmother—still surrounded me. It seemed that nothing in my environment could be faulted. No one detected the extent of my loss because servants were expendable. And anyway, I was five, going on six, about to start school; I no longer needed a nursemaid.

THE HOUSE THAT I remember is the one my parents built in 1954 and that we moved into when I was nine months old. We moved from Selborne, a suburb of East London, South Africa, into the house called Antonville, in Devereux Avenue, Vincent, about three miles from the centre of town. Almost an acre of land had been bought for five hundred pounds and the house designed and built to my parents' taste with enough space for a growing family. My father's legal practice was busy. I was fully cared for by Rosie, my Xhosa nursemaid. The servants all wept on moving day, 'the new house was so far away, out in the country'. The bus service was infrequent and their family homes were far away. Three women servants, my Rosie Khuselo, Sara du Plessis and Katrina Fortuin, the cook, lived in the servants' rooms that formed one wall of the courtyard. Two African gardeners lived down the back garden in their own tiny cottage.

The kitchen occupied the largest area, with a walk-in laundry room, separate scullery area, large walk-in pantry and an eating nook that the whole family could sit in comfortably. The huge Esse coal stove filled the wall overlooking the courtyard and in the East London summers, we sweltered as it burnt round the clock. Flowers, rose gardens and rockeries decorated the front and sides of the house. At the back, a vegetable section, fowl runs and an orchard supplied virtually all our food. Run-off from the roof went into an underground concrete tank to water the whole garden.

In 1958, when I was five, my youngest brother Paul was born. We became a family of three girls and two boys: Mark, the eldest, was fifteen, Anita was twelve and Michele was eight. Mark attended the Jesuit boarding school in Grahamstown, about two hours north-west of East London.

One morning in those preschool weeks, Mother was at the kitchen work table, cutting meat from a huge chunk. From time to time, she sharpened her big knife on a steel and wiped it before she continued. After a while, she sharpened a smaller knife, positioned a stool at the table in front of a small board, and invited me to help her cut the fat for rendering. I climbed up, but the knife slipped from my hand. So I stood alongside, but not too close to mother, who waved her big knife around when she addressed the kitchen maids. Bits of meat fell from the blade into Askim's slobbery jaws.

The crash of a package landing on the scullery bench top announced the daily arrival of the messenger from Garlicks department store:

'Anything to return, ma'm?'

'It's there, Alfred. How are you?'

'I'm fine, but how is this *thombazaan* (girl)? I haven't seen her for a long time. Getting big now, always at the nessery. Hello girl, are you not going to school today? Hey . . . can't you speak this morning?'

'She is very quiet at the moment, Alfred, no talking, no English, no Xhosa.'

'*Shé*, but she is my Xhosa girlfriend—*N'toni.*' He used the interrogative they affectionately called me because I constantly asked '*N'toni le* (What is this)?'

'I'll see you next time. Bye', and he was gone.

'*Dis nou 'n* forward *kaffir, Medem* (Now that's a forward kaffir, Madam)', Sara cut in from where she had been cleaning shelves behind the pantry door.

'You shouldn't speak like that', Mother said.

'*Nee, Medem, ek is 'n coloured. Ons* trust *hulle glad nie* (No Madam, I am a coloured. We don't trust them at all).'

'No Sara, they aren't all like that.'

'*En ek is nou so* happy *die vet nenny is weg*...(I am so happy the fat nanny has gone) the child copied *die swart maniere..* (the black ways), *kwela* music and dancing. Has Madam seen the child dancing, how she sways her bottom, lifts her flat feet and slams them down on the cement without feeling the pain, like them? No, no, we must make her white again.'

I wandered out of the kitchen into the courtyard, past my gramophone in its green case lying abandoned in the corner, and sat down on the step outside the middle room, my Rosie's room, where I'd sat and been fed fingerfuls of *samp* and beans from her enamel plate. The room was empty now; Gladys and Thandiwe had gone with their mother. *Tata* Weelie, Rosie's husband, would no longer come in the back gate in his chef's whites with a handful of Wilson's toffees for all his children.

Bony fingers grabbed my arm and Sara interrupted my reverie to announce, in Afrikaans, that we were going to the shop. 'Put on your *slip slops* (thongs).' We set off down the long driveway that curved through an avenue of crepe myrtles with flowering pink floribunda roses beneath.

We crossed the busy Main Transkei Road and went into Norman's Delicatessen, where Sara bought a loaf of bread and a marshmallow fish for me. An old granny was sitting behind the dark-haired woman who took the money. She wore thick, blue-tinted spectacles, and blue eye shadow drifted from behind the lenses onto her temples to blend with her mauve hair. She cackled away non-stop in familiar sounding Arabic, but was definitely not as glamorous as my Granny Isabel. The shop was always busy; brown people were served before black people and whites before everyone else.

From there we went to Mr Chen. 'Ching chong Chinaman', Sara said, and bought two Lexington cigarettes for a tickey. Tiny Mrs Chen was dusting and cleaning in the shop, dropping strange aspirated sounds to the old granny sitting in the corner with a new baby on her lap. This was number seven, Sara was to tell Madam, '*en Linda, die* biggest *is net eight* (and Linda the eldest is just eight). *Die Ching Chongs* are very busy at night.' Sara lit up a Lexington as we left the shop, offering me a drag. I can't remember when I first began smoking in the courtyard; it was something the servants and I had always done.

We continued on down the road. Sara didn't mind my not talking. She carried on a monologue about all the people we passed or had dealings with. Mostly she was rude about them. 'Cheeky Sara is short-tempered', my mother had once said, and no one disagreed. All the children received frequent slaps and scoldings from Sara.

Sara sniffed the air: '*Ruik na coolies hier* (Smells like coolies here)', she said as we entered Mr Patel's emporium. He came around from behind the high counter to see what Sara was pointing to. His black hair gleamed with oil and he wore a stiffly starched and pressed white coat. Bending down to me he asked in a sing-song, 'And what does the little girl want today?'

'*Nee, niks* (No, nothing) Patel,' Sara cut in. 'I am looking for garlic and one of those pink joss sticks.'

In the corner of the shop, clouds of perfumed smoke hung around some brightly coloured statues and pictures just like the plaster saints in all the bedrooms at home. An old lady with white hair pulled back into a bun was bowing and waving her hands in circles and then holding them in front of her chest as if to pray. She did this a few times and then stepped out into the sunlight in front of the shop. The shining gold trim of her draped skirt, the perfume and the smell of spicy food dazzled me, but Sara broke in on my enchantment, dragging me away from 'coolie things', '*huis toe* (home), I must go and light that joss before the *tokoloshe* (evil entity) comes to bewitch me tonight. It's *mos* (of course) full moon'.

At home, I walked through the kitchen, wandered into the entrance hall and sat down in front of the glass cabinet. An Indian client had given my father the longboat with its princess and many rowers carved from one ivory tusk. The intricacy of the carving absorbed me and I noticed that each oar even had a pattern carved along its toothpick shaft. I looked at the palm of my hand and spread my fingers, measuring the length of those oars. The princess sitting under the canopy wore a veil and a dress just like the old Patel woman. A man stood to one side holding a palm leaf over her. Looking in on this scene, I imagined myself at the princess's feet, hearing the sounds and smelling Mr Patel's shop here in my home.

SATURDAYS WERE SPECIAL. I accompanied my father to the Post Office to fetch the mail and to open the big office in town. I knew all the staff in that office and loved handing out the sorted mail to the relevant people. They gave me peppermints, chewing gum and even a drag on a cigarette, when I asked. This Saturday the phone rang at half past six in the morning. My father answered ' *Ja, sersant, dankie. Ek sal netnou kom.* (Yes, thank you sergeant, I will come right now).'

'We'll do the mail today as usual, but first we have to go and bail out du Toit at the Cambridge police station.' He spoke to my mother in Arabic, and added something about a '*hubdie* (black woman)'. My mother 'tsk tsked' loudly.

At the station the sergeant greeted my father like an old friend and even leant over the counter to me with '*Môre meisie* (morning girl)'. We waited while papers were signed and my father wrote a cheque. The warder opened the big gate and a weedy-looking white man slunk out before the gate clanged shut. My father spoke sharply to him in Afrikaans: 'To prison next time'.

Then there was another sound. It held me at the door and I stopped dead. My father pulled me gently, but I wrenched at his big hand as the weeping grew louder '*Hai, Hai!* (No, No!)' He picked me up and rushed to the car, started the engine and swung the big Chev out into the street. In terror I managed a soft '*Ntoni?*' perhaps hoping he wouldn't hear. But he came straight out with, 'They're whipping the women. Why? Because they're black'.

For the first time in some days since Rosie had gone, I spoke: 'Stop them, Daddy, please'.

'No, we can't.'

'Please, please, Daddy.'

'Don't be a lunatic. You want us to go to jail, too?'

'Please, please Daddy, someone will be killed,' I began to jump up and down in the back of the car, crying.

He made a U-turn and raced home. He pulled me upstairs and took me to my mother, who was still in bed. My head was spinning from the experience at the cells. I went into the sitting room and lay on the floor behind the sofa, pressing my hot feet into the cool wall. Confusion left me trembling for a long time after.

IN THE AFTERNOON, my Granny Isabel came over from her house around the corner for the usual preparation of the Sunday lunch. She inspected the diced meat in the refrigerator and decided which vegetables and herbs were required from the garden. '*Tai, ya immi, khalli jibi* (Come, my darling, let us bring) vegetables from the garden,' and we set off, each with a basket. Granny had the sharp knife. Holding my hand she sang '*banadoora,oo bussell, ba`doonis oo naana* (tomatoes and onions, parsley and mint)' all the way to the beds. Sucking the breath in through her clenched teeth she enthused: '*Shifti? Shoo kwayis hal bami...tai, nitfie kusbara kammen* (Do you see? How lovely the okra is... here, a little coriander as well).' I held a basket out to receive bunches of coriander and spring onions. Red tomatoes waiting to be picked tumbled into our hands.

Back in the kitchen, I took up my position at the work table and was shown how the tomatoes were to be chopped. Imitating Granny's every move, I listened intently to the Arabic running commentary. The kitchen maids fetched and carried implements and ingredients, cleared away and remarked in Afrikaans, 'Granny, she is learning to cook but she still doesn't want to speak.'

Turning to me Granny asked, '*Shoo?* (What) are they saying *ya immi* (my darling)?'

When the maid repeated it in English, Granny rebuked her sharply.

WALKS WITH GRANNY in the garden were regular and comforting. She told me stories along the way of her cooking preferences and experience. It was on one of our rambles that she told me how she'd made her first *laban* (yoghurt) in South Africa with *rowbee* (yoghurt culture) taken from Lebanon in 1910.

'*Tai, ya immi* (Come my darling),' her mother had called her as she packed trunks and tea chests for the voyage to Africa. '*Fee rowbee* (Some yoghurt culture)'. She handed over a small fabric bundle rolled in a piece of damask. 'My older sister Mary sent her husband to the markets in Damascus to bring back linen and table linen for my trousseau, all real Damask which your mom uses now. Your grandpa, you didn't know him. He only ate perfect food. My mother knew that if I didn't make *laban* with the flavours of the *blaird* (homeland), he'd refuse to eat it. He'd be grumpy and make my life all alone over here, hard. So I carried the first starter for the *laban* dried in a cloth. When we got to Queenstown after all those months of travelling, I boiled the milk and put the whole cloth in, wrapped the pot in blankets and left it overnight. The next day we ate Lebanese yoghurt in Africa. It is from that beginning that your mother makes *laban* every Friday.'

Granny held my little hand as if to seal the jewel of memory that she was passing on to me. She realised what I know now: loss and separation from her motherland and culture engendered a deep appreciation of the mundane in the life that she had left behind, and as she taught us about our foods, her joy and hope in the new generation eased her loss. Writing this, I suddenly realise that the olive cloths in which I break fresh green olives before pickling, were part of Granny's trousseau from Damascus, all those years before.

WE VISITED MY aunts' and uncles' vegetable patches and Granny would comment on the quality of the produce, snapping off a leaf here and there and passing it to me to smell or taste. I learnt from that time how to select herbs or produce for what we were going to cook. She taught me, almost inadvertently, from when I was about five years old, always to use my nose first. To this day, I don't taste while I am cooking.

On Saturday afternoons, when my older sisters were being shown the techniques of preparation for our Sunday lunch, I was supposed to be a spectator. My sisters soon left but I stayed on to learn.

THE HOT SUMMER weeks before I started school in January found me in a vacuum. I had no sense of anticipation, but I was pleased not to be going back to Mrs Davis' nursery school where George Yiangou hid under the daisy bush next to the tap and pounced on the unwary, his four-year-old fists at the ready.

Sometimes I sat at the back gate of our garden with Cook after lunch. She'd lower her bulk onto the footpath, light a *zol* (hand-rolled cigarette) and chat to passers-by. An African man with a white face and ginger hair often stopped with us. One day, he took my hand and put a lucky packet ring on one of my fingers. 'When you are older, I'm going to marry you,' he said.

Katrina started to sing, '*Beautiful beautiful brown eyes... I'll never love blue eyes again*' and she guffawed and slapped me on the back. 'Whoa you lucky girl. Somebody loves you already,' and I looked up at him with all the pleasure of being wanted. I rushed inside to show my mother.

'Albino* says he's going to marry me when I'm bigger.'

'Oh, is that so?' my mother mused. 'Poor fellow, he's lucky to be alive.'

*Albinos are Africans born with a white skin due to lack of skin pigmentation and the story was that they were drowned as babies because it was believed they were a sign that an evil spirit was involved in their birth.

2

Sister Johanna to the rescue

My eldest brother Mark had apparently been sent away to boarding school when I was two because it was believed that he could become homosexual if he lived in a house with so many women. When he came home for the holidays, he'd load his pellet gun and shoot moles in their underground runs. He'd fish out the corpses, skin them with his penknife and hang the pelts on the vine pergola to dry.

'The poor moles,' I wailed.

But he countered my protests with, 'There you are, your dolls can have fur coats now.'

No one objected to his hunting games. In fact, my parents spent a lot of time and money searching for remedies for the mole problem. His pellet gun became an object of debate, however, when the neighbours at the back rang to complain that their flock of white pigeons was dwindling. My mother then realised what the barbeque smells that came from the kitchen in the afternoon were. 'You'll have to stop him, darl,' she told my father.

'What for? They're a bladdy nuisance. You yourself said they were eating the seedlings.'

'It's not right. They aren't ours. Please tell him not to.'

My eldest brother, it seemed, could do no wrong in my father's eyes. Sara would be more agitated than ever with him around. '*Los my, jy's woelig* (Leave me, you are troublesome)', she'd complain.

Then he'd harass my mother in the kitchen. 'I'm hungry, give me food, give it to me right now.'

On Monday when Alfred, the messenger from Garlicks came again to collect and deliver the appros my mother had ordered, I wasn't there. I'd been taken to school, to class Sub A at the convent. Sara had helped me to get dressed in the blue tunic and white Panama hat. She put a sandwich into my brown suitcase and took me to the car where mother and my two older sisters, Anita and Michele, were waiting. They teased me on the way and baited me with taunts of 'sour-face' and 'lemon' and 'can't you even smile and be nice?' I wondered what school would be like and whether I'd be smacked. Anita had described canings handed out by prune-faced nuns.

We joined the crowd of parents and children outside the kindergarten building, Mother greeting those she recognised. I held the suitcase tightly and surveyed the unfamiliar faces level with mine. There was no Gladys, no Thandiwe. All, like me, wore hats and shoes. I'd never worn a hat before, and shoes only rarely. There were no trees or gardens around the old buildings; this was a school in the centre of town. The chaos of strangers and the noise of trucks and buses in the street felt and sounded like rocks tumbling about inside my skull. I desperately wanted to go home, back to my garden and the people in it. I wanted my grandmother. I said I could stay home and learn to cook, but Mother said I'd be no better than the dog if I didn't go to school.

Leaving the sea of blue hats and white faces, I went to the iron fence, pushed my face into the bars and stared at the lines of African commuters walking from the bus terminal. My eyes came to life as I searched profiles and faces. It had grown quiet around me. Mother was in earnest conversation with a nun who then approached me with her hand out, speaking in accented English, 'Hallo, I am Sister Johanna.' My glassy eyes, frozen after their fruitless search, looked past her smiling face. A small pause, and then, '*Ach kom, liebes kind* (Oh come, dear child),' and the soft hand drew me back into the crowded room where parents and children sat on tiny chairs waiting for the teacher to take charge.

Sacred Heart Convent was in Albany Street, near the top end of town, just off Oxford Street, the main thoroughfare. The school backed onto Buffalo Street, which ran all the way down to the produce market and beyond, across the Buffalo Bridge to the suburbs of West Bank and

Parkside. Trucks and buses ground up and down from the bus terminus to the market. Noise levels in school were high and the buildings were decrepit. I remember the smell of old sandwiches and stale socks. Rats and cockroaches, nurtured by the humidity and schoolyard scraps, rushed in and out of holes in the walls. Tree roots cracked and mounded the surface on the netball court.

My first day at school is carved into my memory: I was afraid, alienated and desperately longing for something familiar. The physical loss of Rosie's comforting back on which I'd spent my first years plunged me into a silence invaded by my kindergarten teacher. Sister Johanna was a twenty-one-year-old Dominican nun fresh from Switzerland to her first posting, a convent for white girls in a seaside town in South Africa. Her accented English and my initial refusal to speak English put me once more into a familiar place, a place where English was not the mother tongue. With Gladys and Rosie, it had been Xhosa, with Granny, it was Arabic and from Sara, Afrikaans accompanied the slaps, which emanated from her 'finished nerves.'

Sister Johanna was determined to teach me, and reach me she did. She smiled a lot and encouraged us to be energetic and outgoing. Her extramural activity was Red Cross and we watched her as she taught bandaging and first aid to the older girls.

Granny Isabel always came over in the afternoons when we came home from school. In winter, on Fridays, when we all washed our hair, Granny helped with the drying, using the new hand-held Wella hairdryer. Anita, Michele and I sat on the bed and took turns to stand in front of her as she held the dryer. No more towelling tangles and shrieking as intractable knots had to be cut. She combed out the longer bits gently and stroked, patted and fluffed as she saw fit. I loved to feel her hands raking through my hair and tapping my head as she went, all the time telling us how lovely we were.

SOME MONTHS INTO my first year at school, I began to make friends with my classmates, all of whom were English speaking. Judy, whose parents had a timely escape from Hitler's genocide, was very shy and had a head full of brown curls. Her mother spoke very loudly in a Czech accent.

'Tsoody, Tsoody,' she sang out, calling Judy, from the school gate at home time. We noticed each other early on and our friendship grew over many years, to the present day. Also in my first year of school, Rossy and I became friends. She lived across the road from me; her nursemaid, Betsy and my Rosie had taken us for afternoon walks in our pram days.

Most days, during kindergarten, I caught the midday bus by myself from school in the centre of town and walked home up the hill. I did not spend a lot of time with my brothers and sisters. Anita and Michele were closer in age and interests. Mark was away at boarding school and Paul, frequently ill as a young child, was very close to our mother. Only in later years, did Paul and I develop a conversation around shared interests and attitudes.

My sisters finished school sometime later in the day. On Wednesdays, when I stayed back for ballet, my mother collected me by car. The floor-boards in the hall were old and spikey and we had to be careful of falling over as we'd get splinters in our hands. Our teacher, Miss Milly Ogilvie, a stringbean old maid, was from England. She looked like a stick of *biltong* in her black tights and leotard with a black bun on her head. She spoke perfect English and 'Oh deahed' repeatedly as I fell over and upset the whole row of cygnets. The lessons and my inability couldn't last and eventually my mother allowed me to stop ballet. I returned to my *kwela* records and wind-up gramophone in the courtyard.

One day my father collected me from school and took me to Reggie Pillay's radio and music shop in the North End close to town. It was a noisy crowded area next to the bus terminal where Indian businessmen traded in goods Africans bought on their way home to the tribal areas. He smiled broadly at me in my convent uniform. 'So this is the *kwela* dancing girl from Vincent.'

I beamed proudly.

'What record would you like today?' He held up a green record sleeve, 'This one's always popular—Spokes Mashiyane and his pennywhistle.'

'...and I need some more needles, Daddy.' I clutched the paper roll of stubby gramophone needles and he put the record into his briefcase.

Sara was in charge of me in the afternoons and as long as I contributed sometimes, I had free access to her Lexingtons. After school, I'd rush to her room and light up behind her bedroom door. Afternoons in the courtyard continued without Rosie and Gladys but with cigarettes and whoever came by to visit Sara and Cook. Sometimes when money was short, Sara rolled some Boxer tobacco in brown paper and I puffed on that as happily as on Lexington or Gold Dollar.

In my second year at school, 1960, the Convent moved from the centre of town to Vincent into the old Red House Hotel, three hundred metres from my home. Originally a luxurious family home built by a German businessman Mr Malcomess, in the early twentieth century, it was subsequently converted into a country retreat for the gentry. The property came up for sale in the mid-1950s and my parents encouraged the nuns to look at it as an alternative to the existing crumbling old school. Later I was told that my parents had clashed with the Irish Monsignor, the bishop's representative in East London. Monsignor said the planned move was wasteful. 'In Ireland', where he came from, 'schools stayed in the same place for ever.'

My sisters and I were very happy to be able to stay in bed a bit longer and stroll up the hill to school in two minutes. Our dog Askim sometimes followed us along the *crocky* road, as we called the unmade lane that was a shortcut to the convent side gate. We entered past a soughing clump of she-oaks that grew luxuriantly on a patch of low-lying marshy ground. To the left, a double row of benches in an avenue of English oaks was an ideal lunch spot. At the far side, the barracks that served as servants' quarters were hidden by a trellis and creeper. The African staff who lived there went home to the black townships at weekends. Behind all these buildings there were extensive vegetable gardens. The nuns grew cabbages for sauerkraut, butter lettuce, something we'd never seen before, kohlrabis and other European favourites that reminded them of home. There was only one South African nun in that convent, among German, Dutch and Swiss.

In 1961, the additional school buildings and convent enclosure where the nuns lived were finally completed and an official unveiling was held. The Bishop came from Port Elizabeth and nuns and priests came from all over the diocese. The Knights of da Gama wore their shiny sashes and medals, flags were flown, the de la Salle College boys' pipe band played and there was a great deal of pomp and ceremony. Photographs show my father walking beside the mitred Bishop and my mother, a few paces behind in hat and gloves. The procession, led by a pimply college boy carrying a tall crucifix, went through the whole school with incense and prayers. During the week, the nuns held an open morning for our mothers to view their enclosure before it was finally consecrated and locked.

That morning the mothers were allowed to take the pathway across manicured lawns and flowerbeds to the French doors on the terrace. One-hundred-year-old palm trees stood at the front entrance. Circular art deco windows on either side let the eastern sun bathe the quadrangle in the early morning. A winding staircase with wrought iron balustrade led to their cubicles on the first floor. Once the resident priest arrived, the chapel with stained glass windows, mahogany wood panelling and prayer stalls would become our weekly confessional. The recreation room was across the hall.

'At night the nuns sit for an hour after dinner doing embroidery and they are allowed to talk,' my mother told us. 'The room is bare except for a few wooden tables and chairs.'

I could see my mother wondering about that. Mrs Quick was forever at our home rearranging the furniture and recommending new lamps and paintings. The windows of the recreation room looked out to the aviary of budgies in a grove of African plum trees. Hundreds of wild birds sat on the cage wire and set up a cacophony as they feasted on the fruit and left white piles on the seats beneath.

'Simple, plain and white,' my mother said when we asked her what the nuns' enclosure was like. 'We can learn from them. Those women have come all the way from Europe to teach you girls. They have given up their homes and families and sleep with nothing but curtains between them, no carpets and no possessions. We have to be grateful to them.'

From the outside, however, the building still looked like the country retreat it had been.

A stone replica of the Lourdes grotto faced the east windows of the convent. A two-metre white marble statue of the Virgin stood inside a cave; in front, goldfish swam among reeds in a small pond. Sometimes teachers marched their classes there for a fresh air devotional break. We'd stand in front and sing, 'Ave, Ave Maria' or say a few Hail Marys and return to our rooms a little quieter.

The music department in the new school was at the top end of the grounds, a row of quaint rooms with leadlight windows and slate paved verandas deep in needles dropped by giant old pine trees. In standard one, my third year, my short-lived piano lessons were abruptly terminated. Sister Marion had been on at me for weeks to practise. She even confined me to the practice rooms next to the parlour patrolled by Sister Auxilia. I sat for what always felt like hours, practising scales. When I faltered, old Sister Auxilia would shuffle to the door, put her head round and ask, 'Vy are you shtopping now? Keep goink please.'

'Yes Sister,' and I'd plonk on till I was released.

One day I almost smashed the piano stool when my curiosity got the better of me. I'd stood on it to lift the piano lid and peer inside. There I saw hundreds of mothballs to stop moths and mice from eating the felts. I breathed in rather too deeply and felt myself swoon but recovered in time to resume playing before I was discovered. The air was heavy and the smell saturated all the music teachers' habits. More than anything else, my memory is of naphthalene. I was never much good at practising and ultimately gave up piano lessons. That day I turned up for what was to be my last lesson, and sat at the piano next to Sister Marion. The contralto screech of her colleague, Sister Cletus, came through the walls from the adjacent room, a singing lesson in progress.

Sister Marion jabbed me in the side, 'You are like a sack of *mielies* (corn) at this piano. Sit up straight; you *haf* not practised,' her German accent was more pronounced when she was angry.

Affronted, I stood up, 'I will get my father to sue you for defamation.'

Incensed, she shouted, 'Vot are you saying, child?' grabbed me by the ear and threw me out of her room.

Hurt and ashamed, I rushed out, tripped and plunged face first into the gravel on the driveway. I wailed loudly to no avail. I decided to wait for someone to pick me up and continued to sob till another German accent in long black robes stood over me. '*Ja*, periwinkle did you haf an accident?' I looked up at the elderly monsignor. He bent down and lifted me by the shoulder and carted me back to my classroom. Snivelling, my face full of grit, elbows and knees grazed, the first aid box was brought out and I was dabbed with something that burnt my skin, making me look as though I had been blow-torched and couldn't go to school for a week.

'Only poor old Monsignor would have called her periwinkle,' my mother had said at the time. 'She is the least like a periwinkle of all the children. Sister Marion said she deserved to fall and would not be picking her up, she made such a racket.'

Sometimes I walked home with Rossy and Linda who also lived near me and we spent hours chatting and playing after school. Now and again, I invited them to join me in my garden for a smoke. Down the back garden a row of coral trees stood between us and old Dr Robertson's. When we'd collected all the fallen orange lucky beans, we'd push ourselves through the fence into the thick and almost impenetrable clump of old mulberry trees whose branches bowed to the earth. We lay on our backs in those green caverns to be spattered with the staining juice that oozed from those pendulous purple berries. Dr Roberston couldn't hear us. The technology of the day lagged behind his deafness, but when he caught sight of legs or hands that stretched beyond the canopy, he'd part the branches to peer at us and chat. After a polite while listening to him and accepting boiled sweets—we were after all eating his fruit—we'd rush back through the fence. We would go and sit in the fowl run for a smoke. Rossy and Linda's parents would never have allowed them to spend time around servants' quarters. Also, Sara and Cook chased us away when we had friends over. 'Go, go and play. Leave us alone to rest.' Only when I was alone could I be part of life in the courtyard. There was no mystery for me there. I took things as I saw them. When I went inside the house, I soon noticed that the amusing or troubling experiences I related were met with blank expressions.

Sometimes we'd go over to Rossy's. The grand Cape Dutch style homestead stood on huge grounds that had been part of a farm. From stables at the back corner to the sweeping curve of the driveway where we pushed and rode bikes to the front, we found plenty of settings for discovery and mischief. We climbed the fence into Mr Maggs's garden next door. Past the tennis court, there was a large round fishpond into which we stared, like we'd seen the dogs do. But after Rossy fell in, we were banned from staring into his pond and stayed at her place. Rossy's green cubbyhouse set among tall trees in the front garden was her preserve. Her three older siblings never came near us there. However, the house itself was far more fun. We poked about for hours in the six upstairs bedrooms, two of which were attic rooms. The long vine-covered veranda onto which the rooms opened overlooked the wide sweep of lawn to the swimming pool. In the attics, musty smells led us on in our excavation of long undisturbed boxes of satins and silks. Downstairs in the children's nursery, Fräuli, as we called their governess, tried to enforce Swiss rules of formality on English children in Africa. When we had a snack at the nursery table with her, our manners had to be as if we were in the formal dining room. We soon grew bored with boxes of children's treasures and we'd plonk tunelessly on the spinnet that stood in the hall outside the guest suite as we peered through the crack in the door to see who was in there and what they were doing on a hot afternoon.

At Rossy's the dark kitchen was bossed by Betsy, the cook. At four o'clock she set the tray with a china cup and tea to be delivered upstairs to Madam. The drying rack hanging so far above our seven-year-old heads reminded me of pictures I'd seen of English country manor kitchens. The butler's pantry next to the kitchen had a walk-in cupboard into which we sometimes locked ourselves to steal tins of Canadian salmon which we ate with tiny silver coffee spoons taken from the butler's chest. Fräuli would have had a fit if she'd seen us. We only ever climbed the tall avocado tree in the kitchen garden once. We had smoked ourselves blue and Rossy fell to the ground in a coughing fit. I realised that my fowl run was much safer for smoking.

The dining room with its long table and high-backed tapestried baronial chairs hosted the formal Christmas dinner that I once attended. It was a quiet sedate affair as we were waited on by maids who served from the left and cleared from the right, standing to one side until the next course. The food was English and as quiet as the people who ate it. My mother impressed on me how fortunate I was to have a friend whose mother had an inherited title and whose father was a mining heir. 'They are so cultured and civilized', she said, 'while we are so hysterical and loud. You can learn from them, Cecillo.'

In 1961, when I was eight years old, we visited my father's brother, uncle Victor and his family in Kroonstad. There, I was introduced to their grandmother, my great-grandmother, Emily Yazbek. Emily Azerach had been born into the Zarifi banking family in Constantinople in 1869 and was married to my great-grandfather, the widowed, Tamar Yazbek.

At ninety-two, she still lived alone, doing her own housework, 'for exercise' she said, and caring for herself completely. We walked through the large Edwardian house with its wraparound verandas to Gran-gran's bedroom where she was having her afternoon rest. One by one we bent over and kissed her as our parents said our names. She stopped me and held me with her gaze then turned to my father and announced in Arabic: 'She is not from you—she is a friend.'

My mother laughed, 'No Granny,' she said. 'This is Cecile, our third daughter.'

Gran-gran dug her finger into my chest, 'No, this one is a friend. Look at her hair, it is so fair.'

I was so upset. Granny and all those short dark people spoke words I also spoke and understood. I wanted to be one of them: I *was* one of them.

On the way back to our hotel, my sisters teased me: 'You see, she's adopted,' they chanted. 'No one wanted you. Now we have to live with you.'

I consoled myself thinking Gran-gran couldn't have known about the finer things in life, like my light brown hair. My mother's mother, Granny Isabel, whom I would be seeing again in a few days when we got home, loved my hair which she would comb, while stroking my head saying, 'You are pretty. You look like us.' Then years later when I fought with her in the kitchen and told her to shut up, she added, 'But your nature is difficult like them—Yazbek'.

3

Bobby Shafto and other friends

Bobby Shafto's gone to sea
Silver buckles at his knee
He'll come back and marry me
Bonny Bobby Shafto

Bobby Shafto's fat and fair
Combing down his yellow hair
He's my love for evermore
Bonny Bobby Shafto

TRADITIONAL SEA SHANTY

'It was you.'

'Twasn't.'

'It was, so'.

'Nooo, it wasn't,' I wailed

'Yes, it was, it was you. You sat on his knee and sang *Bobby Shafto* to him.'

'That's enough from there,' my mother said as she crossed the kitchen.

'But she did, Ma, remember? He tapped his foot up and down and she rode on his knee like a cockhorse to Banbury Cross.'

'Whoo, they're not shy now, Madam,' Sara said. 'Last night I had to push them into the sittingroom.'

'Yes,' my mother said and turned to my sisters. 'Cecile had to lead you older ones in to say hello to Advocate Hannon. Now I can't shut you up.'

The big liquor cabinet had been opened; fancy glasses and the blue ceramic bottle of whisky were on the table. Sara had brushed our hair, washed our faces and dressed us in our church clothes. I went straight up to Advocate Hannon and curtsied like I had done to the mayor at the Christmas concert. Everyone laughed. Then we were shooed out so the adults could talk.

BACK IN THE breakfast kitchen, I waited for my mother to tell them to stop but my sisters persisted till their boldness ran away with them. 'You fell in love with a drunk when you were six years old.'

Deeply ashamed I hid my hot face in the crook of my arm, their taunting expressions hanging behind my closed eyes.

My father strode into the scene 'Whom are you calling a drunk?'

My sisters froze.

'Come on, own up,' my father demanded. 'If it's Bill you're referring to, he was not a drunk. Anyway, that's a very insulting thing to say about someone who has a sickness.' He sat down at the table to join us for breakfast.

'But he was drunk, daddy,' Anita said. 'We saw him crawling down the hallway from the guest room.'

'Yes,' Michele chimed in. 'He was saying "I want my daddy, daddy, I want my daddy" and he was like a little baby.' My sisters both giggled. I'd also seen a little of that but had been chased back to bed. It was scary to see a big man in white shirt and shorts with long white knee socks crying real tears, his face all red.

'He was a gentleman,' my father asserted, 'a real English gentleman with a drinking problem. I see plenty of them at AA when I have to give talks.' My father was a mentor to people with drinking problems and regularly visited AA meetings to give motivational talks.

'Do they all have such yellow hair and white skin?' I asked.

Bill looked so different from everyone in our house and courtyard—like Ben, a judge who had also come to stay when he had to give up drinking.

'No, they are all colours and sizes. Liquor can be a problem for anybody.'

Anita had been sitting with her head resting on her hand, listening intently, when she broke in with, 'Daddy, what is rape?'

'When a man asks a woman to do something and she says no and he does it anyway.'

My father began to eat very fast, 'Come on, you'll be late for school.'

BILL HAD COME straight off the ship he captained. The priest from the Missions to Seamen had rung late one night. 'Of course,' I'd heard my father responding, 'he can stay in the guest bedroom 'til he's dried out. Two weeks should do it.'

At meal times he sat next to my father and we'd see his hand move slowly across towards Daddy's whisky glass. 'Er, Er,' my father would clear his throat. Then 'Uh huh,' and finally a loud 'Bill!'

I preferred him to some of the other night emergencies. One was a Greek man who told the police he couldn't speak English. They described him as 'an Arab or a Jew or some foreigner.' So they brought him and his stash of suspect cigarettes to my father. A few weeks later, the police appeared again in the night with two Lebanese men charged with illicit diamond buying. When the news items appeared in the paper describing the suspects' nationalities, my father gave everyone he met a lecture about 'People. Real people. What's the difference where they're from or what language they speak? They're just people in trouble.'

Bill was kind to everyone. One night while he was still with us, a woman with three little children came to our house after midnight. She was crying and we all went to peep. Her one eye was closed and she had a big purple bruise over the side of her face. That was the only other time I saw Bill cry.

'Please Daddy, let them sleep here,' I begged.

'Where? There's no space.'

'The whole downstairs playroom is empty,' I suggested.

'Don't be silly,' he said, 'there're no beds there.'

'Where will they go?'

'The police will fetch them. They need protection. That's not our business.' He sent us all back to bed. I wondered for days about that woman. I pictured her sitting on the edge of the kerb, loops of her tattered brown hair pinned up, feeding scavenged food to her babies. I wondered where she had come from, perhaps the flats near the beach where so many poor people lived? Or maybe she lived in the block with the woman who'd lost her eye last Guy Fawkes and wore a black eye patch?

I asked Bill about her and he said, 'There're plenty of good people around. Someone will help her.' He seemed to be so sure of that, I soon stopped praying for her.

Bill gave us all sorts of gifts like silverware with his ship's crest, vases and ornaments. I took a heavy silver matchbox holder to my smoking club in the fowl run. It gleamed from all the Silvo that I rubbed on and polished it with, sniffing the fumes until I saw my face clearly in its shine.

WE WERE SO glad when my father's Aunt Martha came to stay in the guest bedroom. At least there'd be no more drunks or lectures from my father for a while. She was an extremely devout woman and walked around with a long rosary over her arm, praying while she knitted pullovers and jumpers at top speed.

In her seventies and possessed of excellent posture and health, she opened our eyes to the benefits of exercise and healthy living. Maybe it was from Auntie Martha that my father learned and taught us that if we smiled into the bathroom mirror, first thing in the morning, we'd be happy for the rest of the day. So that was added to our list of 'positive' practices. Every night, before Auntie Martha went to bed, we'd hear bumps and thumps coming from the bathroom. I peeped through the frosted glass in the bathroom door and saw her do hand stands and star jumps before settling into the bath. She stayed for some weeks teaching my mother to make muffins, which she called muffets (our word for nose pickings), and praying every day for all of us and her own children. My mother found this devotion trying but Auntie's dowdy dress, manner of speaking and praying fascinated us children. She was so different from all of the other aunts around us.

My father loved all the praying. 'She's so holy. It'll teach you people a thing or two,' he had said shortly before she arrived. This was a counterpoint to my Granny Isabel, who said loudly and often in front of my father, and perhaps to rile him, 'Religion and church—that's for children.'

One night at dinner, while Auntie was still with us, Michele asked whether we thought the story of Adam and Eve was true. My father exploded and ordered her to leave the table. 'But Daddy, we discussed it with Sister Clare today at school.'

'I don't care who you discussed it with. It is written in the Bible and the Pope would have told us otherwise, were it so.'

PEOPLE WERE DRAWN to my father: successful businessmen, debtors, eccentrics and many in trouble. He lent an ear and a loud greeting to all. Mr Milewski, a Polish migrant with a tragic European past, ran a knife-sharpening business near his office.

He gave my dad a copy of his book, *With Garlic in Your Teeth*—a migrant's story. There was also Ginger Lightfoot, who lived in his blue van that he parked in bushes near the sea. He had nowhere else to live. 'Hello Ginger,' father roared and waved from the car on our way to the beach.

Occasionally Eugene Soffiantini visited. He'd arrived in South Africa from Italy in the 1930s. A gifted hairdresser known as a ladies' man, he worked out of a small salon in the centre of East London. When the Second World War broke out with its accompanying scarcity, he concocted a men's hair oil, *Eugene's Brilliantine,* and made a fortune. He then bought acres of prime land and built himself a castle overlooking the winding Nahoon River. The castle was a collection of red-brick buildings crowned with a tower—a shoddily built replica of something out of old Siena. At school, we spoke in hushed tones about the castle and the scary man who would set his pack of Great Danes on any intruders. The park-like gardens inside the forbidding baronial gates were overgrown and untended. One of my classmates, who lived down the road from the castle, spoke of terrible howling and shrieking that came from those grounds when the moon was full.

'Darl, it's that bladdy man again. Can't you tell him not to come here anymore?' my agitated mother whined as Mr Soffiantini came up the steps to the dining room terrace. He walked straight in through the open French doors. 'Joe, Joe,' he crackled, his husky voice matching his mussed hair and general unkemptness. His deeply lined face looked as if it needed to be opened out for the day after a night in a confined space. He was a short, creepy sort of man. Askim, tail wagging and salivating, met him at the door. Mr Soffiantini shoved the enormous garlic sausage he'd been gnawing into Askim's greedy jaws. When he thought the dog had had enough, he returned the sausage to his own mouth. The smell was overwhelming. '*Sies*, darl, now he's making our dog stink of garlic. It's disgusting!' my mother fumed from her vantage point at the bedroom window.

'Mr Soffiantini is going to get tapeworm,' I told my father. The thought that he could die from it gave me hope that he might no longer visit us.

Just like Ginger Lightfoot and alcoholic Bill, Mr Soffiantini was given a few minutes private time. Nonetheless, my father was irritated and marched up the hallway to the dining room muttering, 'I wonder what that bladdy man wants now. Poor bugger is so crazy.' Mr Soffiantini brought the same scuffed brown leather Bible with a rusty dagger or an ancient revolver concealed in the centre. 'Swear, Joe, swear on this Bible and this knife,' he'd hiss in a hoarse stage whisper. He clearly was more than eccentric.

I watched wide-eyed but my father ordered me out, 'Clear off. Go away Cecile. I have business to conduct.' With my father in the room, I'd have felt safe enough to remain, but I was always sent out and therefore unable to answer all of the questions my older sisters plied me with. But somehow I did find out quite a few things as I was growing up. It was no wonder then that when he saw me, my mother's brother, Uncle Mickey used to say, 'Here comes the seven o'clock news. Tell us the latest, Cecile.'

My parents were invited, on more than one occasion, on guided tours of Soffiantini's castle. Usually they were to accompany notables, such as the chief magistrate or the head of the traffic police. Mr Soffiantini wanted the community to see and approve of his lifestyle. His guests left their cars outside the gates and at the appointed time he'd meet them in a black DKW. He would drive the party through the grounds, sometimes over clumps of bush and through shrubbery, as he lost the way in his excitement. At the front door, he would lead the group up the sweeping concrete stairway. The inside walls were mostly unfinished and nothing was painted. He had decorated the stairwell and landings with paintings of nudes and erotic statues, all his own creations. On the top floor, just before the tower room, he opened the door to a luxurious bathroom. I can imagine my mother, clutching her throat as she tried to stifle the scream she knew would come when he pressed the pedal on a cloven hoof that was one of the feet of the bath. He had designed it so that the bath would be up-ended and the contents—water and last night's woman—would be tipped three floors down into the dungeon beneath.

'You'll have to go to confession now because of those filthy pictures,' my father told my mother on the morning after their latest tour.

'What are they?' I pressed.

'Disgusting,' my mother scolded.

Mr Soffiantini's visits became less and less frequent until all we knew of him was gathered from snippets in the newspapers about court appearances as he was charged with traffic infringements and other minor offences. The last we heard of him was a piece in the newspaper describing a charge of cruelty to animals. Apparently he had tied two horses to the back of a VW beetle and begun to drive down the main street when he was intercepted by police. He died not long after that and left everything to his daughter, herself a gifted hairdresser who took up solitary residence in the castle.

'When I'm calling you oo oo oohoo oo oo
Will you answer true oo oo oohoo oo oo...'
Or was it *'Jerusalem, Jerusalem, lift up your voice and sing...'*

Sing sing, keep singing. People will say, 'My, what an exuberant fellow he is.'

I can hear my father's heavy, weary footfall as he climbs the stairs but his heart is fit to burst with the joy of coming home.

'Hello Daddy,' we rush to the top of the stairs.

'Hello my darlings.' Then very loudly, 'Hello darl.' A long sharp whistle flies in and out of his mouth. He puts his bag down in his room and heads in the direction from where he heard, 'Hello darling. How are you? Come and eat.'

This was how I remember my father coming home after a day at work. If the client was a woman with an alcoholic or abusive husband, he'd sing very loudly. 'That poor Cheryl Brown,' he'd say, using a false name. If the clients were rich businessmen needing a lawyer because of too much success, he was quieter. 'Those bladdy rogues don't want to pay their tax.'

When Auntie Victoria, his middle sister, died suddenly at fifty, he didn't sing at all for weeks.

MY MOTHER WAS strict about not entertaining my father's clients at home. 'The office is for work and this house is for family and friends.'

One day, the parish priest asked my mother if she knew Mrs Almassy. It was a difficult question to answer without betraying confidentiality. Mrs Almassy was a client whose husband had left her for a 'Zouz Efrican blonde tart,' as she herself told us later.

My mother got round it by asking, 'You mean the elegant woman with the marble skin and the matching hats who always sits in the front row at mass?'

'Well she is going to be alone this Christmas and I was wondering...'

'All right Father,' my mother responded, 'I'll invite her to stay with us.'

So my father introduced my mother on the phone.

'Eva, this is Joe here. How are you? My wife, Bertha, has something to discuss with you.'

'Hello Mrs Almassy. I am pleased to meet you on the phone. Would you like to meet me at Garlicks tea lounge one afternoon this week?'

SO IT WAS that my mother and grandmother, full of hats and gloves, and I went off to town to meet Mrs Almassy over English tea on Garlicks veranda. On the way there, my mother suddenly stopped the car at a corner on Oxford Street.

'Why did you stop?' Granny demanded.

'Because I can't just leave her there,' my mother said pointing to an ancient waif standing on the road.

'She's poor. She must find her own way,' Granny asserted.

'But Granny she nearly got run over,' I said, getting out to help her into the car as my mother had instructed me to do.

'Why doesn't she stay at home if she can't see? These poor are so stupid.'

My mother blew up, 'Mommy, how can you say that?' Turning to the back seat she asked, 'Where did you say you lived, dearie?'

'A peck 'ows.' Her gummy speech was barely intelligible.

'Cecile, ask her to say it again slowly to you, or even give her this piece of paper to write it on.' My mother seemed determined.

'You think she can write?' I said, looking at her fingers which were knobs and stumps arranged all over her hands.

'Lochs ow plecks pass ketching tsrayn, tsrayn.' She tried so hard.

'Sounds like train.'

My mother swung the car round and headed for Belgravia Crescent which ran past Southernwood railway station. Crawling at a snail's pace, she asked 'Is this where you live?'

'Ye, mayve.' She seemed at a loss.

'Cecile, get out and walk her up and down till she recognises her gate or the path.'

As I took the old woman from the car, Granny started again, 'The car, my clothes, they'll smell like her.'

'Mommy,' my mother continued emphatically, but by then we were shuffling along the pavement.

'What's your name?'

'Ammy,' she mouthed rather loudly.

Her hair was what my mother always called a rat's nest when I got up late. Her sleeve, poking through the crook of my arm, was starched with ages of snot and a dribble ran from the corner of her mouth.

We stopped at a small brick cottage. She pushed me lightly 'p yere'. I started to walk up the overgrown front path and she cawed 'O o,' shaking her head. I decided to let her lead me and we made our way through knee-high weeds to a door standing ajar at what I took to be servants' quarters.

She leaned towards me as if to kiss me. I squeezed her arm.

'Gaw vlesh yo,' and tears washed her face.

I hurried back to the car, hating to look around.

They were still at it. 'Stop it, Mommy,' my mother shouted and she accelerated down Oxford Street.

At Garlicks, Mrs Almassy was unmistakable in all her European finery. Her navy blue hat with a cream chiffon swathe picked up the design of her dress and matching full-length coat perfectly. Her narrow feet nestled in cream Italian patent-leather high heels. She held a white glove in a gloved hand, showing off a giant ruby surrounded by seed pearls. Her limp, bare hand made the cluster of diamonds on her ring finger look even heavier. As we walked in, she stood up, towering over us and extending her hand in greeting, a red gold signet ring on her index finger. We sat on the veranda that afternoon.

Over cups of tea and scones, my grandmother repeatedly asked, in Arabic, '*Shoo* (What)?' as she struggled to understand the heavy Hungarian accent.

My mother nudged her every time. 'Doesn't matter. Leave it.'

I stared as politely as I could at this woman who shed tears into lacy handkerchiefs over 'zat dorty rot viz zat blond voomun.' Mrs Almassy agreed to come and spend Christmas with us. Upon hearing that she was to share my bedroom, she turned to me and pinched my cheek, 'zis gorrjuss gel.'

'WELL, DARL, SHE'S agreed to come,' my mother told my father after our meeting. 'But I am going to need extra help with all the people and meals and laundry.' So Bernie, a niece of Minnie the housemaid, was brought from a small village in the Transkei. She was about fourteen, and according to Sara, 'not a real coloured like us; she looks nearly black.' She worked alongside Sara making beds and preparing for our guest.

A few days before Christmas, Paul and I went with Mother to town to collect Mrs Almassy from her flat. We rang the bell and she led us into a gloomy chamber. From the radiogram, an operatic aria was being shrieked. She tiptoed across the room, holding a cigarette in her mouth as she turned the music off. Olive green brocaded-velvet drapes were drawn. A small glass and bronze lamp at a round table with a floor-length red velvet cloth revealed the outlines of heavy antique and French style furniture. 'So depressing,' my mother muttered as we waited for her to bring the luggage. She emerged from her bedroom with a brown and black leather suitcase, matching hatbox and toiletries bag. Somehow we got it all down in the lift and into the boot. When Jackson came to get the baggage from the car, he whistled and said,

'Yoo, yoo, another *nonquase* (madam) coming to stay.'

We always ate dinner as a family in the kitchen, but when Mrs Almassy came to stay, we ate in the dining room. We sat for hours listening to stories of Zsa Zsa Gabor and her other Hungarian friends, and how she and the 'dorty rot' had walked over hills and rivers to escape the communists. They wore hiking trousers and boots, carrying knapsacks to look like trampers. Except that underneath the black bread and stinky cheese were handfuls of gems, rings, bracelets and necklaces that would have made Aladdin think again about that cave. They ended up in a camp for displaced persons in Austria until they asked to be sent to South Africa. As Mr Almassy was an expert in textiles, they came to East London with its blanket factories.

Sara made many attempts to get us to leave the table after dinner so that she could go off-duty. One night she pulled the cloth out from under our elbows as Mrs Almassy held us spellbound with European escape stories.

Breakfast was in the kitchen. She wore a French nightgown over the lacy night dress and satin high-heeled slippers, no make-up, her skin moisturised with liquid paraffin. For breakfast, 'A raw egg, just zat, my dear. For ze srort. As a singer, I must keep my voice.' After throwing back the whole raw egg, she made a loud, deep sound and then a contraltoish 'Whoo.' The maids in the scullery giggled, but we at the table were just amazed.

Dressing for the day took most of the morning. Nails were painted, eyes lined and hair sprayed. Light perfume, cigarettes and a gold lighter went with her to the sitting room. By then, the mid-morning tea tray was brought in.

That Christmas, my father had commissioned Mr Pepper, a church stalwart who ran the small shop selling holy cards, rosaries and other tokens, to build us a nativity scene. It was a major construction, almost as large as the dining room table, the village of Bethlehem, there in our dining room, with real soil from the garden planted with succulents and aloes among which brightly coloured plaster shepherds guarded flocks, and farm animals grazed. A white-plaster angel on a tall stake stood guard over the stable where Jesus was born.

On Christmas morning, we went to the early mass. We always sat in the second row. The diminutive pair of Misses Waberskis sat in front of us in their colourful pillbox hats. The Romans sisters, an equally small pair of Lebanese women sat in the back row of the church. At the top of his voice, Daddy's lungs seemed set to burst as he let rip with 'Faith of our Fathers' and Mrs Almassy sang out long and loud next to him.

'Darl, do you have to sing so loudly?' my mother nudged him, conveying Father Muckley's glare from the altar. But he had heard the organist pumping air for the next 'Ave' and he was off, running with the hymns like someone possessed. Mrs Almassy's height was enhanced by heels and large hat. This, combined with the volume she and my father put out, accentuated my mother's shortness.

I sat on Daddy's right in church. He splayed the fingers of his hand on the prayer shelf and his pinkie caught mine. Our game had become a habit. My brand new missal, with the mother-of-pearl cover, was open at the creed. A sparrow flew into the church. As it ducked and weaved through the high rafters, it dropped a runny grey pile on my prayer book. Daddy's pinkie came down on mine like a vice and held firm until I no longer showed any sign of squealing.

At home after mass, we sat in the dining room next to the Bethlehem scene and opened our gifts from Mrs Almassy. Anita received a large sapphire ring in a gold French setting. Michele unwrapped a slave ring with sapphires and diamonds. My red jewel box contained a set of five Greek gold rings set with turquoise. The previous night Mrs Almassy had invited us to sit on her bed with her as she poured out the contents of her jewellery rolls and boxes. She watched as we tried on and admired rings and trinkets, all with her encouragement, and when we'd gone to bed she had chosen and wrapped them for us.

We were stunned. 'Eva, you spoil my girls. You shouldn't.'

'Gels must hef jems. You,' she turned to me, 'got five because you share your room viz me.'

'Eva, please,' my father began.

'Joe, I don't vont to hear it. Zis is a vunderful Christmuss for me. Better zan any viz ze dorty rot.'

We took her home on Boxing Day, into the heavy silence of that brocaded flat.

BERNIE STAYED ON as Sara had become used to her help in the laundry. In mid-January when schools began, Bernie went home to the Transkei, taking my rings, my first gold jewellery, with her. She did not take my sisters' presents, only mine. I wept with fury.

'See, she's not a brown person like us. Brown people don't steal,' Sara intoned.

I didn't believe any of that and went to tell mother of my loss.

'Well, there's nothing we can do. Imagine how horrible the police would be to her if we lodged a complaint, how terrible it would be for those poor people if we were to send the police after them to look for a ring.'

'But I loved it so much. It suited me.'

'You'll get plenty more in your life. Just think how she must have felt as a teenager. She saw you and your sisters with so much and she had nothing. She is happy now in the village. She has a pretty ring.'

'Yes, but it's mine,' I wailed.

'It *was* yours. Let her have it now.'

I went to my room to think about that. No. I would never ask the police to do anything for me. Imagine if they hurt somebody because of my complaint. It's not right to steal. But if, as my mother said, I let her keep it, it is no longer a theft and she is not guilty of anything. Still, if she came back, I'd ask her loudly, 'Where is my ring? I want it back.'

SARA'S FURY WAS something to be reckoned with and the other maids were cowed by her. One day Minnie, the laundry woman, stood up to her, but within a few minutes we heard Minnie shrieking her way through the house, 'Madam, madam', a stream of blood trickled down her face from a black stiletto heel embedded in her head. Sara had 'had enough' of Minnie. But my mother would never fire Sara because she was a 'fantastic cleaner!'

There was, however, one person who had it over Sara: Jackson. He was one of five brothers, all gifted gardeners who worked for my family on and off over fifty years. Jackson's skills were honed during the regular periods he spent in Fort Glamorgan jail for, among other things, robbery, drunkenness and assault. In prison, he worked as a barman, waiter and trainee chef, but he polished off the dregs in the glasses so was sent back to the garden to learn rose cultivation. We loved him. He had a broad smile and was kind to all of the children. He called all of us girls, 'Mrs Brown' and made effeminate mincing movements behind our backs. He teased my mother gently but once, while very drunk, he shook his finger at her, 'The master, Mr Joe, is going to heaven but you, Miss Bertha, you are going straight to hell, to the devil.'

Sara baited him out loud, 'My daddy says you are a Mau Mau.' This was a reference to the reign of terror by panga-wielding gangs in the 1950s in Kenya before independence from Britain.

One day Sara was cleaning the children's bathroom when Jackson crossed the courtyard on his way to the kitchen with vegetables from the garden. 'Here comes the Mau Mau,' she taunted through the open window. Jackson, having left his muddy shoes and basket at the back door, padded through the house to the bathroom. There was a sharp 'whoo' and then silence. My mother found them. He'd pinned Sara's arms behind her back with one hand and the other was clamped over her mouth. 'Where's the Mau Mau now? I tole you I gonna' fix you.' For Sara, that began the first of many months of annual stress leave.

4

African pictures and whispers on a Wild Coast holiday

On Friday evenings, we'd hear the roar of the engines of the giant motor transport buses as they ploughed their way down the Main Transkei Road, one block away from our home. They carried workers and small farm animals home for the weekend. I had seen them at the nearby pick-up point. The windows and sides of the buses were caked with red dust. Windscreen wipers cleared a small patch for the driver to peer through. People readied themselves: *madalas* with goatee beards sat on the edges of their seats chattering softly. The big women of Africa steadied the piles of *doeks* they wore on their heads, gathered in their many layered skirts and strode aboard. *No'weeds* (One who pulls weeds), as they were called, lit long pipes, chuckling and hawking through brown-stained teeth—'home for two days, no Madam's garden to weed.'

On the roof of the bus, moth-eaten white leghorns in homemade wire baskets squawked and tried to spread their wings to steady themselves as the loading and unloading rocked the machine this way and that. There were no younger men on these buses; they were mining deep underground in *Egoli* (the city of gold—Johannesburg), so many worlds away.

I knew the road the bus travelled to its destination, Umtata. Uncle Michael and Auntie Marie lived in a house next door to their trading store, a quarter of the way to Umtata, in Mooiplaas, a tiny settlement with a petrol pump and a hotel but no other houses. They ran this bus-stop shop alone. Half an hour further down this road was the village of Butterworth, where Auntie Elaine lived. Every couple of months, we went to her house for Sunday lunch.

We took that road to Umtata in the school holidays, when I was seven years old. My mother, who would have preferred a shopping trip to Cape Town or Johannesburg, had reluctantly given in to my father's cajoling. We were to travel beyond Umtata along unmade roads to the Wild Coast, to 'Trennerys', where my father's cousin Tony and his wife, Diana, ran a holiday resort.

Schools closed, and the cavernous boot of the big Chev was loaded with eight people's luggage. My eldest brother, Mark sat in front with my parents. My two older sisters Anita and Michele sat with me, my younger brother Paul, and his nursemaid, Katrina. Mother had wanted Sara to come but she refused, saying she hated black people and 'anyway the *tokolosbe* will get me there in Transkei.'

'St Christopher, pray for us.' The car moved down the driveway . . . 'Hail Mary full of grace' we continued, entering the stream of traffic on the Main Transkei Road. We followed Daddy's nasal lead intoning decades and litanies for protection against a fatal accident. Katrina sat with her eyes closed. We realised the whole world wasn't Catholic when Sara first told us she wasn't. 'Aren't you frightened you'll go to hell because you don't go to mass?' we asked her.

'I'm in hell already,' she snarled, so we never asked again.

The road as far as Mooiplaas was narrow with a few bends and turns, but at least it was tarred all the way. Tall grasses grew beside the road through the gently undulating landscape with few trees. Small flocks of hadedas stuck their long beaks into the black earth and pulled out worms and grubs. Cows settled in the shade of thorn trees and white cattle egrets hopped onto their backs; usually there was a small dam where the animals drank, and if we were lucky, we'd see a blue crane or two. These fenced lands had become white-owned farms and there was no longer any evidence of tribal people having owned the land.

After thirty minutes, we pulled into the bumpy open lot in front of Mooiplaas Trading Store, Prop. Michael Yazbek. A bus with its engine idling stood waiting for passengers who were inside the shop. Under a large old gum tree, a couple of mothers sat on a grassy patch with their babies at the breast. Their *doeks* were bigger than those worn in town, and hundreds of brass bangles covered their legs, which stuck out under their voluminous skirts. They broke pieces off a half-loaf of brown bread on a sheet of newspaper in front of them. Just outside the shop, a couple of older women, their bare arms bangled from elbow to armpit, lit pipes filled with the fresh tobacco they had just received in exchange for their home-grown pumpkins and corn. They had wrapped European-style towels and shawls over their traditional skirts. A few older men, wearing blazers despite the heat, shared a length of *twak* (tobacco) and spat long and far before putting the next plug in their cheeks. We went in to look for Uncle and Auntie, who were serving in the shop. They spotted us at once and made moves to come and greet us. My father put both his hands up saying, 'Finish first. These people are waiting. We'll talk when the bus goes.'

We stood to one side and absorbed the scene: a large old barn filled with African goods and weakly lit by a couple of bare light globes and two tiny-barred openings near the roof.

In the gloom, lines of shoppers stood patiently waiting to be served. Tiny Auntie Marie projected her shrill voice over the high counter, 'Next,' impatiently cutting and wrapping the selected items. Long bars of mottled soap that smelt of carbolic were piled on the counter. For sixpence, a six inch block of that fatty non-foaming servants' soap we'd seen mother hand out in our courtyard at home was cut and wrapped in newspaper. Bolts of blue or brown cotton German-print fabrics were stacked along the back wall. German missionaries had handed out that fabric to the people they were converting in the nineteenth century; locally it was known as *i'jaman*. Auntie measured along her outstretched arm to her nose and charged two and six a length. Two such pieces made a wraparound skirt for a thin person. Mothers with babies tied to their backs by towels and fringed rugs bought precious jars of Vicks Vapour rub. Others bought a tickey's worth of tiny multicoloured ceramic beads from one of the giant bottles. They made these into traditional beaded garments for brides or young unmarried women and a few pieces to sell to white people at the seaside. Huge coils of oozing chewing tobacco added an acridness to the dusty woodsmoke, a smell that burnt our nostrils. Uncle's long knife, its blade worn away from years of sharpening, cut mouthfuls of the *twak* for the men.

We milled about until the last customers got back on the bus, then followed Auntie and Uncle over to their house for morning tea. Their cook had made fresh scones to go with the farm butter. While the adults chatted, we children wandered around the vegetable garden and the fowl run. We examined the blue porcelain eggs Auntie put in the nests to encourage the hens to lay, wondering what kind of magic that was. The lowing of a cow or the bleating of a sheep broke the ear-filling silence. Our noses twitched at the strong dung smells of the countryside. Flies buzzed persistently round our eyes and mouths, sticking to our faces in the hot, sultry air.

Before we knew it, my father was hurrying us to the car: 'We still have two hours to drive.'

My mother seemed relieved to be on the move away from such isolation. 'I wonder how they sleep at night. They have no neighbours for miles.'

We headed toward Butterworth, but first we had to negotiate the Kei cuttings: a winding, narrow mountain road that led down into the valley where the Kei River flowed. At a one-lane bridge, that was the post signifying the border into tribal trust territory, Father stopped the car in the shade of some giant old weeping willows beside the river. The customs officers wearing khaki shirts and pants and white pith helmets checked the car for contraband quantities of alcohol and cigarettes, then waved us on. The slow climb up the other side out of the valley was marked by hairpin bends. My mother dreaded this part of the journey and, as usual on our trips to Auntie Elaine for Sunday lunch in Butterworth, she pleaded in a shaky voice to my speeding father: 'Not so fast darling, we'll plunge over the edge.' Eventually she'd become quiet and we'd notice her eyes were closed until we reached the other side.

We children loved the scenery: rolling green hills studded with groups of thatch-roofed mud huts, some with white designs painted around doorways and window openings. *Kraals*, made of tightly packed thorny branches for securing animals at night, were a short distance from the homesteads. Next to each cluster of huts, a small stand of *mielie* plants grew to provide *samp* for the winter. Two or three women wearing the usual armpit to ankle wraparound shift pounded huge wooden pestles rhythmically into a mortar, crushing *mielies* for the day's use. Small cooking fires sent spires of smoke straight up into the still air. Goats scampered and grazed on the steeper slopes. Beside the road, red-blanketed men carrying *knobkerries* under their arms walked in pairs, their bodies smeared with red ochre. 'They crush the lumps of earth, and make a paste for colouring themselves and their blankets,' Father said. They saluted us as we passed and we waved to them. 'These are Red men,' father continued, 'they haven't been to school; they prefer their traditional practices and ceremonies.' My father described some of these as we travelled. 'Remember Max, who worked for us in the garden and who went away at eighteen to become an *abakweta*? He had to live in the bush, away from all his family and friends in a special hut with other *abakwetas*. They weren't allowed to eat their favourite foods or see any women, even their sisters and mothers.'

'Why was that, Daddy?' Mark asked.

'They have to learn how to be men in the Xhosa way. They also practise stick-fighting.'

'Stick-fighting,' he said, 'I'd love to do that.'

'It's a discipline, my boy,' Father continued. 'It is about being brave and scaring but not killing the enemy, although accidents do happen. It is very tough, which may be why Max was so quiet when he came back after all those weeks away.'

We were thrilled to catch sight of a *sangoma* (traditional healer) walking on a hillside path. He wore heavy white beadwork and parts of animal skins and tails. 'When something bad happens or somebody gets sick, the healer orders the slaughter of an animal, usually a white goat,' father continued, ' white for the ancestors and spirits. At a celebration, an ox or a sheep might be killed. That costs a fortune.'

Once father stopped the car and we bought clay cattle from the children at the roadside. 'Give them a bit extra,' my mother said, 'look how thin they are. You kids don't know how lucky you are.'

Butterworth was a small village of about four hundred white people; Africans were often not counted or even mentioned in the statistics and Butterworth was no exception. There were a few churches and a hall that doubled as a cinema. As we passed the large municipal park with rectangular fishponds covered in waterlilies, my mother remarked, 'This reminds me of King William's Town and Queenstown, where I was born. The English built local government towns and always put in parks and ponds.'

Auntie Elaine's house was up the hill above the town and we stopped there for lunch. The kitchen maids pinched our bottoms and cheeks, remarking to one another how fat and healthy we were or 'shame, how skinny,' looking at Michele. We wandered around the garden and clenched our teeth as we stared at the bottles of snakes that cousin Conway kept in the shed.

Tilly, the cook, called us to lunch and after grace, as we began to eat, the bell tolled in the little Anglican church across the veld. 'They must be getting ready. Can we go and see?'

'See what?' my mother asked.

'Conway told us, they'll be doing Arabic dancing in the church,' I said as I imagined fat Auntie Josephine and moley Auntie Evelyn donning chiffons and veils in preparation for the sunset service, when they'd fling themselves around the altar.

'What rubbish. They can't dance. Anyway, people don't do Arabic dancing in church,' my mother said.

'And that is an Anglican church,' my father emphasised.

After lunch, we set off again, wending our way through villages with names like Idutywa, Nqmakwe and Ndabakazi. The lands were not fenced; sheep, goats and cattle grazed all over the place. 'Please don't hit a cow,' my mother said. 'You know how many accidents there are with animals here.'

From the back we begged, 'How long still, Daddy? How much further?'

'Just watch the next bend', or 'Past that tree and another two minutes,' he patiently replied.

Finally we arrived in the centre of Umtata, the largest town of the Transkei, and the traditional home together with the Ciskei, of the Xhosa people. The chaos and the noise of buses, bicycles, some cars, and pavements crowded with street merchants was exciting. Xhosa men who had ridden into town on horseback tethered their animals at the watering troughs and went about their business. Some people were dressed in the same red blankets as in the countryside. Young women, their faces white with lime signifying recent marriage, wore rows of bangles on both arms and strings of coloured beads in beautiful designs.

We picked our way through the town, crossed the bridge over the Umtata River and turned right, following the sign that said: ' Wild Coast, Coffee Bay'.

'Hell's teeth', my mother said, 'now I know why Tony's got an aeroplane. I suppose these are the last shops we'll see for a while.'

'Yes, darling,' my father said, 'but we'll go fishing and collect oysters and the girls can play tennis to their hearts' content. Tony's so excited we're coming. You know how hospitable he is.'

We swayed and bumped, throwing up a dust storm as we went. The scrubby bushes scratched the sides of the car on the narrower parts of the track. My father swore profusely; 'bladdy shit,' he said, about a hundred times. My subdued mother sat next to Mark, who behaved as though he was riding his favourite stallion. He egged Father on as the car scraped bottom and sides. Paul vomited over us in the back and Katrina quietly wiped and restored all.

The bush gave way to a sandy track through clumps of tussocky green grass. From the crest of a rise we saw the sea for the first time and opened all the windows. Our excitement rose, and Daddy began reciting John Masefield who 'had to go down to the sea again', at the top of his voice.

We followed the road until it became a ribbon of black sand that led up to a stone arch on which was carved 'Trennerys', the name of an attractive collection of whitewashed, thatch-roofed *rondavels*. Paved pathways around colourful flowerbeds connected the cottages, all of which led to the kitchen-dining room complex. Uncle Tony and Auntie Diana rushed out to welcome us.

Porters unpacked the car. Michele, Paul and I bounced on the beds in our cottage and peeped through the high little windows while Katrina put our clothes in the wardrobe. Soon mother called us and we followed the maid carrying a tray of tea and scones down to the tennis court. Grey vervet monkeys swung in and out of the trees and the maid warned us not to feed them as once they'd eaten all the sugar, they would bite us. My mother could not relax; out in the country, the African bush was alive, reaching out to consume all of us.

At six o'clock, the electricity generator came to life with a bang and little lights began to twinkle in the gardens. At the same time, a white-coated waiter wearing a red fez just like the one Uncle Ayoub wore in the photos from Lebanon, patrolled the grounds, plonking a tune on the xylophone to announce children's dinner-time. Chambers, the fez-wearer, was in charge in the dining room. The nannies waited for him to arrange the seating and menus. Katrina fed Paul and then, after tidying us, took us to the cocktail bar where our parents sat having drinks in a small group. A short dark woman with moles, a long pointy noise and red lipstick lunged at me and kissed me all over my face. She did the same to my sister but grabbed my brother, put him on her knee and, cooing in Arabic, planted smacking kisses all over his head. 'This is Auntie Rose, Uncle Tony's sister', my mother said as if to explain the lips that employed themselves so promiscuously. We rushed outside as soon as we could and walked with Katrina to our *rondavel.* From behind a low fence, a fox terrier flew at us, yapping furiously at Katrina, who stamped her feet shouting, '*Tula, Tula* (Shut up).' But the dog got even wilder.

Inside our cottage the lighting was weak, but we could make out spiders and swallows nesting in the beams and thatch. This was exciting and creepy, especially when tiny bats stirred and flew out into the twilight. After preparing us for bed, Katrina went to her quarters. 'She'll be fine sleeping with the other servants in their separate accommodation', my mother had said. We never knew what that accommodation looked like; it was always somewhere else, behind kitchens, next to storerooms, across fields.

The early morning was disturbed by the smells and sounds from the kitchen. Mist hung over all the buildings until the sun topped the hills and cleaned up the valley.

The family ate breakfast together, while Katrina stood next to Paul feeding him porridge. We rushed our meal and bounded down the pathway through tangled shrubbery onto the beach. Uncle Tony was waiting to take us in his boat onto the lagoon to show us where the wild oysters grew. I noticed two Xhosa women on the hillside weaving baskets from the long green thatching grasses. I begged to be taken to see what they were doing. 'Afterwards,' my mother promised.

We chugged about the lagoon, my mother repeatedly asking what would happen if we capsized. 'We'll swim,' Uncle Tony said, 'and I'll save you, Bertha'. The water was dark with long fronds of brown weed that concealed rocks on which thousands of oysters grew. In the shallows, dense reed beds made it impossible to reach the orange coloured dunes on which coastal shrubs spread their leaves and flowers in long arms.

After we arrived back on the shore, my mother walked up the hill with me. We waded through the waist-high waving grasses, their seed-heads full and ripening. Blackjack seeds stuck to our clothes and scratched my bare legs. The water below us glistened in the midday sun and the breeze swayed the bull rushes. '*Molo*' we greeted the weavers. '*Molweni*—hello to you', they replied. They sat on a reed mat, cutting, plaiting and twisting long swathes of freshly cut grasses. These were coiled, secured vertically with reed strips, and a basket took shape before my eyes. I smelt the greenness and, fingering the wiry fibres, asked my mother to buy a basket for me to take home. 'No, no, too big, too smelly', she said. 'Please, for my room', I pleaded.

Daily we went down to the beach and out on the water in Uncle Tony's runabout. I longed to sit up on the hillside with those women. I wanted to ask them where they lived, and about their lives, which seemed so different from ours and even from Katrina's.

One morning I slipped away and sat on the hill, a little distance from them. I gave no hint of my fluency in Xhosa. They chatted freely in front of me and even about me, giggling as they mused why this white child wanted to sit there. Then a small girl arrived with a gourd of sour milk. *She sat down and asked them if they'd heard about the snake that had come up the river the other night. It had two bright eyes that lit up the whole hill, drawing the* abakwetas *from their hut. I became curious as she continued. They had seen two river people climb from the belly of the snake. They were picked up by a car and driven away. The snake submerged as silently as it had surfaced. It was the first time they had seen the powerful water spirits, a good omen for everyone.* I watched the women nodding silently and felt myself doing the same. The full moon rose high that night and Auntie Rose's horrible fox terrier howled and yapped. Crouching on my bed, I lifted the curtain and peered through the small window above me. There seemed to be more people about than usual. The pounding of the breakers could be heard quite clearly. *Down at esi Khaleni—'the place of the sound', a cliff with a cleft that waves rushed through when the tide was high—the river people must have been talking on their drums.* Lying back dozing, I imagined I saw the two bright eyes of the river snake shining on the taps at the hand-basin. Paul snored through his blocked nose and Michele blew out through her open mouth. I was so entranced by the snake's hypnotic swaying that I didn't immediately hear the sound of running feet or the barking of Auntie Rose's dog until it was yelping in pain. I shot up to look out again and just saw Chambers' tall figure running away in white dining room sandshoes, carrying a white bucket in his hand. Then I heard Auntie Rose sobbing, 'My poor dog, they've poured hot water on you.'

My heart pounding, I lay back and searched for the snake. Questions piled up in my head. I looked out again, but the whole place had become quiet, the moon covered by a cloud. I fell asleep wanting to talk with those women on the hill. I wanted to sit near them once more and watch the sea flow in and out through the hole in the rock. I wanted to ask them my many questions and tell them about the snake that visited me. My parents knew nothing about things like that.

On the way to breakfast, I saw that Auntie Rose's cottage was closed up and the dog wasn't there. Chambers didn't bring me my porridge; in fact I was glad he wasn't around. I asked my mother what had happened in the night, 'Nothing, my darling, nothing at all.' Mark and Anita looked at my parents who continued the denial. It reminded me of the time early one morning when I had heard soft moaning outside my bedroom window. Looking out, I saw the gardener's girlfriend lying on the lawn with a spike sticking out of her head. When I told the others at breakfast they had said 'No.' 'What?' 'Nothing.' I had gone outside but all I had seen was fresh soil covering the spot where I thought she'd been lying. Someone else would have to explain to me what I was seeing; these white people seemed to hear and see nothing at night.

That morning, no one noticed my absence as they rushed down to the sandbar to collect prawns on the receding tide. I wandered to the hillside, resolving at last to overcome my shyness, talk with the women and ask them my questions. I found no one there. A brown scar on the green hill was the only evidence that people regularly sat there. Even later in the afternoon, the place was as quiet as before.

That night there was a fancy dress party. My mother dressed as a handkerchief girl and my brother and sisters were pirates, but I sat next to my father the whole night, holding onto his belt. He sang and tapped his foot to the beat of his banjo and the hall was full of choruses and cheers. One man enjoyed himself so much that his wife and a few waiters had to carry him to bed. Luckily, in fancy dress as Wee Willie Winkie, he already had his pyjamas on. Katrina took us to bed, my brother and sister snoring even before the clothes were hung up.

We left early the next morning, so that my father could get back to his office. At home I stood by the boot of the car looking into its growing emptiness as the servants unpacked everything, scattering the Wild Coast dust and beach sand in the garden. The smell of wood smoke and freshly cut thatching grass hid themselves in layers of my memory that would continue to surface from time to time.

YEARS LATER, I was to find out that the story of the snake, referred to submarine activity. Early in the liberation struggle in South Africa, eastern bloc submarines made their way, on possibly more than one occasion, up the Bashee River in Transkei. They were transporting trained fighters of both *Umkhonto We Sizwe* (the military wing of the ANC), and the Pan-African Congress.

As a child, I heard one of the women who worked as a cook for an aunt giving a version of her son's firsthand account of such a visit. She was so encouraged by the news that she retired from domestic service and left to join an African women's church group. Their covert support for the struggle provided her with a vehicle to express her strong desires for liberation.

She returned to visit my aunt in the 1970s, stunning my relatives as she raised her fist proudly and sang the songs and choruses of the war.

5

Life stories in the courtyard – 1959 onwards.

Umuntu ungumuntu nga Bantu
You become a person by being with people

ZULU PROVERB

One day in 1960, Daddy came home from town with enormous boxes from South African Druggists crammed into the boot and backseat of his big Chev. He had six large bottles of mercurochrome, twelve crepe bandages, a tiny box of sticking plaster, masses of toilet rolls and one-hundred-and-forty-four packets of Kotex pads. 'What is happening?'

'People are being shot,' my father said feverishly. 'There's going to be murder everywhere and we might have to help the injured.' That was how the massacre of pass law protesters at Sharpeville brought fear into our home for the first time. I remember that when my father was agitated about something, he forgot that I was just a small child and he said things quite baldly. The first time was at the Cambridge lockup when he went to pay bail for his client and I asked him why the women were weeping. From packing all of that into the store cupboard, my father went to the locked filing cabinet in his study and brought out a rusty looking revolver. I started to cry.

'Why? Why? Put it away daddy, please, please.' He put it in the drawer next to his bed, and I never saw it again. My mother, meanwhile, had ordered from Uncle Mickey's grocery store and filled the pantry cupboards to capacity, 'in case we can't go out.' At nine o'clock at night, the siren sounded on the Main Transkei Road, and after that it was very quiet. 'It's a curfew,' my mother said. 'All African people have to be off the streets'. I missed the familiar sounds of the Transkei buses and loud African chatter that I usually heard from my room when I went to bed.

Once or twice after dark, I heard Afrikaans voices in the garden outside my window: 'We are looking for natives without passes, Meneer.'

'We don't have any here,' Daddy announced. 'Bastards,' he said inside his bedroom.

On the way back from school one day, Rossy told me that her parents said the Afrikaners were killing black people in the north of the country at a place called Sharpeville. Linda went very quiet. Her father was Afrikaans but he was a doctor. He wouldn't kill people. I asked my mother about Linda's family, 'Her mother is English, from England and her father is a very quiet man.'

MY FATHER'S LEGAL office in town drew clients from all sectors. Eventually a separate section was created for Africans. The vast number of apartheid laws drafted and enacted by the Nationalist government began to bite. A thick black arrow next to the main entrance of the office, pointed down a dimly lit hallway to the desks where the African clerks presided over document delivery and mail. A row of backless wooden benches was often crammed with African people waiting to see a lawyer. At the end of the day, when the office closed, they overflowed desperately into the courtyard of our home.

The kitchen windows overlooked the courtyard on one side, while the children's bathroom windows took up the other wall. Three washing lines hung between the bench and the row of servants' rooms, the bathroom and the coal cellar. The giant corrugated iron water tank stood next to the gate that led down the steps into the back garden. An enamel mug always stood next to the tap for whoever was suddenly thirsty. My mother warned us not to share the mug with strangers. But I loved the cold tank water and I had been drinking from Rosie's enamel mug all my life.

From the time I was eight years old in 1961, the courtyard began to change. People came down the long tradesmen's path and in through the gate beside the kitchen door. The dogs gave one or two barks but soon became accustomed to the daily procession. Some people shuffled along, weighed down by age or poverty; all were profoundly affected by the myriad race laws being drafted onto the statute books. Women carrying babies tied to their backs with bath towels or tartan rugs wiped sweat from their faces, '*Shoo,shoo*(hot) today, Mama. Please, just some *mielie* meal,' as she unwrapped the whimpering baby.

' She needs milk, Mama,' I suggested.

'I can't Missie, my titties are dry from too much worry and it's too dear in the shops.'

'Please Mother,' I rushed inside to search for some.

The *jirin*, an upturned concrete mortar in which meat was pounded for special occasions, was my perch. On my right, five adults sat tightly together on the bench. They'd arrived in ones and twos waiting 'To see Mr Yazbek, please.' Older men sucking on long pipes blew pungent smoke through stained teeth.

'Today my father is in his office in town,' I said in fluent Xhosa.

'*E`we, thombazaan*. But when we go there those clerks make us wait and come back so much, and we sit there in the darkness of that back office. I don't think Mr Yazbek even knows we are there.'

I went back into the house. 'Those people will wait forever. When is Daddy coming home?'

'Give them some more tea, darling,' my mother suggested. 'You can use the mixed fruit jam for the sandwiches.'

'This child is driving us mad here feeding these people all the time,' the cook complained. 'They keep on coming because they know there's always bread and tea here.'

'They're tired and hungry,' I told cook indignantly, 'they've walked a long way.'

But she would have nothing to do with those people. 'They are blacks and speak Xhosa, and I am a brown person speaking Afrikaans, the whiteman's language,' she asserted proudly.

'Please ma'am...' an excited old man began. 'Hey, who's ma'am here?' he was stopped by a younger fellow, 'this is only a *thombazaan*, a child, a Xhosa-speaking child.'

'Sorry ma'am, er *thombazaan*. I need my pass but the *tsotsis* took it. Please get me a note from your Daddy.'

'To whom it may concern: Peter Molotsi is well known to me. At present he is without a pass awaiting a new one. Do not arrest this man. He is not a criminal. Signed J A Yazbek, Attorney at Law, 24 Gladstone Street, East London.' My father scribbled out hundreds of notes. As I grew up, he dictated to me and then he'd sign. Sometimes women wanted letters: 'To whom it may concern: Do not evict this woman. Her husband has gone to seek work and will return shortly.' African women were not allowed to remain without legal husbands in township houses. Regardless of the number of children or elderly relatives they shared with, when their husbands left or died, they were evicted from their homes by the Bantu Affairs Administration and sent back to the 'homelands' in the countryside.

When my father did appear, stories tumbled out, 'Please master, my son, he was in a fight. Now he's in jail. They will *donder* (beat) him there. Can we try for bail?'

THE COAL TRUCK came every Tuesday. Three African men with jute hoods carried the hundredweight (fifty kilogram) sacks of anthracite on their backs all the way from the street to the coal cellar at the end of the courtyard. They had to lift the bags up and over the top of a high partition. When an older man faltered, I noticed a younger one help him. The stacked coal was drawn three times a day from the chute at the bottom to fill the Esse stove. These men were black from head to foot with coal dust; I only noticed the whites of their eyes. They never smiled. I watched them every week and wondered where they lived, if they ever washed, whether they had children. . . . they seemed so removed from the kind of life with which I was familiar.

One day as I was standing near the kitchen door, the gate flew open as usual and the laden coal men came past me. On the way out, one of them stood and stared at me. He must be hungry I thought and I asked Cook to give him something to eat. 'No. He can drink water from the tank like everybody else. Go. Go and drink there!' and she waved him away. I half followed and watched him taking great gulps, filling the mug three or four times. Finally he threw his head back and finished with a loud 'Aah.' In one movement he wiped his mouth with the back of his hand and plunged his index finger into my chest, ' I want you.'

From behind me, Sara screamed, 'You, you black boy, you want a white girl? *Voetsek* (bugger off) before I call the master.' Sara's eyes protruded even further. I thought she was having a fit. I'd never been afraid before. Suddenly I was caught between this vulcan and Sara's rage. I watched him walk off silently.

The courtyard was my home, where my mothers slept and hung out the washing, ate their lunch and smoked their *zols*. Sometimes when I wound up my gramophone, somebody joined me for a *kwela* (dance). As the sixties wore on, African people laughed at me, 'Whites don't have to know how to *kwela*. It is us blacks. We dance when the policeman shakes his *sjambok* (whip).'

Until I was seventeen and went away to university, I sat in the limbo of that desperate waiting room, and listened to the stories of life in South Africa for black and brown-skinned people, as they talked to me. Partly because I spoke Xhosa and Afrikaans, they openly told me their stories. Mostly, however, I think it was my whiteness that allowed them to hope that, child as I was, I could help.

This backward view into my courtyard childhood makes me shiver now. I was an old woman of eight, nine or ten making tea and jam sandwiches and listening to stories I carried inside, imagining relief was at hand. 'Just make some more tea, my darling,' my mother said with a bittersweet smile on her face. Eventually the intensity of the suffering closed my heart to the people inside the house. They were powerless to relieve or change anything, although my father thought that the rule of law still prevailed and relied naively on the courts to implement justice.

The Nationalist government was going berserk, implementing the apartheid nightmare at all costs. The Race Classification Courts sat regularly, hearing appeals from people to be re-classified in order to live together with husbands, wives or children whose recently classified skin colour disqualified them from their previous identity. My brother appeared once or twice on behalf of people caught in such a predicament. A Chinese was applying to be a 'coloured' in order to live with his wife in a 'coloured' area. The applicant had to pass physical tests just as the Nazis had conducted in Germany in order to establish whether someone was Jewish. In this case, the Chinese person had to have a pencil stuck in his hair to see if it fell out or stayed in. Nostril widths were measured; people wept openly and pleaded with magistrates 'only doing their job'. The ruling regarding their colour could change the course of their lives and those of their partners and children. We knew families where a dark child had to live in an African area and would sneak home at night to sleep with his family in a 'coloured area'. A white person could choose to be classified as Asian or black or coloured but it was almost unheard of for anyone thus classified to successfully 'try' for white.

My brother was stirred up and came home with the gory details of the humiliation being inflicted on the population. My father whistled, 'Gee whizz, Markie, this is tragic. These people have gone mad. No wonder all the Chinese are going to Canada. What a loss of brains for this country.' At one stage, racial counting was so detailed, there were three hundred listed Chinese people in the whole country.

Initially my father and brother thought they were doing a service to those who wanted to live together without the threat of prosecution, but it wasn't long before the firm declined to take on further cases in that court; they had lost faith in the capacity of the legal profession to work with integrity within the system.

IT WAS OUR understanding and our experience that no Lebanese had been allowed into the country after 1948, as the nationalist apartheid government decreed that we 'were not white enough.'

In the 1960s, a ship docked in Durban harbour after sailing down the east coast of Africa. A Lebanese man who disembarked was sent back aboard and not allowed to remain overnight on land as 'he was too dark-skinned'.

6

Auntie Susie makes fun

Our neighbourhood lives were interwoven with cousins, aunts and uncles. Auntie Susie, Daddy's youngest sister, was an especially loving figure married to a withdrawn Maltese. Uncle Joe grew up with his large Maltese family in Cairo in a community of expatriates during the reign of King Farouk. His sisters danced at the famed Gezira club frequented by Farouk, along with Hungarians, Jews, Greeks, Italians and others, most of whom left Egypt when Farouk was deposed and Nasser took power in 1952. Susie's marriage to Joe after the death of her mother Florie was not always easy. They went to live and work for a time in Tanganyika (Tanzania) and returned to South Africa, adding Swahili to the Maltese, Italian, English and Arabic that Uncle Joe spoke. He travelled away to do engineering contract work from time to time while she worked as a bookkeeper in my father's office and brought up three children, my cousins, Antoinette, Charles and Joanne.

Uncle was often moody; he roared at my cousins and I was afraid of him. When Joanne was a baby, he picked her up and swung her by her hair as Auntie pleaded in Swahili with him to stop. My father had built a semi-detached cottage around the corner for my Granny Isabel. Auntie Susie and her family lived in the other half. Once when I was staying at Granny's, I cooked myself scrambled egg and went to the garden to pick some mint. Uncle saw me through the kitchen window and when I returned to my feast, he had smothered it in Tabasco sauce.

Auntie sat relentlessly at the piano, played and sang and taught us to do the same. When the first of our cousins got married, she assembled us to practise until we could perform Handel's *Where ere you walk* from the choir loft in St Patrick's church.

At mass on Sundays, Auntie could be mischievous, especially if her old friend, Father Lawlor was the celebrant. From the front row, she'd look him in the eye and pull her skirt up slowly to reveal her knee and then she'd grin, Uncle jabbing her hard in the ribs. When the collection was taken for the sick-priests' fund, on more than one occasion, she produced a box of aspirin from her handbag and put it in the plate. Her irreverence and her jokes were a great distraction, perhaps, primarily for herself. As children, we watched her with glee but knew we were not to copy her.

I OFTEN SPENT Friday or Saturday night with Granny in her own cottage, and early in the morning, while she was still asleep, I'd creep through the kitchen door to Auntie Susie's and climb into bed with Antoinette, who was my age.

Sometimes, when Granny went out, Antoinette and I dug into the box under her bed and pulled out her old spectacles and false teeth. We'd put them on and, pretending to be Granny and her friend, Auntie Halia Mukheibir, would conduct spitty Arabic conversations with each other, waving our arms around, calling Charles, 'Sharl, Sharl, *habeebie t'burrnie* (darling bury me).' Those were the times that Uncle Joe threw back his head and laughed uproariously.

Auntie Susie would always gather us round after lunch and tell us a story. That day, I sat with my cousins at her feet in the living room. We heard how when they were children, Auntie Susie and my father and their sister Victoria were driven around Kroonstad, where they lived, in the big black car by the Nazareth House chauffeur. 'We looked out on our school friends walking in the streets but we were being driven because we were *special* children, living together in the big house with lots of other children. The Nazareth Sisters took care of us.' Auntie was four, Daddy was seven (my age as I sat there that day) and Auntie Vicky was nine.

'Your father was a toughie. When I asked him if he *foossed* (farted), he would pull my pigtail and I'd cry, but Sister Philomena would pick me up and pat me and say: "Joey, be kind to your sister", and he'd be good until she left. Then he'd start *foossing* (farting) again.'

'But where was Auntie Elaine?'

'Oh, she had left school and was working with our mother, your Ouma, in the family sweet shop because our Daddy was dead.'

'Why did he die?'

'Because he was so good he had to go to heaven . . .'

Sitting there, all our fathers and mothers intact, we thought how privileged and special our Aunties and Daddy were because they only had Ouma and they had lived with the nuns.

The truth was that when their father died suddenly in 1923, their mother, Grandmother Florie, was unable to care for them and run the shop. Auntie Elaine left school when she was twelve to work with her mother, and the three younger children went to the Nazareth House orphanage for seven years. The Nazareth Sisters are the closest to a mendicant order in the Catholic Church. When I was growing up in East London, they visited my home every year in December. Two reticent Irish women clad in blue habits, white veils and leather sandals regardless of the weather, came in for a substantial morning tea—cheese sandwiches, fruit cake and butter biscuits. After regaling my mother with tragic stories of their work at the Home in Port Elizabeth, sandwiches and cakes were parcelled up for them to take away. Then my mother would ask in conspiratorial tone, 'Have you been to my husband's office yet, Sister?'

Sister Brigid's hairy top lip would rise showing long white teeth, and her eyes would twinkle with a broad smile, 'Yes, thank you Mrs Yazbek. We have been there.' Her positive tone referred to the annual donation my father gave them. I had seen the nuns at my father's office. He made a fuss and once he nearly hugged a flushed Sister Clare who flinched and retreated as he enthused his thanks for the years of care he and his siblings had received.

UNCLE JOE WALKED in on Auntie Susie's story about the orphanage, carrying a bunch of flowers from the garden and announced it was time to go to the cemetery and to visit an old family friend, Mrs Abdo, who was sick. We piled into the car and set off. Joanne was too young to go visiting, so she stayed at home with Esther, her nursemaid.

'We are going to see Great-Auntie Abdo round the corner,' Auntie Susie said. 'She is very old but look for the angels fluttering their wings by her bed. They are ready to carry her to heaven.'

The Victorian house had huge rooms with high ceilings and wooden floors. Small stained-glass windows were covered in layers of lace. In the gloom we could barely make out the shrivelled person in the high iron bed. Her white hair on end, she wailed, '*Shoo ell han* (What do they say of) Rodney?' Her sons sat around chatting and drinking tea. As we left, Auntie Susie said, 'She always wants to know about Rodney, her grandson the priest. She's not long for this world, I hope.' I pictured her sons one by one, kissing her goodbye as she lay back, rosary twined around her fingers and Father Rodney sprinkling her with holy water. Those angels would carry her, like all dying people, into the arms of Jesus.

From there, we drove to the Cambridge cemetery to put flowers on Ouma's grave. We parked outside the black gates and, following the avenue of tall cypress trees, walked past the caretaker in the front garden of his cottage: '*Goeie middag* (Good afternoon)'.

'Hello *Meneer*', we replied, but as usual Uncle Joe didn't say a word. He never greeted people or even responded to them. I used to think he lived in his own world and found other people annoying; in sharp contrast to my father who spoke to everyone, wherever he was. We headed down the main cemetery drive, surrounded by graves as far as the eye could see. Angels, broken pillars and huge crosses with a few modest headstones in between, covered the hillside. We came to Sandro's grave. He had been an articled clerk in my father's law firm when he died suddenly in a car accident. It was a beautiful Italian marble headstone with his Mario Lanza face in one corner. We stroked the smooth marble and patted his picture; his young face in this place of old people frightened us, so we gave him a flower from our bunch.

From there we turned left, walking under the towering pine trees, our shoes crunching over the fallen cones. The soft whooshing of the breeze calmed us as we settled on a deep bed of needles, while Auntie Susie went ahead to speak privately with her mother, our grandmother. We watched her approach the top end of the grave under the huge cross, pull a few weeds and remove the vases for washing and refilling. When she reached the foot end, we gathered next to her and knelt down together. She moved her hands around and over all accessible parts of the grave, her lips soundlessly speaking to Granny lying under the gravel blanket. Out loud she began, 'Mommy, how are you? Are your feet cold? Let me rub them for you my darling', and she would start picking at the small blue stones, raking them with her fingers and then smoothing them with her whole hand, caressing Granny's feet. 'Does that feel better, Mom? I'll get the girls to do your flowers now.'

It was very quiet; there were no other people around. The screeching of the tap as we turned it on to fill the three gravestone vases almost scared us. We cut the taller flowers: roses at the top 'for Ouma to smell', violets for 'her heart which ached all her life' and bright daisies for her cold feet.

Standing up, Auntie moved to the head end and raked more stones into a heap into which she embedded the vase of roses. Walking backwards, she rejoined us and together we prayed Hail Marys and Hail Holy Queens. Then we children wandered off, taking care not to stand on anyone's head or toes as we read their names and dates. Periodically we glanced back, but Auntie Susie was still kneeling, and Uncle Joe, a statue, was still standing to one side. We continued our prowling among other people's relatives. Some of the graves were covered in glass domes packed with plastic flowers faded by the sun. A few new graves had fresh flowers. When we saw Auntie stand up, we rushed back to say, 'Goodbye Ouma, see you next week. Keep warm and remember that we all love you lots.' We walked away from the grave slowly backwards at first and then, cuddling close to Auntie, we propelled her up the hill to the car.

Ouma had died long before we were born, but Auntie Susie still spoke to her in the photographs on her dressing table, and in the cemetery.

When we got home, she put the kettle on and called out to Esther and Joanne. There was no reply, and when we went to look in the maid's room, the door was locked. We playfully called 'Joannie' under the arms of the weeping mulberry tree and behind the half tank where the tortoises were kept, but we held back when we saw how seriously Auntie Susie and

Uncle Joe searched and called for her. It was a long time. Uncle drove round the streets; Auntie Susie walked into the bush next to the house where the drunks always sat drinking meths until they fell over and lay dead drunk for hours. The search hung over us like a cloud—where is she? where are Esther and Joanne?

The calls began to get frantic, 'Where is my little girl?' whimpering, 'Where is my child?' and then desperately, 'Where is my baby?'. Auntie wailed like someone discovering she'd lost a limb. I wondered if that was how she had cried when she had those miscarriages in the doctor's rooms in the country. She always told us how precious we were because not all babies were born alive.

Uncle Joe came and stood mutely next to her in the middle of the lawn. Her face got whiter and the circles round her eyes darkened as she quietened to croon softly to herself. Every morning she kissed the statue of St Anthony in her bedroom—a thick layer of red lipstick covered his sandalled foot. He always found lost things for us. But that day St Anthony and even St Jude, patron saint of hopeless cases, were forgotten in the desperate search.

Then Esther walked through the front gate holding Joanne's hand. Joanne stood barefoot on the slate pathway that led to the front door. Esther melted into the background. Auntie kneeled down in front of her and gazed into her face. 'My child, my baby'. Then silently, she keeled over sideways onto the ground.

We older ones watched from a distance. Uncle Joe carried Auntie up the stairs and laid her down on her bed; she'd wake up eventually.

Joanne tripped and danced into the middle of the lawn to join us in our game of catch around the birdbath, until we collapsed into the thick grass. We lay and watched the clouds floating overhead. I carried my story all the way home up the hill through the gardens into the house, anxious to tell my mother that Joanne had been lost and when she was found, Auntie had fainted and Uncle carried her to bed. But my mother waved her hands in front of her face and I felt her push my story away.

In retrospect, I ponder the relationship between my mother, the youngest, prettiest sister in her family, and Susie, my father's youngest, prettiest sister. My mother led a charmed life while Susie showed us another side of life with hard work and suffering. Yet she had a great sense of humour and many light-hearted family memories emanated from her. As Susie aged and lost her looks, she enfolded all who visited her in a simple, warm love.

MANY YEARS LATER, in faraway Sydney, I was vacuuming my house one morning when thoughts of Auntie Susie stopped me in my tracks. I couldn't continue my housework. So I sat at the dining room table and wrote a card to her, enclosing a tiny gold guardian angel someone had given me. 'Dear Auntie, I have the feeling that you need this more than I do right now. Know that I am thinking of you at this moment.' At that exact time, Uncle Joe was having a stroke in the bed next to her. Paralysed, he was nursed day and night for eight years by Auntie, herself over eighty when he finally died.

A couple of years later, Auntie herself was in the nursing home fading to the last shards of a life of light and love. Amidst all her physical pain she was refusing to die. The family discussed what could be holding her back.

'Hello Auntie.'

'Hello my darling, I love you so much.'

'Thank you Auntie, I love you too. I am phoning from Australia to thank you for all the love you gave me when I was a child with Ant, Charles and Joanne; later too, you never stopped loving me. I have felt it all my life. You have been a mother to me.'

'Oh darling of my heart, you deserve our best love always.'

'Thank you, Auntie. Now it is your turn, finally after all these years, to take your rest. You have loved us all into life; it's all right to go now. Daddy is waiting for you over there with your mother, my Granny Florie and everyone else. Goodbye Auntie, thank you. God bless you. Go now Auntie, goodbye. I will never stop loving you.'

Three days of silence followed until Auntie breathed her last.

But she has never really disappeared—she is so present to all of our family in our conversations.

'Ceelore,' Charles, her son, calls from his Malmesbury farm full of dogs, cats, horses and any others that are abandoned. 'Ceelore,' he drones, an African-sounding lilt to my French name.

'Happy New Year, *Galeelie Zumboortik,*' and we both scream with laughter at yet another of his mother's or my father's made-up words. This one is supposed to be affectionate—like 'darling of my heart' or something else floral.

'Ceelore, don't forget to write about the plays we put on in the garage.'

'Whew. Thanks Charles,' relieved he wasn't going to remind me of the cupboard games we later went to confession about. Antoinette and I were the fairies in pink toe shoes and tuille skirts while Paul and Joanne were the elves.

'Yes,' he continued, 'and I was the goblin who jumped out from under the table, stamped my feet and pointed spells at you.'

'Oh Charles, I was never frightened of your roaring, but I think you were afraid of me as I constantly tried to kiss you.'

Perhaps, being a goblin, he was supposed to learn 'manly' ways and I'd stop trying to kiss him . . . it was with my cousins that I had a childhood of games, dressing up and play-acting. When I went home, there was the courtyard, always full of people.

7

Jesus died and rose in Queenstown

Easter was a special time: my father went to play bowls in the regional tournaments in Queenstown. Haseebie and Ross Khoury, who were on the ship to Africa with Granny Isabel, had remained settled there and, in my grandfather's opinion, had been a more acceptable class of person for his family to mix with. Whenever we went to Queenstown where Auntie Phyllis, my mother's sister, and Uncle Joffe ran the Waldorf Tea Room, my mother made sure we saw Haseebie.

We stayed with our cousins and had full and noisy holidays in a country town in which it was safe enough for children to wander around and ride bicycles. My parents stayed in one of the hotels in town, sometimes the Windsor owned by Mr Haas, a German who kissed my mother's hand in greeting while we children chanted, 'Hello Mr Arse,' to our parents' chagrin.

On Good Friday and Easter Sunday, we attended the services in the Cathedral of Christ the King on the hill. Bishop Rosenthal had raised money in his hometown in Germany to build this edifice. In the years of its construction, my father had taken us on walks to watch the progress. From Germany the bishop had procured a mosaic artist who was also a nun. One Saturday afternoon, we watched her in her white habit, sprawled on the floor of the empty church as she arranged a myriad tiny glass tiles into the three-storey mural of Christ the King that would decorate the wall behind the bishop's throne. Bishop Rosenthal was a silver haired good looker who swanned about in his black Mercedes Benz, flashing red silk stockings and holding out a huge square diamond for us to kiss every time we saw him. Sometimes his family visited from Germany and, on one occasion, he and a niece were invited to a Lebanese family for dinner. Mrs Sahd served a dish of *kishk* (fermented yoghurt soup), a foreign taste to most people. The niece leapt from the table at the first mouthful and sounds were heard in the hall before she reached the bathroom. 'Stupid people trying to show off with our food,' my mother lectured. 'It is important to realise how different all our food is and to keep those really exotic tastes for people who know about them.'

The cathedral had a crypt where previous bishops and priests were entombed with bones visible. We went down there once or twice but it was from the choir loft, three storeys above the congregation and level with the head of Christ the King that we got the best view of Bishop Rosenthal on his throne during mass.

After the Good Friday service, when we'd kissed the feet of Jesus on the cross, acknowledged our sins and prayed for the conversion of the Jews, we went to Auntie Phyllis's house for hotcrossbuns.

Easter Sunday High Mass—altar boys who'd been drilled in swinging thuribles without scattering charcoal all over the sanctuary, mile-high beeswax candles in gold candle sticks and a resplendent choir transported us from a town in Africa to the Vatican. From on high we watched the service and dreamed of the Easter eggs and sweets we'd given up for Lent.

After mass, we stood around outside as our parents greeted and chatted for what felt like an eternity. From time to time, a short dark woman would step out of a huddle and grab a child to kiss generously and juicily. My mother had more cousins than we could count, all perfectly groomed and with large bright lips. The exception was Haseebie, who although always beautifully presented, was sedate. She lived on a wide oak-lined street, in an Edwardian stone bungalow with plenty of leadlight and woodwork. That Sunday, she wore a silver grey mantilla that matched her hair. We had watched her going to receive communion with the utmost devotion—both hands clasped in front of her chest, eyes closed, mouth open to receive the wafer. She returned to her pew with unequalled solemnity. Everyone stood back for her. She glowed with a sanctity that matched her slow quiet speech. After mass, she stayed back to pray alone. Outside, she joined the gaggle, 'Berta,' 'Haseebie'. She kissed my mother. 'Tanks God, Jesus,' and she bowed her head deeply, ' is risen after what he went through on Friday. How are you all? Please come and have breakfast tomorrow while the men are at bowls. Joan and Julie will come too.' She referred to the Chemaly sisters who ran a glamorous dress shop downtown.

So on Easter Monday morning we all went to Haseebie's home for breakfast. We stood on the veranda as she welcomed us, *'Hamdulillah la salami'* to her home, always a gentle and generous hostess. Fresh rolls tumbled from her ever-baking ovens onto the lace tablecloth set with bowls of gleaming *labne* and the blackest olives, crunchy cucumber and red tomatoes just picked from her own garden. Lush green ferns filled every corner of the room, and the mantelpiece was covered with photographs. From at least five frames—her first son who had died of leukaemia before he turned five—stared at us. 'That darling child,' my mother said as she passed her hand over each picture. 'He nearly took his mother's mind with him,' she whispered to her sister Phyllis. Only a daughter remained and she was at nursing college.

Haseebie fed us profusely. 'Breakfast, not the whole week's meals,' Phyllis laughed as she plunged her knife into another knot roll.

Haseebie spoke gently with a soft Arabic accent, 'It's lovely to have you all at my table,' and she looked long at each of us as she spoke.

'You go to so much trouble,' my mother said.

'Nothing is too much trouble for you,' she replied as she went back to the kitchen to refill the teapot or the breadbasket. For dessert, she went to the vine outside the dining room and picked fresh crystal grapes.

Whenever she left the room, my mother and the other women ran a parallel conversation discussing the tragic litany of loss Haseebie had experienced. Most recently, her husband Ross had died suddenly. 'Heart,' they whispered.

'Tsk,Tsk,' my mother shook her head. 'They were so close.'

Joan and Julie, unmarried and childless sat quietly with sad eyes.

SOME YEARS LATER, in East London, my brother and I went to town with my mother. She parked outside the old Webster's Tea Room at the top of Oxford Street. The stained glass windows of the facade masked the faded interior. Mother's high-heeled shoes clomped across the wooden floorboards. We couldn't see anyone in the gloom. My brother lunged at a packet of Golden Grain potato crisps but my mother was oblivious as she made a beeline for a table in a dark corner. Haseebie sat there, so quiet and reduced that I almost didn't notice her. Strands of what was left of her crinkly grey hair were plastered to her head, barely enough to form the familiar bun. She was fingering the rosary draped across the table, her lips moving soundlessly over the open prayer book. 'My darling Berta,' she whispered more slowly and quietly than I remembered. My mother bent over and kissed her but she put her hand up as if to repel a hug. She touched my brother's cheek and then mine with her cold, bony fingers. 'See, it took this to get me to East London to see you again. Why didn't I come before, when I was well?' She began unbuttoning her blouse, '*Shoofee* Berta (See) what they're doing to me,' and she revealed red scars and black radiotherapy tattoo lines across her breastless chest.

'Oh Haseebie,' my mother whimpered, putting a lace handkerchief to her red nose.

'I come here every afternoon for a cup of tea. It is a short stroll from the hospital. I like the noise and traffic of Oxford Street—Queenstown is so quiet.' In that tawdry tearoom I thought of her gracious home and the comforting smells of her kitchen. ' It takes five sorrowful mysteries to walk here from the hospital.' She continued, 'Tanks God, Ross has gone already; he doesn't have to see this.'

'I'll come again,' my mother promised.

We went home and tears rolled down my mother's face as she told Granny Isabel, 'How much more does one person have to suffer?'

When the treatment was over, Haseebie went home on the train and died not long after.

8

Great Aunt Eugenie's recipe for making boys

It was a weekday afternoon in the summer. I was still in junior school. My mother had surfaced from her after-lunch rest to take a phone call from Igea.

'Berta, can I comin' up?' the familiar Italian voice of her good friend came down the line.

'Sure,' my mother said. 'I'll get Katie to make us some tea.'

I knew the routine. This happened a few times a week. After her rest, my mother rearranged her hair and make-up, changed her clothes and, carrying her sewing basket, went to sit in the lounge. Granny Isabel and one or two of mother's friends, especially Igea, would be there.

My mother sat on the sofa spreading the contents of her basket out next to her. She did hems, lingerie straps and other alterations that, 'we short people have to make to clothes made for tall English women'. Granny took up her crochet and produced squares for yet another rug. I was often an unwelcome participant in those afternoon tea times and was sent off on spurious errands at every opportunity. As I passed the lower entrance to the sitting room, I'd hear the conversation hurriedly take off in hushed tones, catching the odd 'Did she?' or 'Who?'

Granny knew I eavesdropped from there and when something really spicy came up she'd call 'Ceeeceel' in a deep voice as if to flush me from my listening post. It was how I found out that my best friend Lucia's mother was 'an unusual woman', how the Queen and Brolly families swapped husbands and wives permanently, and Mrs Springs had the gin bottle brought in with her morning tea tray. The fact that all these people had daughters in my class at school burdened me with secrets I could never share with my friends.

This particular afternoon, Igea seemed to have news and I was agog.

'Berta, you bin in King William's Town again last Sunday?' Igea asked.

'Yes, it was that Kennedy girl's final profession.'

'You mean the one called Sister Jezebel?'

'Genevieve, Igea, Sister Genevieve. Jezebel was not a good girl,' my mother said.

Suddenly I piped up, 'She was dressed like a bride with a veil and flowers and her cheeks were very red. Then the nuns took her veil away and Mother Fremunda chopped off her hair with a huge pair of scissors right there in front of us.'

'Yes,' my mother said, 'her mother cried when she saw that. It was so sad.'

'And Mark kept on whispering loudly, "what a waste of a girl, she's so pretty", and he was nudging you, Mom,' I said, 'I saw him.'

My mother loved going to those profession ceremonies, she always dabbed her eyes with a lace handkerchief; we went to quite a few of them, but my dad never came along. He played bowls on a Sunday morning.

Igea continued, 'I heard, did you hear about the Netters? The divorce case is over but dey so good to zose keeds, adopting, loving like zere own.'

'Uhm, Uhm,' my mother cleared her throat intrusively.

'Cecillo, go and fetch me a reel of pink cotton from the top drawer of the chest next to my bedroom, please.'

I went down the long hall, picturing Lisa Netter and her brother John hanging on to a wire fence around some kind of run as they waited for someone to choose them. My father had told us about orphanages where children without parents waited to be taken home. Our nuns had an orphanage nearby at Izeli and once a year the children came in a bus to our school and we took them out for the day. My father wanted them all to come to our place but Sister Johanna said we could only have five.

I wondered if Lisa and John had been in Izeli.

Ordinarily I'd have rummaged around a bit in the drawers to see if anything new had been added, but I was in a hurry to hear the rest of the story and wrenched them open before slamming them shut. The Netters sang in the church choir. Mr often read from the altar while John served mass. Mrs was on the Catholic Women's League with my mother and Lisa was in the Holy Angels with me. When we were bigger and turned twelve, we'd become part of the Legion of Mary like my older sisters.

I couldn't find the pink cotton so I took a reel of red instead. Deep in contemplating the Netters, I heard my mother exclaim 'Whaaat?' as I approached the lower sitting room door. 'She never did it?' I slowed down about to call out, 'She never did what' but stopped myself in time. 'See refused. See refused him. See still a virgin, *perche* zey adopting; it was told in the court.'

'Yee, she must have had a headache for fifteen years,' my grandmother said.

I walked into the room that was suddenly quiet. 'No pink cotton,' I handed my mother the reel of red.

'Are you sure?'

'I looked in all the drawers,' I said.

'You would, you nosey parker. You leave my chest of drawers alone. Go and ask Katrina to bring in the tea tray,' my mother commanded.

I waltzed over to ring the bell behind the curtain. 'No,' she said. 'Don't do that. She'll only come and ask what we want. Go outside and tell her we are ready for tea.'

I left the room reluctantly. I knew Mother Mary was a virgin and that made her very holy. She spoke to angels because she was a virgin. Was Mrs Netter so holy? Did she speak to angels? I'd have to ask Anita, my eldest sister, about this. On the way to my bedroom, I saw my mother's chest of drawers outside her room. If I couldn't sit in the lounge, I might as well find something else to do. I knew the top drawer very well. It was packed with needles, pins, tape measures, reels of cotton and scissors of all sizes. Nothing much in there for me. The next drawer had notebooks and servants' identity documents and a black leather diary. I flicked over the soft green cover of a notebook and went to the drawer below. Belts, looked like hundreds of them, curled up tightly like garter snakes ready to jump out if one was released. Next drawer, quite good, I thought. Scarves, gloves and mantillas, real ones my mother had bought in Spain, blue, brown, white and a black one with shiny beads on the flowers. Mantillas were for church. I lifted my face and posed this way and that trying to look holy. But the thought that if I was a virgin and angels suddenly came to speak to me . . . I slammed it shut. The bottom drawer still had the same collection of gifts I'd seen last time. A few embroidered handkerchiefs, cakes of perfumed soap, bath salts, sticky tape, ribbon and paper. Nothing new. Mother hadn't replaced the lily of the valley bubble bath I'd pinched some time before. It was a pretty bottle that I'd emptied completely into the bath. I wasn't punished by my mother as God had got in before her, Anita said. I had had to sit on the bathroom floor in a bowl of lukewarm bicarb water to quell the fire that burnt for hours between my legs.

I went back to the second drawer with the notebooks. Each brown pass book that African servants carried had a photo inside the front cover. Jackson Nqandu looked out at me, not smiling but still showing his huge white teeth. His brother Alan looked as though he was being choked, his puffy face glared at me. In the black leather diary I saw a list of servants' names: Johanna Botha, Siena Harris, Rosie Khuselo. My nursemaid Rosie, there was her name. I hadn't seen or heard of her since Mother sacked her before I began school. In 1956, when I was three years old, Rosie had borrowed fifteen pounds for a funeral. It wasn't crossed out and there were no subtraction sums under it like the ones under Siena's twenty-five pounds she'd borrowed for false teeth. I wondered if that was why my mother hated Rosie. Bang. I shut it. My eye fell on the green notebook that I'd seen so often but never bothered to investigate. Its scrappy cover and dog-eared corners stuck out among all the other important looking leather-bound books. Inside, the pages were filled with lines of dates, a tick or a cross underneath each one. I flipped through but it all looked the same to me. At the back of the book there was a recipe like so many others for Mrs Bennie's biscuits or Mrs Mulholland's fruitcake.

This one was headed: Auntie Ginny —Boys. Three cups warm water, two dessertspoons bicarb. Stir well and wash thoroughly before and after. Underneath, there was a big cross next to 28 May 1953—my birthday—and below that a big tick on 19 February 1958—my brother's birthday. What was my mother cooking 'before and after'? I stared at the page so intently I didn't hear her pounding footsteps down the hall. 'What are you doing in my chest of drawers? Give me that book at once.' She snatched it away, slammed all the drawers, even the closed one and stormed back to the sitting room. 'I wondered why the tea tray never came and what you'd got up to', she shouted over her shoulder.

My face was hot. Why did she shout like that? I'd seen Rosie's name in the book in the drawer, and my birthday and my brother's. I had an interest in her books. I skulked back up the hall to look for Katrina in the kitchen but was stopped by the laughter from the sitting room. Peeping through a slit in the folding door, I saw my mother holding the green notebook as she related the initial failure of Great Aunt Eugenie's recipe for making boys.

'Oh, Berta, you so good, you so funny, but you got your second boy', Igea cackled.

'Oh Igea, Auntie Ginny promised me it would work but then I had Cecile.'

'Terrible, she was,' my granny added. '*Gibit tlet banet* (she had three girls). The *rahbet* (nuns) came downstairs to talk to her but she was very upset.'

'Oh Berta, but she's so nice, so clever, such a good cook,' Igea offered.

'Yes, but I didn't know that then. So when Mother Guntilde came down from the convent, I offered Cecile to her. I told her, "Do the blessing, Mother. I have three girls, the church should have at least one."'

'You tink the blessing work, Berta, like Auntie Ginny recipe?'

'I don't know. Mother went straight down to the nursery and did signs on her forehead, heart and feet. I was better after that.'

I felt creepy and wondered how I was supposed to be. Maybe those recipes and blessings didn't really work. My four-year-old brother and I were fighting over my dresses and he was dancing on his toes like all the girls in my ballet class.

GREAT AUNT EUGENIE, or Auntie Ginny as we called her, was my father's aunt. Her grace and gentleness was a gift to our large family. She was married to Willie Chemaly and they had three daughters. When she finally produced a son, women sought her advice. Family legend ascribes a recipe to her. Her son, Francis, a blond, blue-eyed rake, was much admired by the young women in East London in the 1940s, among them Pam Lipworth who remembers they nicknamed this snappy dresser who drove sleek cars, 'Wolf'. He was a best man at my parents' wedding. His fair looks suggested a genetic wobble. Did he carry something the Crusaders had left behind eight hundred years before? Or did he confirm the Turkish ancestry of his grandmother, Emily Azerach?

9

Summertime ~ days of feasting and fighting

In September, Mother went down to the summerhouse in the garden with all the seeds for the summer crops. Jackson and his brother Wansile showed her the empty beds that they had prepared and they discussed what to plant where. All the little brown packets of seeds from last year were put out on the table and they decided which were still good and which should be thrown away. I followed mother as she dropped each packet of seeds on the bed that would be its home.

'Peppers and eggplant need a lot of sun. Plant them here, next to the onions,' she told Jackson. As spring wore on and before the weather got too wet, Jackson would harvest the swelling onions and hang huge plaited bunches in the garage to dry. We walked around and Mother's garden shoes collected inches of thick black loam that she had to scrape off before she went back into the courtyard. My bare feet were heavy with the soil that clung to them, and the smelly manure made me squeamish. We stood together at the bottom of the steps to the kitchen, Mother wrestling with the foot scraper while I gouged at the mud on my feet with a stick. A minty smell rose as we brushed the bush that flourished in that wet corner. *Mielies* were being planted to grow as usual into a tall screen along the edge that bordered the barbeque area. The ears would be ready when the warmer weather arrived. My father loved selecting a cob, tearing it off the plant, peeling the leaves back and putting it straight onto the fire. While it grilled, he'd stroll through the beds, pick a few young peppers, carrots and radishes, wash them at the garden tap and crunch enthusiastically. He'd whip the ready cobs off the grid. '*Shoo, shoo*' he'd tumble the boiling hot cob from hand to hand, grabbing a sizzling bite in between. When he'd had a few cobs, accompanied by ice cold beers, little corn germs clustered on his stubbly chin. He licked his fingers, 'the best food on earth'. My mother looked sideways at his lip-smacking pleasure.

The summer school holidays from early December to mid-January were as one long Christmas in our home. Relatives came from all over the country to be at the coast where we lived. We had six weeks of feasting, noise, talking and crowds of excited children.

Preparations for Christmas itself began in August when my mother ordered a young turkey from the farm. It was put into its own section of the fowl run. My friend Rossy, who lived over the road, came to play most afternoons. We spent hours wandering in the back garden together. We'd creep into the fowl run and talk to the white hens, then, avoiding the bantam area because they were so cheeky, we'd sit near the turkey and wait for it to talk. It was such a large bird in comparison to the rest of the poultry that we were certain it had some special wisdom to share with us. Only when we were much older did we realise it was actually on death row.

The regular Christmas order was placed with the Greek grocer in Johannesburg. Tins of olives, tahini, burghul and fresh spices arrived by rail a few weeks later. We had to go to the goods window at the railway station to collect them. Sometimes mother went overboard with the ordering and a huge railway delivery truck pulled up outside the back gate. A man in overalls came to the back door with bits of paper to be signed. Then his assistant would wheel a trolley up the long pathway and into the scullery. Mother would phone Granny, '*Portas* order has arrived, Mom'.

The two women opened tins and bags, sniffing and tasting, inviting us children to join them. We volunteered for an olive or a few pistachio nuts but scrunched our faces and made retching expressions at the smell of the *kishk* (fermented yoghurt powder). 'So fresh,' they enthused. 'Look at the greenness of the *za'ater*' or 'How red is this summac'.

Jackson stood to one side in case he had to lift any of the heavier boxes or bags. He was never offered a taste or a sniff. He had a big knife to cut the string on the burghul sack and a tin opener to open the five kilogram tins of black olives swimming in a dark oily liquid. Looking into the open tin, I thought that if I fell into it, no one would ever see me again. It was as murky as the underground water tank in the garden where my brother Mark sometimes swam.

Granny and my mother looked like they were in heaven. Katrina kneaded dough to make fresh Lebanese bread to have with the olives and strong white cheese. The scullery maids cleared out and scrubbed the pantry. Betty washed the ceramic containers; Sarie climbed the ladder while my mother, standing below, used a long cane to point out what was to be placed where. The glass jars had all been polished and shone with their oily contents. Mother then brought her big bunch of keys and locked up the smaller containers of Turkish Delight, pistachio nuts and almonds. We peered through the wire mesh covering the cupboard doors. Later we learnt how to make a small hole in the edge, lifting out whatever it was we wanted and replacing the mesh. Many times, Mother opened tins to find the contents had been removed through the underside. In her storming fury she accused us all of being gluttons and thieves.

In October, Betty and Sarie emptied and washed the cake tins in readiness for the freshly baked Christmas cakes. Jackson stood on the pantry ladder and looped strong cables near the windows to hang the Christmas puddings. I loved making the puddings and cakes with my mother. We'd collect and boil as many silver tickeys as we could find. Mother hauled out Mrs Slade's grey bible of cooking which guided us in English foods foreign to us. I remember the consultation and research around Yorkshire pudding and the conclusion, 'That is not for us; too doughy and tasteless.'

It didn't go well with *Laban Immu* (lemony yoghurt stew) and *Mahshi Malfouf* (meat-filled cabbage leaves) also served with lemon and mint. Mrs Slade guided the washing, sorting, chopping and soaking of the Christmas cake fruit. On mixing day, after my fingernails had been cut and my arms scrubbed I plunged my arms into the mixing bath, almost to the shoulder. The dog knew I'd be spilling bits: he stood patiently drooling great saliva strands until required to clean up a splash. Katrina was in charge of the cloths for the puddings. She had boiled them and hung them out in the sun. Then she laid them on the kitchen table, blobbed the mixture on top before I pressed the money in. She drew the large bundles together, tied them up and immersed them in the turkey pot full of boiling water. After a few hours of furious boiling, the hulks were hung in the pantry to mature till Christmas. While the steam was building in the kitchen, the rest of the soaking fruit was poured into a giant bowl. Countless pounds of butter, eggs, sugar and flour were added. Between generous sloshes into the mixture, Mother covered the bottles of brandy with a towel in case Katrina was tempted.

Twenty-five cakes later, she wrote the labels. One for the nuns, one for the brothers, one for the hospital, one for this auntie and that and even one for us. Since we had two stoves, an electric one and the original Esse coal stove with four ovens, the baking was over in half a day. As they came from the oven, cups of brandy were poured this way and that. Daddy was inconsolable when told 'No, these cakes are not for us; we eat too much.' One night I saw him take a knife into the pantry, cut the heart out from the underside of one cooling on the shelf, and stuff it into his mouth.

My grandmother saw him coming from the pantry and screeched 'Yee, Joey, what you bin doin?' My mother's rage shot tongues of fire through the house, but Daddy said, 'There is nothing nicer on earth than fruit cake, just warm from the oven.'

It reminded me of their encounter over the bamboo boxes of Lebanese cakes shipped to us by a cousin in Beirut. Piles of sticky nut pastry oozing syrup shone in the dim light of the pantry. We all snuck in quietly to poke our fingers deep into those sweet snacks, imagining no one else knew. One Sunday afternoon, my father was at it in the pantry when he heard my granny shuffling her Chinese slippers into the kitchen. Provocatively he tossed a giant *Borma* cake, all glistening syrup packed with pistachio nuts, high into the air to be caught in Askim's slobbering jaws. Granny shrieked, ' Yee, Joey, *shoo am tamil halla?* (What are you doing now?)'.

'Nothing, you old cow,' he muttered under his breath. My father always told us of his hardworking, suffering mother and in the same breath referred to my mother's mother, Granny Isabel, as an old bag.

Summer holidays arrived when school term ended. My father came into his own, closing his office and spending early mornings taking us swimming and walking on the deserted beach. We bodysurfed in the waves and he came out looking confused, reaching out saying, 'Where are you, my darling? Is that you Mark?' knowing full well it was one of the girls. He could hardly see a thing without his glasses and joked with us about his 'blindness'.

We watched him doing all sorts of arm and leg swings and squats accompanied by voluntary and involuntary sound effects. He showed us how to do deep breathing then punched the air around him, probably remembering his boxing days at university. His exuberance and *joie de vivre* washed over everyone; even at dawn he'd have us singing along with him or reciting Wordsworth or Shakespeare.

Leaving the beach, we imitated the vigorous way he dried himself, and raced to the car. Sometimes, hunger overtook him on the way home so we had to stop at the cafe in the produce market for a meat pie. We loved that, all the more because my mother was so disgusted with our taste for 'minced horse or cat or whatever else they put into that brown sludge.'

In mid-afternoon, surfacing from his siesta, Daddy pranced on tiptoes up the long hallway past the bedrooms singing, 'We are dainty dancing fairies'. We'd follow him to the veranda where he told interminable stories that contained villains and angels. He had his favourites, and I say his, because in retrospect, he seemed to enjoy story-time as much—if not more—than we children. There was Mahlouf the tiger with giant claws, who climbed onto the rooftops to avoid the rising river of human blood his savagery had caused, and the wicked queen who bit off children's heads, adding to the river of blood. But he always ended every session with Charlotte and the fairy queen who sprinkled gold dust on her pillow to make her wishes come true, keep her safe and give her sweet dreams. As the grandchildren arrived, we saw him re-enact the same stories full of the original gruesome and loving characters.

At sunset he would take us back to the beach to walk quietly along the wide rock shelf and paddle in the rock pools. Anemones waved their tentacles and closed around our fingers. Prickly green sea urchins clustered next to mussels and periwinkles. Tiny fish darted through the colourful jungle of seaweed fronds. Hermit crabs scuttled across the shelf like women in high heels with big hats at a horse race. My mother laboriously pushed her sore feet along in the soft sand in an attempt to strengthen and improve her dropped arches. We never swam after sunset when sharks came foraging close inshore in those subtropical waters.

As Christmas approached, uncles and aunts arrived from the interior of the country. Our extended family of cousins, inhabited towns and *dorps* (small towns) with names like Indwe, Dewetsdorp, Dordrecht, Graaff Reinet, Odendaalsrus, Kroonstad, in the deep heart of Afrikaner Africa where they were somewhat marginalized but to a much lesser extent than the original family had been at the turn of the century. When we got together, however, the comforting heart of our identity was awakened. We gathered around those heroes—doctors, lawyers and other educated members of our family—and felt ourselves to be validly established in the wider society. Although we no longer needed to be invisible—being in school and having our parents in business, and all speaking with South African accents—we continued to gather to affirm who we were, where we came from and what we believed. Our common genetic heritage was evident not only in our physiognomy, but most obviously to an outsider, in our interactions. We were said to be loud, we were enthusiastically alive and we posed a serious challenge to what we jokingly called 'Jewish Geography', referring to the convoluted interconnectedness where a couple of brothers might have been married to a couple of sisters. The family had a network and most were able to read a connection straightaway: for example, Auntie Ginny's sister-in-law married her brother Michael. In short, everybody knew everybody else and sometimes, their business as well. For some who were learning the ways of the new world and growing a teensy bit of reserve, this became embarrassing and tensions arose.

The wider East London family (including my mother's brothers) accommodated as many cousins as they could in their homes, while their parents stayed in beachfront hotels. My mother had particular facial expressions, like pursing her lips tightly or rolling her eyes when certain members of the family on my father's side were mentioned. Someone was 'worse than any mother-in-law'. Another was, 'a spoilt princess in her

Johannesburg frocks' and someone else was 'a devil with money—he has more than anyone in the family and nobody knows where he gets it from'. When Granny had been up north, she saw 'houses with nine carat gold bathroom fittings, two-storey-high crystal chandeliers, Italian marble floors and European grand pianos'.

My mother and my older sister Anita, faced with all the visitors, were in a panic over their summer wardrobes. They paraded in 'appros' from Garlicks in front of the long mirror, looking at each outfit in the eyes of this or that aunt or cousin.

'Now we must be careful not to look like Auntie Josephine and Selma who bedeck themselves as if for an audience with the queen, overdressed and painted. Remember the engagement party last year when they sat like royalty and spoke to no one.'

Michele and I lay on my parents' bed watching, while Granny hovered with a tin of pins and the tape measure.

'That's too severe,' my mother said to Anita. 'You'll look like Auntie Mary—a man dressed up as a woman; remember to take care with the eyebrow pencil.'

Discussing the vast numbers of shining bangles and gleaming rings the visitors wore, I heard Granny say: 'They live so close to the gold and diamond mines, they must get them cheaply.'

'Knees, ugly knees; can you lengthen this one, Mom?' and Granny would get down on the floor, unpick a little hem, put pins in and examine the effect.

If it was a long session, Mother rang the bell next to her bed. The board in the kitchen with all its little windows indicated where the summons was coming from. Katrina appeared to take the order for a tray of tea.

They went to the hairdressers daily to repair the ravages of sea and sun. My mother talked to my sisters about whose hair was dyed too black, whose was too red and whose was too long, as if our visitors were walking examples of do's and don'ts.

We children watched the pouting and raised voices that went with certain conversations. 'No, no, you've got it wrong,' my mother said. 'We Lebanese have got flat heads and our hairdressers must be careful of the way they cut around the crown.'

'What rubbish!' someone else snarled. 'Speak for yourself. My head's not flat at the back'.

My mother was adamant, addressing my father's sister, 'You Yazbeks have got Turkish blood: look at those blue eyes and flattened heads.'

Then someone rose indignantly and stormed to the kitchen to 'get a glass of water'.

'Just ring the bell'.

'No, I'm hot in here.'

Perfectly manicured hands and polished fingernails were used as pointers to the maids, who ran themselves ragged doing mountains of washing and hanging out fifteen or twenty beach towels at a time.

When mother's deaf cousins came from the Karoo, we watched fascinated as she signed in a mixture of English and phonetic Arabic. They had all grown up together in Queenstown and mother was an expert in sign language. When Johnny Chemaly became blind as well as deaf, mother took his hand and 'wrote' on his palm. He replied in a slurring nasally monotone.

Mother told us, 'Listen carefully, and you will understand.'

When our cousin Barbie who had Down syndrome was difficult, we copied Mother's way. We didn't hold back; rather, we pulled her along, coaxing her to play with us. Eventually she'd take herself by the hand saying 'come Barbie,' and follow. She was my age and we included her in everything despite her bowed head and arthritic, stubby fingers. She spoke to no one except herself, echoing whatever she heard going on around her. 'Look Barbie, John's naughty. Woo woo—he's going to get a hiding.'

Anita and Michele and some of the boy cousins rested upstairs in the afternoon, told jokes, drank beers from under the bed and smoked cigarettes out the window. When I lit up in front of them they slapped me. I ran back to my smoking hideaway in the fowl run. A few my age tried to puff with me, but they coughed so much, I thought they'd get us found out, so I smoked only with those who could hold their breath. I never let Barbie smoke: her parents would have killed me.

Before we'd experienced the shame of Catholic confession, we hid in the closets and showed one another our developing bits, allowing exploratory fingers and curious eyes to roam and prod. The laundry maid found us as she was packing away the washing.

She clapped her hand to her mouth 'Haa, what are you doing now? I will tell madam.'

'Go,' someone said, 'we dare you, she won't believe you; so wa wa and twenty-four, shut your mouth and say no more'.

'We aren't allowed to talk to our maids like that.' I said.

'Why not? She's just an *ousie* (African woman). She hasn't been to school.'

'Don't be cheeky to her.'

' That's why my dad says you people are *kaffir boeties*'

'My mother will kill your dad for saying that.'

True, the arguments raged back and forth as my liberal family met some of the less tolerant attitudes head-on. As the years went by and the rift widened, we were even called communists. But at the end of the day, we were all just family.

MY MOTHER'S MOTHER, Granny Isabel, had specific demands regarding adherence to recipes—her recipes. Dishes were described disparagingly or otherwise, depending on their origin and whether a Beirut or a mountain village recipe was followed. Granny had no time for any variation in the spicing or herbs added to particular dishes.

Having had it drummed into our heads to 'eat up, eat up, there are starving children just down the road,' we were shocked one day to see Granny scraping her plate emphatically into the fowl-food bucket. One of my aunts had done something 'Mexican' with poultry and when Granny tasted it she declared it to be 'rubbish, not food'.

As the numbers grew, my mother noted with relief that some cousins would be spending the day with the other side of their family. A brother of one of my aunts had fourteen children, so from their house alone, twenty-one could arrive for lunch. Granny and my mother planned the Christmas Day menu. Others added what they felt good at but pork was completely taboo until my older brother and sisters married Hollanders and it was allowed on the grounds that it was their traditional food. But my mother kept as far away from it as she could and said ' *Sies*' through clenched teeth when anyone mentioned it.

We always had hand-rolled vine leaves, hundreds, boiled in two large pots. On warm spring afternoons, after Granny had had her rest, I strolled with her to the grapevines. We'd pull the long tendrils of new growth toward us and pick the third leaf, if it wasn't too small, and on to the sixth from the tip. If the November winds had already arrived, we had to stop at number five as the next ones would be too tough. Granny talked all the time in a mixture of Arabic and English, '*hayda, la*—not that, this one' selecting the most suitable and discarding the tough ones. The day the leaves were to be done, Granny took the little parcels out of the fridge. Chopping boards were laid out on the table with the giant dish of minced lamb, rice and spices in the middle. The fresh leaves were blanched in boiling water and my job was to separate them, hang them over the side of the dish to drain, then pass them around.

Mother and Granny talked non-stop about who had arrived, who was yet to come, the suitcase full of money someone had forgotten in the study.

'Whose is it?' I ventured.

'Shut up.'

'So much money, they could have been robbed.'

'Where? What money?'

I persisted, 'I saw it, the snakeskin suitcase with all the green money.'

Finally my mother laid down, 'It's gone, and it never was there, anyway.'

As the pile of rolled leaves grew my mother's face got more red.

'Ooft, sometimes I think we should all stay in our own homes for Christmas, each with his own family.'

As cook, Katrina had been taught the authentic recipe for the turkey stuffing—minced lamb, onion, rice and spices. She threaded the string onto a long mattress needle and stitched the cavity closed, binding legs and wings to stop them from falling off as it boiled for hours with whole onions, red wine and spices in its own special cauldron.

I remember the time we hosted the Christmas feast for the whole family at our home. It was also the last time we raised our own turkey. On a hot afternoon I met my father down the back garden walking toward the fowl run. 'Go inside, lock up Askim and you can all watch from the bedroom window.'

'Watch what?'

'Don't ask, just follow the big girls.'

So I went to their bedroom and stood at the window with its view over the lawn and beyond. Then I saw Jackson coming up the garden with the shiny black turkey under his arm. Its legs were tied together and he tied it down on the lawn. My father stood back and took aim with his revolver. My eldest sister burst out screaming, 'Stop! Stop!' and raced outside to retrieve her cat which was sauntering toward the tethered bird.

We resumed our positions at the window, my sister's arm and cheek bleeding from her struggle with the cat. My father cursed loudly. I saw Jackson turn his face away grinning, and coyly clasp his hands behind his back; the gun was jammed. Gruesomely, Daddy picked up the axe, stunned the turkey with it and then chopped off its head. We watched the pile of shiny black feathers writhe and gyrate. Then Jackson picked up the bleeding headless corpse and took it to the courtyard to be prepared for the pot. 'Poor thing' my mother said. No one told me that that was the bird Rossy and I had been sitting with day after day. Even after we'd eaten it and it was no longer in the fowl run, I didn't make the connection.

Preparations continued in the heat and oppressive humidity. Seven women worked in the kitchen, cutting and chopping, washing and clearing. My brother Paul was on Betty's back and Mary had her own baby tied on. Katrina visited her bedroom frequently as if to escape the heat and the clatter. When she took the roasting pan from the oven to turn the meat over and a leg of lamb skidded across the kitchen, my mother burst into tears and rushed to tell my father 'Oh hell, darling, she's at the bottle again, we should never have set the drinks table so early.'

Auntie Elaine arrived at the back door, walking all the way through the kitchen calling, 'Hello. Happy Christmas, where is everyone?' My father ushered everyone onto the veranda. By one o'clock, almost fifty people chatted, had drinks and embraced those they hadn't seen all year.

Auntie Elaine went into the music room next to the veranda, sat down at the piano and in her rich contralto sang *Coming Home* and *Macushla*. Uncle Charlie then sang Italian arias. When one of my cousins took her turn singing American spirituals, adults glared and slapped children holding index fingers to pursed lips. Granny went into the kitchen to check on the preparations and scuttled out looking sheepish as the by then thoroughly uninhibited Katrina told her to '*Voetsek*'.

We moved in a chattering mass from the house to the side garden and up to the top lawn where the long row of tables was laid under the trees. My father's voice boomed from the top of the table, 'In the name of the father...' to my mother at the far end. Grace was followed by a brief moment of silence, a speech of welcome to all, especially those who had travelled. Eyes were dabbed for absent friends. Those dead, too sick or too far away to be there were all named.

The maids brought out the food on huge trays. Jackson stirred the embers on the barbeque and my father roasted his fresh *mielies*. Empty bottles filled the trays going back to the kitchen. We ate heartily over some hours. I ate so much *babbaganouje* that my mother told me I was digging my grave with my teeth.

Toward the end of the main meal, while the maids cleared away and prepared the Christmas puddings, my father took out his ukelele and sang, 'Nobody loves me, everybody hates me, I'm gonna eat some worms'. We children clustered round him grimacing our disgust. The adults had all lit up cigarettes and were quiet for the first time. Daddy played on into a song about how sipping cider through a straw can accidentally get you a mother-in-law. He looked across at Granny and she waved a 'go-away' at him. The mood was quieter, even pensive, over Turkish coffee, conversation punctuated by the sound of roasted pumpkin seeds being cracked between the teeth.

People started to drift off at about six o'clock. Families passed through the kitchen taking their empty bowls and pots with them. My mother whispered something to Katrina, who was half asleep on the bench in the courtyard. She swore loudly in reply but heaved herself back into the kitchen to finish clearing up. 'Yessus, white people are greedy. I have to go back and stand in the kitchen to guard the left overs,' she complained.

During December we doubled up happily, but after a few weeks we wanted our space back. Tetchiness grew into tearful explosions at the slightest thing. 'The days of feasting and fighting are here' my mother said, swallowing another Bacon's headache powder.

One morning I woke covered in red spots. I had a terrible headache. I went through to my mother's bathroom to look in the mirror.

'Measles,' she said. 'I think you've got measles.'

By the next day I was worse and I had a high fever.

'I'll have to call Dudley,' my mother said, referring to our GP. He arrived about midday, walked into my room and sat down on the bed to open his bag. Next minute, my mother lay down on the spare bed and said, 'Oh Dudley, I've got pains in my chest. Can you listen to my heart please?' He glanced across and carried on examining me. When my mother related how Dudley had to examine her too because of chest pains, my aunts rolled their eyes and laughed. 'Not again, Bertha, you're so nervy', one of them said referring to the last time Paul was sick and she'd done the same thing.

Sometimes, we'd go down to the harbour on a Sunday and watch the cranes loading open pallets of gold bars into the hold of the Union Castle mail boat. Two railways policemen with revolvers in their holsters stood guard. Eventually, under pressure from my mother, my father booked Christmas cruises to Durban and back on those luxurious ships. We'd board on about the twenty-third of December, sail to Durban, have an English-style Christmas in port there and sail back a few days later. Usually we arrived back when the fuss had died down and some relatives had even gone home. My mother was more peaceful and the holidays continued more quietly.

THE TRIPS TO Durban had a different kind of excitement. It was a subtropical Indian Ocean port city with a varied population speaking languages not heard in our part of the world. It was there when I heard a rickshaw puller speaking Zulu that I recognised its similarity to Xhosa and sometimes even ventured a little conversation. My father spoke some Sesotho and engaged in nostalgic reminiscences about the totally different grass plains of the Orange Free State where he was born.

We visited the Indian market where my mother discussed the relative merits of 'mother-in-law's tongue' or 'devil's dance' curry powder before purchasing some for Cook. She even managed a short lecture on the social evils of garlic. The storekeepers just smiled wryly back at her.

One summer holiday we could not run away. It was in the early 1960s and my father's first cousin, Madeleine, and her husband, Jean Arsan, were coming to visit from Beirut. She was a glamorous Lebanese matron and he worked for Alitalia at Beirut International airport. They had three children. The eldest, Joseph, was my age, then Antoine, and finally, little Madelaine or Mimi, as they called her. First, they spent time in Kroonstad, in the north of the country, with my father's brother Victor and family. Then they came by train, to us at the coast. For them it was a mammoth trip and Madeleine wept all the way; in the time it took, they could have travelled from Beirut to Moscow! My mother rustled up Great Aunt Eugenie and the three of us went to the railway station to meet two, short Middle Eastern looking people, bubbling Arabic sounds on the platform. East London was not used to such obvious foreigners. Everyone, porters included, stared as we bundled them into the car and drove home. The week of their stay was filled with large family parties, *meza* and long breakfasts.

I watched Madeleine turn her long black hair into ringlets and emerge daily looking like a Parisian model. She pinched my cheek a thousand times with her red fingernails and said '*shoo hilwe* (how beautiful)', but next to her, we all felt colourless and dowdy. Their visit increased my mother's visits to Garlicks.

As a result of this visit, my parents then went on a trip to Lebanon with Auntie Elaine. First they went to Rome, to mass in St Peters hoping to catch sight of the Pope, holding rosaries and cards aloft for blessing. In Beirut they visited the homes where their parents and grandparents had been born and in front of stone doorways, they wept the same tears of the exiles they'd grown up with in Africa. The slides of their trip described the culture we came from: when they arrived, the twenty-one gun salute by the Beirut police force at the airport; my father kissing the whole row of medalled and braided officers and overdoing it as usual, by extending a kiss to the customs officer who coolly stepped back to indicate the *faux pas*; my father's uncles Philippe and Ayoub, the latter in red *tarboosh*—an Ottoman honorific; hordes of first cousins that looked like us. This memory always fills my mother with chagrin as she retells of the pitiful 'reception' we gave them on the East London railway station.

When my parents returned to South Africa, I took up correspondence with my cousin Joseph. He was a medical student at the American University in Beirut. We communicated for eleven years. In the last letter I received from him, the cousins had joined a militia during the civil war and gave a long description of how the Virgin Mary had appeared in a vision. She had instructed them how and where to lay the booby trap. They were able to kill twenty-three 'of the enemy' at once. God was with them and their platoon. As a pacifist and in the South African context, I found this horrifying.

OUR LEBANESE IDENTITY is expressed in our interactions as well as our food. For some, there was—and still is—the strong community around the Maronite Catholic Churches in Johannesburg. Generally, however, we spoke remnants of Arabic language in a culture that marginalized our ancestors. But because of our looks the question continued to arise, 'Where are you from?' In questioning my mother and grandmother about their early days in South Africa, it was the gaps in the stories that caught my attention. I sought the memories they had concealed, even from themselves. It is this lack of an historical identity that afflicted members of succeeding generations, myself included, with a cultural dissonance in the South African context. It also facilitated the shift by some into an over-emphasis on material possessions and cosmetic beauty because those were areas where they had commonality with the wider society and where they no longer felt so different.

10

Dorps and cities – frontiers of identity

When my cousin Antoinette and I were eleven-years-old, we went to spend a holiday with Auntie Victoria. Auntie Victoria, my father's middle sister, had married Nompie Chemaly and they went to live in the small Orange Free State village Jagersfontein where they owned trading stores. In 1871, Jagersfontein developed around diamond mines, where some of the largest natural diamonds were found. When we visited there, the mine was long closed and it was reduced to a dorp with about thirty houses for whites and an impoverished township for Africans, with a few essential shops. Uncle had the grocer and Auntie ran the corner shop right next to their home. Their son, Norman, had a trading store in the township, where he sold blankets, paraffin, candles and other necessities to the African customers.

The Dominee (church minister) would come into Auntie's shop, '*Môre Dominee. Hoe kharra met u?*' She'd play an Arabic pun to make it sound as though she was interested in the functioning of his bowels. Auntie wore chunky rings on her fingers that always held a lighted cigarette.

We stayed with our cousin Norman and his Afrikaans wife, Mariaan, in their tiny two-bedroom cottage just near Auntie's home. It was the first time that we had had to use a long-drop toilet with smells and flies that held us back almost until we returned home. Norman and Mariaan had been childhood sweethearts, marrying the year before, when she was seventeen, five or six years older than us. An Afrikaner in the family was a new experience for us.

We spoke to her in a mixture of English and Afrikaans. In the mornings, she'd bring us cups of coffee heavy with condensed milk as we squashed up in the single bed we shared. Frost lay white on the unmade footpath and the window was misted from our warm breath. We snuggled together barely able to breathe under the weight of seven blankets as we tried to keep warm. Mariaan stuck her feet in under the covers with us and lit a cigarette for me as well. Her long black dyed hair snaked around the white skin of her throat. Thick winter pyjamas covering her skinny body almost hid her tiny breasts. She rubbed our backs for us and fiddled with our hair. She was like a gentle older sister. She had five younger brothers and sisters and they all loved her.

'When are you going to have a baby?' I asked her.

She sighed and slumped. 'Maybe *die Here* (the Lord) knows.'

She looked so sad while Antoinette was giving me donkey bites on my leg with her strong toes.

During the day we wandered the unmade roads of the dorp looking in shop windows.

'Look at that skinny model with the black hair. Looks like Mariaan,' I giggled.

'*Ja,*' Antoinette agreed. ' My ma says she's thin like that because she's got diabetes. That's why she can't have kids. You can't ask her about that.'

'I didn't know.'

'*Ja*. And she has to have an injection every day.'

'How d'you know? I'm going to ask her to show me.'

'You can't do that. My mother told me she gives it to herself in her leg and we're not supposed to know.'

'That's what I like about your mother,' I said to Antoinette, 'she always tells us the truth about things.'

We visited Auntie in the general store. She leaned over the counter, her strong arms supporting her ample breasts.

'*Ja,* hello you two. Where are you off to now?'

'Just having a walk, Auntie.'

'How many cigarettes have you still got, Cecile?' Before I could answer, she produced a packet of Van Rijn, 'Here, in case you run out. Share them with Mariaan, hey?' She thrust a handful of Chappies bubblegum Antoinette's way. 'You're not such a smoker, like the rest of us. Want some chocolates too?' Before she could reply, Auntie gave her a bundle of Chox bars. We left the shop huddled over our bounty.

'Thanks Auntie, see you later.'

'And don't forget you are all coming to eat with me tonight.'

'*Ja*, Auntie. See you at five.'

We strolled over the common where clumps of arum lilies—pig-lilies in Afrikaans—flowered. We crossed a little wooden walkway over a stream, followed its course for a few yards till we heard the sound of a cow bellowing loudly coming from an old wooden shed just ahead of us. Inside we found a young farmhand standing next to a wet and shiny beast, the size of a hippopotamus. We saw a *derem* (intestine) hanging from the cow's bottom and dragging on the ground. Sticky brown liquid ran down into a pool between its back legs. I was mystified and the farmhand looked at us sideways. He had a long stick and poked the animal from time to time, 'Come, come,' he said in Afrikaans.

'What you doing?' I asked him. He stared back at me as if he didn't understand.

'He can't speak English,' Antoinette said. So I tried again in Afrikaans and he frowned at me but still didn't answer.

'So there you are,' Cousin Norman grabbed us. 'Off home with you. That's too rude for girls like you to see.'

'What?' I asked.

'Never mind,' he said

I lost interest. Guts and blood might be rude in Jagersfontein, but for me it was just disgusting.

'The cow is having a baby,' Antoinette announced.

'Oh good. Let's go and see,' I rushed.

'Oh no you don't,' Norman insisted.

'But we saw it already,' Antoinette intoned.

'Well you're not seeing anymore,' and he pushed us past the gate into Auntie's house.

They were all in the sitting room, the paraffin heater blazing with a black enamel kettle whistling on top. Uncle and Auntie each had a huge glass of whisky while the rest of us drank coke.

'Hello *liefling* (darling)', Norman greeted Mariaan stroking her neck and giving her such a long kiss I thought they were trying to make babies right there. She wound herself around him and they sat holding hands right next to me. Norman's sister, Veronica, smiled at us through the gap in her front teeth from a life-size photo on the wall. She had curly hair, dark eyebrows and wore big hoop earrings. Auntie Susie called her 'Mrs Bandaranaike' and we liked that because it meant someone else had a funny name like ours that no one could spell or pronounce. Next to that was a wedding photo of Norman and Mariaan kissing. It made me shy to look at for too long.

We followed Auntie to the small kitchen at the back of the house. A bowl of chops and chips sat on the big black wood stove. She dished up for us and we helped ourselves to salad. She looked often at our plates, 'Eat enough. Norman and Mariaan can only give you Marie biscuits if you're hungry in the night.' Uncle Joe and Auntie Susie picked us up the next day and drove us home to East London.

A year after our visit to them, Mariaan had the first of her babies. But she died quite young as a result of the diabetes.

IN 1965, MY father, mother, sister Michele, brother Paul and I went on a holiday to Cape Town. One morning, in Truworths in Strand Street, my mother bought a dress, a light colour, was it cream? The short, dark-haired woman who served my mother said, 'It looks good with your colouring, very suitable for *Yom Tov*.' Outside on the street, clutching the dress among all the other packages, my mother remarked that she'd never met a Jewish shop assistant before.

Returning laden with purchases to our holiday flat in Sea Point, we jumped on board a foreshore bus and threw ourselves into seats as the vehicle lurched about.

Suddenly the woman in front of us, also short and dark, turned around to my mother, 'Been shopping for *Yom Tov*?' My mother looked quizzical and the question was repeated.

'No,' she replied, 'just shopping. We're not Jewish.'

'You are,' she insisted.

Quietly my mother said, 'We're not.'

The outraged woman pointed to the cross around my mother's neck, 'I know your sort, masquerading as *goyim* (non-Jews).'

'What are you talking about?'

'Scared, so you're wearing a cross.' Then she stood up, leaned over us and shook her finger, 'It's Jews like you, trying to hide, but we'll always find you.'

I looked at the woman and was afraid. Then I thought, *she's mad; doesn't she know that we drink Turkish coffee, eat za'ater and have Christmas?*

The memory faded into the streets of Sea Point that I knew so well. Hairdressers who, in the days of very short styles, cut my hair to within an inch of its life, Italian ice cream shops and the café that we snuck into one lunch time while my father was doing business in the city. My mother and I shared an enormous Greek salad full of feta cheese and giant kalamata olives.

My father got back to the flat before us and when we walked in he was furious. 'Wasting bloody money eating out,' he scolded. But I remember my mother enthusing over the cheese, olives and very red tomatoes. My father could be such a spoilsport when we did things without him.

THE MEMORY OF this Cape Town holiday unfolded recently after a Sunday bagel evening at a friend's home in Sydney. I became convinced I'd met my friend's mother, Eva before. She sat quietly; her well made-up pale face and dyed coiffure rang a faint bell in my memory.

In a clipped South African manner she said, 'I'm from Norvalspont.'

'Norvalspont,' we echoed. 'We've been there, a one-horse dorp near the huge Hendrik Verwoerd Dam. You must have been the only Jews there. Etienne Leroux wrote a story that featured *Die Lesbiese Gifmoordenaares van Norvalspont* (The Lesbian Poison Murderess of Norvalspont).'

The room giggled while Eva's bosom shook with amusement that eventually left her body in a delicious laugh. 'Oh, is that so?' she said.

'We passed through on one of our trips to family on the farm but saw no murderesses or lesbians.'

In my mind's eye, I saw a landscape murdered by the searing Karoo sun: brown hills and flats pocked with rocks exuding relentless heat; drought-stalked thorny scrub poking through bleached skeletons. From that desert, blossoming Eva had inched her way to Cape Town until eventually she found herself on another continent, Australia, in a lushness she'd never imagined.

I went home with the mystery of where I could have seen Eva before. In the middle of the night, after I'd gone to bed, the dream picture came to me. She was the shop assistant in Truworths in Cape Town who sold my mother the dress 'for Yom Tov' in 1965. Thirty-five years later that chunk of frozen memory containing a vocal seeker of lapsed believers and a kindly saleslady thawed to reveal its contents to me and water my quest for identity. Silently, I thanked that angry woman on the bus who frightened me all those years ago. Because of her, I stored the memory of the day Eva sold the frock to my mother, and realised that in our small world, we are sometimes gifted with comforting friendships that take years to register.

Not long after the bagel afternoon in Sydney, Eva's husband died. We gathered in the Jewish cemetery in North Ryde. Eva, following custom, picked up a shovel and dropped clods onto the coffin in the grave. It was a sound that I doubt any beloved could ever forget. Names on the gravestones of wandering Jews from Galicia in Romania, Lodz in Poland or Ploemyan in Lithuania, who ended up under the ground in North Ryde. I wished that on top of their allotted span, they could have lived all the years they'd lost behind European barbed wire. I looked at us: once we were strangers, Jews, *Goyim*, Lebanese in the divided margins of South African society, *Land'smener* now united in Australia.

THE QUESTION OF our looks and identity pervades my memory of growing up in an apparently Anglo town like East London. Of course there were all sorts of people around us, but to the mainstream, they were often not as visible or important. After the incident with the Jewish woman on the bus in Cape Town, we made jokes about our Semitic noses and how we experienced the best and the worst of those worlds of otherness.

Every year we received Rosh Hashana cards and then a couple of months later, Christmas cards. None of this bothered any of us. But when troubles erupted in the Middle East, I detected concern and sadness in my parents. My mother regularly wrapped giant parcels of clothing and fur coats which she sent to cousins in Lebanon, who became personally known to us only later, after mutual visits.

The 1967 Six-Day War was a painful time. That summer, in East London on the Orient Beach with our cousins from the Free State, local Jewish people staked their sun-baking space with Israeli flags. We had been brought up to be suspicious of all flags and flag-wavers. When we were given flags at school for Republic Day, my parents both said, '*Kharra djaj*, it's all *kharra djaj* (bullshit).' On the beach, my mother sat tight-lipped. We felt awkward.

IT WAS WHEN we went for our school uniform update that things became clearer. Mendy Liebowitz and his wife ran Suburban Supply Store, the school uniform shop, halfway up Devereux Avenue. Their eldest daughter, Maureen, was in school with us and filled our Christmas concerts with her soprano rendition of *Oh Holy Night*. Her father was a passionate musician and sometimes conducted the school orchestra. Whenever we went in to the shop, my mother loved to banter with Mendy and joke about Sister Cletus and her contralto voice. Mrs was quieter, although she sometimes added a comment. She wore a wig and my mother thought it was because she wasn't very stylish. We later found out that it was because they were Orthodox Jews.

It was a few months after the war had ended when we went in, as usual, for our uniforms. Michele, Paul and I needed a whole range. It was a tragic time for the Liebowitz family. Their older son Harold had volunteered in the Six-Day War and was killed driving an ambulance in the Golan Heights. My mother attempted to offer her condolences. Mendy was quiet and just sort of nodded, but Mrs turned away to the back without saying anything. Perhaps she was overwhelmed by pain, but my mother was upset. She paid him and he handed over the parcels. As we moved to leave the shop, my mother turned around and in a loud voice said, 'Mendy, we have all known one another for a long time. I want you and your wife to know that my family is not at war with your family. We all live here and if we spread this conflict to the world beyond, there can be no peace. We have to be larger than these endless wars.'

Back home and my mother told my father in heated terms about 'this bloody war and people's triumphalism and people's grief' and a whole lot more. 'Our children knew nothing about hate until this moment,' she fumed. 'Those poor people will never get over the loss of their son, and for what?'

FROM EARLY ON, perhaps when I was ten, I ran errands in my father's office. I snooped all over and dug files out of the archives in the dusty back office. It was there that I first saw Queen Victoria's seal and the signature of Sir George Grey, the colonial secretary on title deeds of land awarded to local chiefs after the nineteenth century Frontier Wars. I went to ask my father what it all meant and his reply was, 'The Queen of England didn't realise that these people had been on this land and owned it for hundreds of years. She thought she was giving them a gift.' In fact the effect of her land grants was that Xhosa chiefs were given much reduced parcels of land and white encroachment continued unhindered.

When I passed standard six and was just thirteen, my father allowed me to learn the office switchboard. Nancy Pretorius, the operator, taught me patiently to master countless extensions and nine incoming lines. She had been born with a hole in the heart but, as a Jehovah's Witness, she was not allowed to have surgery that would have entailed a blood transfusion. All her fingernails were enlarged and purple, and although only thirty-five, she was soon to die of heart failure.

One day while Nancy took a break, I ran the system and accidentally cut my brother off. His office door flew open and he exploded from there into the reception area, jumped clean over the counter and lunged at me. I stared at him as he fulminated, eyes popping, Adam's apple leaping up and down like a mad piston. I didn't hear what he said as I slipped out under him and went to the bathroom. The other front office staff must have told Auntie Susie. She opened the door and stood close to me patting my back, 'It's all right darling, we all make mistakes. Markie's just got a bit of a temper. Don't let him upset you so much otherwise you won't be able to work here.'

I needed the work. Every Saturday, my father paid me five rand and I went to Mrs Winnet at the Strand Bookshop next door to order a book I'd read about or seen. My mother had organised for Mr Pepper, the man from church who'd constructed our large nativity scene, to make a bookcase for my bedroom, as the one shelf I had was already full.

11

Meneer and Mevrou on the taal farm

The line of them is long. They tread
on my heart. They walk through my bones.
Their feet pass through my ribs. My head
is as air to them. They walk on stones
beneath me and their limbs are slick with rain.
It is the rain that sent them and their tread
comes on and on. They carry sticks and pain,
skins and bones, and they, the living dead,
walk through my heart. They tread on it as though
I were not there. They are not here for me
but for the fire from the cave, below
the aeons of dust - below, where it burns free
of change. This is why they come. They go
through my heart to the ash hearth below.

Ancestors at Wonderwerk
Mike Cope

Wonderwerk is a cave near Kuruman that has been continuously inhabited for a million years.

I can imagine that when I was born, the first unfiltered voice I heard was saying, '*Gut, Gut, eine schone Tochter* (Good, a beautiful daughter,)' as German Sister Jadwiga held me up for my mother to see.

Maybe before I was born, my mother and grandmother's Arabic conversation came to me underwater, 'Berta *ajerken*... Berta if you have another girl...' or maybe, 'try something that hides the tummy a bit more.'

Or then it could've been Sara, in Afrikaans, '*Medem, wil Medem hê*... Would Madam like me to dry Madam's feet,' after she'd washed my mother's back in the bath as I'd seen her do before my youngest brother was born.

I imagined being carried in my watery hammock around the garden. Beside the rockery, I might have heard Jackson in Xhosa, '*Gomso, Wansile*... Tomorrow Wansile is coming to help me shift these big rocks and plant the proteas.' Inside the house, my father, stroking my mother's back, 'Darl, you look beautiful with that new hairdo,' in plain English.

I wander around the garden of languages of my early days. I pick memory upon memory to arrange on the page. Words come in short sentences, the voices speaking their original languages. The sounds breathe in my mind and I can't answer the question: What language did I hear first? Did Granny say, '*T'i breenie* (bury me)' when I was born or did my mother weep as she birthed a third girl instead of the son she wished for? Tears and laughter common to all language ring in my memory and are as essential to an infant as the many other shaped sounds.

Language and life in South Africa were accompanied by signs particular to place and time. Xhosa and Zulu were spoken by the most menial workers. Afrikaans was spoken by brown people who had minor status and whites who were often policemen, public servants or in the positions of authority that state legislation reserved for them. We all had to attend a school of our first language. Therefore I had no Afrikaans friends. Arabic of course was never to be spoken in public if one wanted to be accepted. My mother berated my grandmother repeatedly when they attended functions at our school, 'Speak English,' hard nudge, 'Speak English!' But Granny lapsed frequently as she enjoyed commenting about Mrs Reilly's ugly hat or Mrs Bolton's big feet.

Surrounded as I was by all these languages, I was nearly seven before I fully realised that I was a white person with all the attendant constraints and privileges that that would impose on my life. My parents tried to ensure we were fluent in both English and Afrikaans, the latter essential to qualify for university entrance. They spoke English to us and we all spoke Afrikaans one day a week. Weekly the maids led us, astray as it turned out. Their pronunciation was an informal ethnic dialogue on its own and betrayed our contacts to 'pure white' Afrikaners. So it came as no surprise when my elder sister began to have difficulty with Afrikaans at school. This academically unacceptable style had to be urgently repaired for matriculation exams.

'I WONDER IF Betty Kok still lives on that farm outside Queenstown?' my mother mused. 'She was just a few years older than my sister Phyllis and also went to the convent. Betty rode her bicycle to and from school everyday and we thought she was so sophisticated because our dad wouldn't let us ride bicycles. Phyllis told me that she's retired from teaching and tutors students in Afrikaans. Students stay with her and *Meneer* for a week at a time on their farm speaking, reading and writing the language. I think you can go with Michele,' my mother decided.

'Phyllis, how is everyone? I want to send Michele and Cecile to the *Taal* Farm. Does Betty still do that?'

'Hello, is that you Betty? I heard from Phyllis that you are still teaching live-in students on the farm. Do you have space for two of my girls?'

'That's a brilliant idea,' my father enthused that night at the dinner table. 'You're so lucky,' he turned to my sister and me, but his excitement had not communicated itself. 'You'll be fully immersed in the language for a week. Your exams will be a cinch after that.'

'It's fine for you to say that,' my sister whined, 'you are used to Afrikaans people but we don't need the language.'

'Afrikaans is the language of power in this country. We all have to know it. I was too poor to go to any other university but the Afrikaans one in Bloemfontein. Now, I'm in the pound seats because of that. Many of the present government ministers were in college with me. I can talk to policemen, magistrates, any Afrikaners in fact. They admire me for it.'

'But if they knew what you thought of the government, they'd hate you,' I said.

'Look,' my father continued, 'we all have to live together in this country. We are human beings with the same needs for housing, jobs...'

'That's all very well for us to think like that,' I interrupted, 'but the government doesn't see anybody but Afrikaners as human. The rest of us are dogs.'

'Now remember,' my mother warned us, 'those are respectable, traditional Afrikaans people. I don't want any nonsense or bad reports. No cheek and just keep quiet when you don't agree with something and that goes especially for you, Cecile.'

I began to dread the prospect because my only experience of traditional Afrikaans people was with old Mrs de Wit across the road. She and her husband had retired from their farm, which was in the same district as our *Taal* farm. In her spare time, *Mevrou* did sewing alterations and we often had to pop over the road for pinning or measuring. The house smelt of animal fat, which she rendered and made into soap. She taught me how to make traditional Afrikaans *koeksusters* and was especially keen that we spoke Afrikaans. When she heard we were off to the *Taal* farm, she became enthusiastic about correcting and improving our pronunciation.

'*Dis nou 'n wonder* (that is a wonder),' she pursed her lips and nodded her head. 'To think that when I was young we were not allowed to speak or learn Afrikaans. Now they are teaching our language to the English people.' She then told me about her family who had been interned in British concentration camps during the Boer War and how Afrikaans only became recognised as a language in the Cape Province in 1925 almost twenty-four years later.

MY MOTHER AND Paul were booked to come with us on the train to Queenstown. Auntie Phyllis, my mother's older sister, would pick us up at the station and drive us to the farm.

'Gee, Granny, I'll miss you,' I said as she watched me sort out clothing for the trip. 'Don't you want to come and stay with Mommy and Paul at Auntie Phyllis' place and then you can come back with us when Daddy fetches us?'

'No, I'll go another time. What's this farm you said you're going to?'

'We have to learn Afrikaans, Gran, so that we can go to university.'

'Yee! I tell you, this country belongs to *bubeed*–black people and Afrikaners. We don't belong here. One day they will fight over it.'

'You shouldn't say things like that to the children, Mommy,' my mother chided.

Granny raised her voice, 'Why? What's the matter? That's the truth. You want to hide the truth from them. These *bubeed*, terrible; Afrikaners, terrible; *Ingleesie* (English), you can't trust them. They don't say what they think.'

'Don't say that, Mommy,' my mother pleaded.

'I'm old, I'll say what I like.'

'So how did you learn English, Granny?'

'It was your mom and Auntie Phyllis: they nagged me a lot after your grandpa died. I had to read *Little Women* a few times. Then they asked me questions about it. After that,' she said, 'I fell in love with reading.'

When we visited Granny for afternoon tea, we'd find her engrossed in the latest James Hadley Chase or some Mills and Boon. Sometimes, a strong burning smell lingered in the air. Granny had incinerated her most recent read: the luscious sounding adventures of the buxom *Angelique* by Sergeanne Golon, 'to make sure the girls don't find it'.

WE SET OFF on the morning train in our first class compartment. The third class carriages were for black people only and they sat on bare benches day and night. No compartments or beds were provided, even on the three-day journey to work on the gold mines in Johannesburg. The train crossed mountain passes and went through several tunnels on this five-hour trip. After the first hour, everything was covered in soot. A young waiter came through from the dining car to take orders for tea or coffee. His once white apron covered food-stained trousers and shirt. My mother scolded him angrily, 'How can you work with food and look like that? Your dirty clothes are disgraceful. First go and change your apron and wash your hands, and don't forget to wipe that tray. Then we'll talk to you.'

He slunk out of our compartment and my mother continued her tirade, 'They only want to employ white people and so we have the dregs serving us. If they made the job open to the best person for it, we'd have a much better class of waiter. Forget about the colour.'

We sipped milky South African Railways *moerkoffie* (boiled coffee) in thick white china cups and ate our Lebanese bread with yoghurt and olives. 'Keep the marmite sandwiches for later in case you feel sick,' Mother told Michele.

The countryside was changing from green coastal bush to the drier edges of the Karoo. Aloes with bright-orange candelabra flowers dotted the rocky hillsides. At each railway siding, the train stopped to collect milk cans and goods. African children ran alongside waving and shouting and my mother threw coins from the window. 'Look at them, poor things, they've got no shoes. In winter it snows and there's black frost in this area.'

The train raced the last few miles from Essex to Queenstown. Huge old willow trees grew beside small dams. 'We used to have Sunday picnics here when we were growing up,' my mother reflected. 'After my father died, Mickey, who was sixteen, took over the driving. He crammed all of us into the Ford. I used to be so nervous, we'd fall around in the back when he took the corners. Once we found a spot we liked, Granny took out the picnic—lots of fruit, *kibbe*, fresh bread and salad and we'd spread it on the car bonnet. After lunch we would laze about under the trees and Granny and my aunts would play cards.'

'In the old photo albums in the study,' I said 'there are scenes of picnics like that and people playing a board game.'

'That was *taoulie* (backgammon). Ooh! They used to fight and shout and the loser often tipped the whole board over,' she chuckled. 'You make me tell you these things. Now we are almost there. Get the bags together.'

It was a still sunshine-filled autumn day in Queenstown. The platform was crowded with people getting onto the train for the long haul to Johannesburg. Auntie Phyllis collared a porter for the luggage and marched us off to her car. 'Look how wide the road is,' I exclaimed.

'Yes, they were made like that more than a hundred years ago so that the ox wagons and the bullock trains could turn around,' my aunt filled in. I tried to imagine the people of that time, women in long dresses with bonnets tied under their chins and pipe-smoking men with long beards wearing *veldskoene* (hide shoes) and hats of the same material.

Auntie's cook, Kesselina, was a devout middle-aged woman who lived in the local African township. She was the only person in the world who could tell Auntie what to do. '*Môre,* Miss Bertha,' she greeted us. 'How are you? How is Granny?'

'All well, thank you. Granny says hello and hopes you are still bossing Miss Phyllis around.'

'Yes, she is the Medem, but she is a young gel next to me. I can teach her a lot.' Kesselina laughed and went back to the kitchen to bring out the lunch of stuffed vegetables and salads, all from the big gardens at the back.

The twenty-minute drive to the farm passed very quickly, especially as Auntie and my mother teased us about the wicked witch who was going to be in charge of us for the coming week.

'What colour is her hair?' I asked.

'Bright red and long,' Auntie said, 'and she has fingernails to match.'

'Does she still ride her bicycle?' my brother asked.

'Of course not. She's a grown woman now. She has a bright red sports car.'

We stopped at the farmhouse where a short woman was waiting for us. Her grey hair swept into a chignon, she wore a blue dress with stout walking shoes

'Hello Betty, how lovely to see you again,' my mother and Phyllis greeted their old school friend.

'How the years have flown,' *Mevrou* said. 'To think I am now teaching your girls and my daughter is finishing her doctorate at university.'

'Seeing you on your bicycle all those years ago, I would never have imagined this day,' my mother said. The last words in English had just been spoken.

Mevrou approached my sister and me, extended her hand and said in Afrikaans, 'Please say goodbye to your mother and aunt because they must go and we must begin.'

My sister and I shared a large bedroom with three other girls, while around the corner two older girls, Tessie and Jane, were in a smaller room.

We all went to Anglican and Catholic private schools and had some resistance to learning Afrikaans.

Tessie's English grandparents were citrus farmers in the Kat River valley not far away. One of our maids at home, Minnie, grew up in that valley and she told us how the farmers used to dump the oranges in the river when they were too cheap. Her granny had once gone to a farmer to ask if he'd give her the oranges for the children instead of throwing them away. But he got his headman to chase her with the dog. I wondered if Tessie's grandparents gave their surplus to the farm workers and their families, or did they also throw them in the river? I began to ask, but then changed my question. 'Do the farm workers and local people also like to eat oranges?'

She answered, 'Yes, they used to steal a lot but Grandad installed high voltage electric fences all around the orchards.'

'You mean people get shocked if they want to pick an orange? Do they die?' one of the other girls asked.

Anyway, Tessie was used to being on a farm and she took us on a quick scout of the homestead yard. *Mevrou* had beautiful flower gardens around the house. An old fashioned climbing rose covered one side of the glass walled conservatory next to the tennis court.

Meneer came up from the lands at five o'clock and we prepared ourselves for the evening meal. The huge dining room with its mile-long table was brightly lit. The maids carried in dishes and platters containing a real country dinner of meat, rice, potatoes, vegetables and gravy. We bowed our heads before starting while *Meneer* said grace '*Ons dank U Here* . . .' Dessert of homemade ice-cream and stewed fruit followed the main course.

'Oo, the ice-cream is delicious', I turned to *Mevrou*.

'Yes and if you speak English, then you won't get any ice-cream.'

Meneer put the radio on for the seven o'clock news. 'Listen well because I am going to ask you what the man said.'

I felt uncomfortable. The news was bound to be full of propaganda and what this and that minister had to say. 'After negotiations in London, Bechuanaland and Basutholand will become independent from Britain by the end of the year. They will be called Botswana and Lesotho.' This was 1966.

'What do you think of that now?' *Meneer* asked. 'Do you think black people can make a government?'

Tessie, piped up, 'If Britain thinks so, maybe it is a possibility.' She's brave, I thought, but *Meneer* and *Mevrou* know her English grandparents and I suppose she can say what she thinks.

Then *Meneer* pronounced, 'But what do the people in Britain know? They don't see the black people walking around without clothes, wearing only animal skins. Let us read the Bible.' He took the big old leather-bound family Bible off the dresser and opened it at the place where he'd last read. '*Psalm honderd vier-en-viertig* (Psalm 144): Blessed be the Lord my strength, which teacheth my hands to war, and my fingers to fight . . .'

Night after night we had South African Broadcasting Corporation news and then a Bible reading. My real comfort was the giant featherbed which no one else wanted because it was so high. I pulled a chair up to the side and climbed onto it, sinking into the thick mattress. Once I pulled the feather quilt over me, the darkness gave me a private space to think my own thoughts about all these challenges to my diet, my language and my religion.

Next morning the wake-up bell rang at half past six and we assembled in the dining room for a seven o'clock breakfast. 'Be ready by eight o'clock in the conservatory. We are going to study and write.'

At mid-morning Grieta brought the tea tray in from the kitchen. We stopped work at midday and went for a short ramble along the farm road. Tessie showed us how to tell the time and plot directions using the sun and a few natural landmarks. The African children all spoke to us in Afrikaans. None of them knew how to speak Xhosa and I was disappointed.

After a dinner-sized lunch and a short rest, '*Kom, kom,* let us wander in the riverbed.'

Mevrou set a cracking pace, waving a stick around and poking at items of interest along the way. Plenty of sloughed snake skins, 'Yes, very poisonous cobras and puff adders,' she warned. The banks were pocked with holes and tunnels, rodent towns where meerkats lived.

'Look at this stone,' my sister blurted out.

'Remember, Afrikaans, otherwise you won't get any ice-cream,' *Mevrou* cautioned. 'What you have there is a Bushman's knife. Look how sharp it is on one side.' We began to search for other signs. 'Yes, the Karoo plains were full of Bushmen. The caves have their drawings and thousand-year-old fireplaces. I'll show you tomorrow.'

After four o'clock tea, we played an hour of tennis. *Mevrou* wore her peak cap and a whistle round her neck. She sat in the umpire's perch and called, '*Stroop vyftien* (love fifteen),' or '*Gelykop* (deuce)'and finally, '*Pot* (game).' At the end of our week we got a 'certificate of proficiency in playing tennis in Afrikaans'.

The next day, after an early finish to the morning lessons, we set off across the riverbed to the Bushman Cave in its specially fenced camp. None of the herders or farm workers crossed here, 'Bewitched', they said. We picked a path through the long dried grass, constantly on the lookout for snakes. The absence of animal dung or any signs of human traffic gave the place a wilderness feel. A stunted tree grew from a large jutting rock overhead and we noticed the shallow cave beneath.

It took our eyes a moment to adjust to the light change and to see the rock paintings. A giant yellow eland materialised in the centre of the rock face. We were awed and the quieter we became, the more pictures we saw. A group of men with eland faces were doing the eland trance dance to one side. Beyond them, hunters carried bows and arrows to the hunting ground. We stood in awe, as if the priest had opened the tabernacle in chapel and we were waiting for communion.

'Yes, this is a Bushman's church,' *Mevrou* said. 'They ground the orange rock into a powder then made it into a paste to do the painting.'

When the sun told us it was well after midday, we ambled back dreamily for lunch. I felt as though I'd been looking through mother's View master, completely transported into another world. My sister nudged me, 'What's a penis in Afrikaans?' We had to wait to get back to our dictionaries to snigger about the exaggerated bottoms and penises in the Bushman drawings. Our resentment at being exiled to learn Afrikaans surfaced especially when our poor vocabulary frustrated our whisperings.

The last day of our stay, *Mevrou* indulged us with a special afternoon tea of homemade cakes and biscuits. Tessie seemed to be the star of everything and I was envious of her mousy hair and freckles. I supposed *Mevrou's* friendship with her grandparents made her a favourite. Lessons were cancelled for the rest of the afternoon.

About four o'clock, during our free time, we noticed a line of dust along the farm road and then we heard a car coming up the drive. From where my sister and I were sitting behind the tennis court, we watched as *Mevrou* and Tessie went to meet them. Grieta followed carrying a suitcase. Tessie's parents got out and after a few words, they fell into a sobbing huddle with their daughter. They all climbed in and drove away. We were left mystified. *Mevrou* disappeared inside the house and *Meneer* came up from the lands soon after they pulled away.

We found the others in our bedroom staring wide-eyed at one another. 'What do you think?' We decided to wait in the last patches of sun next to the conservatory. We saw *Meneer* come out of the house and go into his study on the veranda. He emerged with a rifle, looked through the sight in different directions. I wanted to run away. I hated guns but was frozen to the spot.

Grieta came round the corner and crooked her finger at us. '*Mevrou* says stay close to the house, you will be eating early.'

In the dining room, *Mevrou* stood at her place at the table. Her nose and eyes were red and she had a big handkerchief bunched in her sleeve, 'Please wait for *Meneer* to come before you sit down.'

He walked in looking grim. 'This morning, a group of blacks attacked and murdered Tessie's grandparents on their farm.' A collective shiver and the sound of breath being sucked in filled the room. Then he picked up the Bible and began to read Psalm ninety-four, 'O Lord God to whom vengeance belongeth, shew thyself . . .'

After a silent meal, we gathered around the fireplace and snatched snippets of conversation with somewhat improved fluency. Then *Meneer* turned on the radio for the regional news bulletin. 'The news for the Eastern Cape follows. A well-known Kat River farmer and his wife were found murdered on their farm this morning. It appears that Mrs Elizabeth Archer was stabbed to death in her bed. Mr Fred Archer's dismembered body was found in various parts of the front garden. Police have issued a warning to all farmers to instruct their workers to inform them at once of any strangers in the area.'

Suddenly *Meneer* burst out with, 'The only solution is to shoot them all.'

My already hot cheeks caught fire and I felt as if I was choking.

One of the others said, 'It's not Christian to think like that.'

Meneer flew back with, 'Blacks are not Christians, they are worse than animals.'

I wondered about *Mevrou*. She always spoke so nicely to Grieta and Sarie; surely she didn't think like that. But her thin lips remained pressed together and her chignon didn't lose a hair. She went to the kitchen to make hot cocoa and my sister volunteered to help.

'The blacks are going to stab you all to death,' he continued. 'But we are safe here because our blacks know that I have all sorts of guns and I will shoot everyone without asking any questions.'

My revulsion of the raw hatred expressed kept me awake all night. Then I began to fear that somebody really was walking around, blade sharpened, ready to cross the hall and slit my throat. Who would recognise me as African with my white skin? In the night of the long knives I would be just one of the enemy. My pulse raced. By morning my head was throbbing and my eyes had sunk into dark rings of sleeplessness.

'Probably flu,' *Mevrou* diagnosed at breakfast. 'Stay in bed until your father comes.' I dreaded having to spend any more time quarantined in this wilderness. It was hard enough dealing with such a contrary atmosphere when I was well. I felt even worse moping in bed when I started to think how many whites in South Africa thought like *Meneer*. The world of my home and family felt so far away. Tears trickled from the corners of my eyes. I wondered why they were so full of hate. Dislocated, I realised that my outward composure was fragile and I would probably attack *Meneer* savagely if he said another word.

Grieta came from the kitchen to help me get ready to go.

My father raced up the drive in his flashy Chev and greeted *Mevrou* charmingly in his perfect Afrikaans, 'Yes, *Mevrou*, I was at university in the Orange Free State. Police Minister Pelser was in college with me. I know many of the government ministers.' My head was swimming and my sister pushed me into the car before I fell over.

'It was a pleasure to welcome your daughters to Koks River. They can come again any time.'

12

Saints and gangsters

Master I am a stranger to you,
But will you hear my confession?

I am a faceless man
Who lives in the backyard of your house…

EXCERPT FROM *THE MASTER OF THE HOUSE*
OSWALD JOSEPH MTSHALI

Taking a bath one night I became aware of scuffling sounds and clinking bottles, just outside the window overlooking the courtyard. Next I heard one of the newer maids drunkenly cursing at Sara, '*Jou poes* (Your fanny).' '*Jouna ook,* (Yours too),' Sara retorted. Then the abuse escalated '*Jou moer* (Your womb—an extreme expletive).' The reply, '*Jou ma se moer* (Your mother's womb),' put the fat in the fire. By that stage almost the whole family was in the bathroom with me, peering through the window. Mark came dashing through and jumped straight out of the window wielding a leather *sjambok* this way and that. Needless to say, Sara was the object of the cursing. She left work yet again, 'because of her nerves.'

She sent Winnie and her daughter Poppy to take her place. At three o'clock one morning, the dogs started barking at the kitchen door. Eventually my father went to investigate. He found a queue of Chinese sailors waiting outside Poppy's door while her cunning mother took their money and encouraged them to wait. My enraged father sent them all packing and returned to bed cursing. My mother dabbed her eyes 'because poor slow Poppy had a mother as wicked as Winnie.'

When Winnie and Poppy left Theresa came to work for us. I was thirteen. Anita and Michele were growing up and I was increasingly alone. Theresa was thin, quietly spoken and looked waifish in our tumultuous household. Her more robust friend Margaret came with her and together the two of them sought to minister to all our needs.

They shared the same boyfriend, Margaret asserting her rights vociferously and at times, physically. Her power was reinforced by a long sip from a deep bottle. As far as I was prepared to know, Theresa did not drink. My affection for her was not to be diluted by such thoughts. I had seen drunken violence in the courtyard where they lived. When there was screaming and disturbance in that world, I accepted it because I had been loved and fed by many mothers in that place from the time I was born.

One afternoon as I was doing my homework, Theresa came into my room and shut the door. 'Can I show you something?'

'Sure, whatever you like'.

She unbuttoned the top two buttons of her cheap blue cotton uniform and extracted a smallish breast. In the centre, above the nipple, I saw death. I wanted to scream. I'd never seen anything so ugly before. The skin was puckered and collapsed inward around a small black mound. Mastering myself I tried to sound confident and light-hearted: 'Don't worry, I'll tell my mother and you can go and see Dr Le Clus'. The truth was that I was so sick and afraid I couldn't tell a soul. I hauled out the enormous plastic rosary that glowed in the dark and for three days I told the beads. Then fear and guilt overtook me: she would surely die if I didn't tell Mother.

So on the Saturday morning I strolled casually into the kitchen and drew my mother into the pantry. There, pressed up against the shelf of giant jars containing the season's olives, I blurted out: 'I think Theresa needs to see a doctor—she has a huge lump in her breast.'

After interrogation, 'How do you know? When did she tell you? Why didn't you tell me before?' my mother sprang into action. 'All right, I'll ring Albert.' She rang her eldest brother, an anaesthetist, who told her that it was too late for a private GP to be of use. He whispered in an appropriate ear, and Theresa went to the head of the three-day queue at the local outpatients' department.

The radiotherapy was debilitating, and most of the time Theresa lay on her bed in the little dark servant's room that faced onto the courtyard. When I came home from school I baked cakes, and Theresa and I would sit and have a cup of tea. She would pinch off crumbs from the big slices I cut for her, a substitute for the cigarettes we'd otherwise have shared. The traditional herbalist whom she consulted suggested that smoking slowed the recovery from cancer, so we restrained ourselves. In my mind she was stronger because of those herbs and our closeness. I willed her to live and imagined, that I was somehow saving her life. She had been a gentle companion to me from the moment she came to our home. From the time she showed me that awful tumour, I felt responsible for her wellbeing. Coming home from school one afternoon, I resolved that we should have our tea in the orchard far down the garden where olive and pecan trees provided good cover. I supported Theresa under her good arm and together we painstakingly made our way down the three steps from the courtyard on to the back lawn. The terraced slopes and the dried out wormcasts added to the difficulty of our walk. Each step took us closer to our spot and further from the divided household where I lived inside and she lived outside in the servants' quarters.

We reached the summerhouse that stood on top of the concrete water tank that irrigated the gardens and paused to gather strength for the four steps down to the orchard path. Oranges, guavas, custard apples and other delights hung from the trees as the season dictated. From where we stood we looked through the long tunnel created by the grapevine on its pergola. 'These leaves are already too tough for Granny. You'll have to help her early next year with the picking,' she said, as if reminding me that I could anticipate the next season's crop but she'd already seen her last.

When she'd first come to work in our Lebanese household she'd been amazed to see Granny going to the vine every second day to select leaves until she had piles for stuffing and rolling. Just to the left of the vine, the knee-high bushes of coriander waved their flower heads in the breeze.

Eggplant, okra and herbs regarded as exotic filled the loamy beds. This was my garden where many mothers had brought me ever since I could remember. Now I was leading one of those mothers down there, hoping to be soothed by the benign spirits of tree and leaf.

There was nowhere for us to rest under the vine, so we headed carefully for the toolbox that Victor had carted to the glade under the olive trees. We perched on the ends and caught our breath. 'The olives are all in bottles in the pantry now,' I said with a mental picture of Victor and his helpers, in April, shaking the trees and beating the branches with rakes and brooms to drop the olives onto the groundsheets.

To the right of us, the gardeners' cottage where Victor and his young assistant lived was partly hidden by a dense clump of banana trees. He had warned us children not to go in among the bananas, but we always doubted the stories he told of the long green tree snakes. I told Theresa the light-hearted part of a small story: how one afternoon, taking our Lexingtons and matches, we went in there for a smoke. I giggled as I told her how Antoinette and I had coughed and spluttered our way through ten cigarettes and then rushed out into the mint patch to eat handfuls to mask our breath. But I couldn't bring myself to tell her of the horror that had flung us out of our hideaway: a small cross made of tomato crate planks standing on a little mound and the name 'Tandiwe' scratched across in black crayon. I had wondered at the time if that was Jackson's baby that had died when it was born. My mother didn't seem to know, nor did it bother her that someone was buried in the banana grove.

I went back to the house and fetched a tray with the tea and cake. I took care setting out nice cups and saucers, dressed the teapot in a cosy made by the nuns and covered the milk jug with a beaded doily that tinkled all the way down the path. We didn't speak much. I watched her looking at each item on the tray and imagined her thinking: 'What would Madam say if she saw her cups and things down in the garden with the maid?' But I knew my mother was tacitly giving me licence to do what the custom of the day prevented her from doing.

It was difficult to tear ourselves away, but the rising wind off the sea and the cooling afternoon sent us back to the house, out of the garden, back to the ceaseless clatter of the kitchen. It was a slow uphill climb.

We were reluctant to resume our allotted places in the household. In the soft, dappled tree light, contrasting skin tones merged, whereas up at the house the background gave us no relief. Theresa would not receive any more radiotherapy. She was going home to her village in the Transkei, where her grandmother was waiting to nurse her.

The bloody wound of her amputated breast never healed; her intense pain mirrored my pain at the prospect of losing her. We couldn't even mention the Saturday morning train that would carry her away. When the car came to fetch her that morning, Victor took the hamper of food I had packed for the journey down the long tradesmen's path to the street. Theresa's boyfriend carried her tiny frame away from the house. She edged backwards into the car, picking her stick-like legs up one by one with her emaciated hands. She managed to move her mouth into the shape of a smile and lift one hand in a gesture of farewell...but my heart was gone from my breast.

My mother sometimes said softly, 'She was a lovely woman, that Theresa. A real saint in the way she died.' I agreed silently, feeling that she had suffered so much that my grief was mere self-indulgence. But I became increasingly moody. My mother often begged me to join her and my sisters but I felt like a stranger around them and their conversation seemed so irrelevant to how I experienced life. As a young child in the courtyard among women who worked themselves to exhaustion to keep our home functioning, I couldn't see myself living the life of a white lady.

The gulf between the servants' lives and the lives inside the houses always struck me. We were taught to treat everyone equally but how could their suffering be allowed to continue while we lived so well?

Maggie was one of the many women who worked in our home. She was famous in our family for her floral language as well as her muscular forearms with which she produced the fluffiest round Lebanese loaves. In a famous response to a comment from my brother Paul about the heat, she retorted, '*Ja Baas, shoo, dis so warm, my doos by sweet ook* (Yes Mister, it is so hot, even my c... is sweating).'

One Saturday morning I was poring over the newspaper at the dining room table. Sun streamed into the room with its view to the Indian Ocean. My mother was finishing off letters she'd begun during the week thanking people for hospitality received on their recent overseas trip.

Maggie came and stood in the doorway. Her face, arms and neck bore the familiar purple patches. Once I had seen Tommy—her tall, powerful boyfriend—and his brother, I stopped wondering where the marks came from. There were tattoos on most visible parts of their bodies proclaiming their membership of one of the most feared prison gangs in the area. No artwork, just brutal carving by metal or glass shards, whatever the screws provided or 'left behind.'

My mother looked up and Maggie burst into tears. She came and stood close to us, holding onto the back of my mother's chair. '*Hy druk my*...he squeezes me, then he forces me so that my underneath parts are sore for days. And even while they are sore, he squeezes me and forces me again.'

'You must say no,' my mother insisted.

'*Nee*, he'll kill me. Even his brother, he'll join in and they'll hit me together. I must do it with all of them.'

I just sat there. 'That's terrible, Maggie.'

'One day he's going to kill me.'

'You tell him from me to stop at once,' my mother scolded.

'He's going to laugh.' She held her hand over her mouth chuckling at my mother, who was completely out of her depth.

The next day, Sunday, a phone call from a public phone, 'I want to speak to Mrs Yazbek,' came a voice in attempted disguise.

'Speaking.'

'I'm coming to kill you. You leave Maggie alone. She belongs to me and my family.'

'Is that you, Tommy? You behave yourself.'

By the end of the week and a few more such phone calls, my mother told my father.

Reluctantly he told the police who were cynical. The brothers were just out of jail after a sentence for murder. '*Ja*, he needs to murder again so that he can go back inside and be in charge of all the gang members in the region,' the sergeant at the station told my father.

The news went round the family that my mother was being threatened. One of my uncles wisecracked, 'Your mother plays the fool with the servants. One day they'll kill her. They're savages.'

While we didn't share those views, prompted by my father, we became more vigilant,

After twenty years, on and off, Sara finally left work permanently in her late fifties, but not before her most famous rout with Maggie. The screaming began in the scullery, '*Jy*… you're not a real brown person like us.'

'What are you talking about, Sara?' I interrupted.

'*Ja*, Maggie, look at her huge bum cheeks, she has to get those pills every month at the clinic. VD, she's got syph'.

'Sara, that is shocking,' I struggled.

But Maggie was better at her own defence. '*Ek, ek* worry *nie*. (Me, I don't worry) I am happy as I am. You are the unhappy one, Sara, screaming and fighting with everybody. It's better if you retire now.' I marvelled at her courage, her dignity still intact in our home.

13

Brides, beauty queens and bloddy fools

Then we were plunged into preparing for a cousin's engagement party. I seethed on the back seat of my mother's brand new Fiat. She and Anita gabbled on and on in the front.

'Now we'll go and see Mrs Antoniotti,' my mother said, 'and ask her if there's anything she can do to shorten that dress without losing the pretty border.'

My sister sat thinking for a minute then turned around to me, 'What do you want to wear to Donnè's party?'

I shrugged, my mouth set hard and my pricking eyes ready to overflow when I needed my tears to quell the fire of hatred that burned inside. I had not wanted to go to Garlicks. I had not wanted to dress up. I had not wanted to have those two babbling beauty queens dragging me around trying to enhance my feminine assets with Elizabeth Arden or her cohorts' help. I knew Garlicks cosmetic department intimately. My mother paid homage there almost every day, taking my grandmother or one of my sisters along. We subscribed to *Seventeen*, an American magazine that would help my mother make her three girls into belles. We read articles on how to swallow food without a sound or ripple on face or throat, how to make big breasts look smaller and a myriad cures for bad breath. I resisted firmly and as time wore on, the more I knew, the less inclined I felt to 'just come along.'

'Nita,' my mother said, 'don't worry now. When she sees all of us getting dressed, she'll want to join in.'

But I wished them both dead; if being female meant trawling through Garlicks every day, I didn't want to have anything to do with it.

I'd much rather have stayed upstairs and chatted with my father. 'Go with them, my darling,' he'd encouraged, 'you might enjoy yourself. At least you might stop your mother spending all the bladdy money on her face'.

My mother revved the engine to life, 'Aren't we lucky,' she said, 'on your father's birthday, he always gives us such lovely presents.'

'I know, Mommy,' my sister said. 'Two brand new Fiats, a blue one for me and a yellow one for you'.

She backed the car slowly out of the garage and then accelerated. Instead of turning the wheel to the right, she held it straight. There was a jolt, a loud bang and the sound of breaking glass. I was shaken up in the back seat, my wooden expression giving way with a scream. We were in the driveway and firmly banged up against my sister's car that was parked directly behind. I looked up to see my father standing on the balcony breathing out through clenched teeth, speechless for once but shaking his head. 'You bladdy women never stop talking. Look what you've done now!'

My mother and sister both burst into tears. 'Oh Mommy, my new car looks toothless now.' She pointed to the smashed headlights and dented front grill.

'I'm so sorry, my darling,' my mother pleaded. 'I don't know what happened.'

'I know what happened. You bladdy fools never stop talking about clothes and make-up and now God's punished you!' I spat.

They turned around and stared as if they'd just discovered me. I quickly resumed my sulk but the relief of an aborted trip to town made me smile inwardly.

'Oh hell,' my mother confirmed, 'Now I'll be without a car while this is being repaired'.

'Why don't we do them one at a time,' Anita offered, 'then we can share'.

'That's a brilliant idea. It shouldn't take too long.'

IN MY TEENS, cousins began to get married. Granny Isabel, who walked in the gardens with me when I was small, had her own story about finding a husband or a wife. 'Life is like a garden,' she used to tell her grandchildren. 'You go in the gate and you see small green plants and you walk on and you see tightly budded flowers and then they open more. You have to pick one at some point. If you leave it too late, they are full-blown and die quickly or you come to the part of the garden, the end where the autumn leaves and dead things show no sign of further growth. By then it's too late. Pick at the right time and you will be very happy'.

The weddings were great lavish affairs much like Christmas, only decibels louder. Hundreds of us, perfumed and pomaded, eating and talking loudly as the non-Lebanese partner's family sat in a small cluster. We were only seriously challenged once when my cousin Renee married a Greek. My generation, the first to marry out, chose among others: Afrikaners, Jews and Dutch, my brother and two sisters marrying the latter. I wonder often about these cross-cultural marriages. We were said to have 'married out', but in truth the marks of our identity and culture were so strong we could never truly become Afrikaners, Dutch or Anglo-South Africans. So our non-Lebanese partners were actually marrying in. The inclusiveness and hospitality of our culture immediately claimed the new partners as sons and daughters. Nothing ever felt lost. Not all fitted in and sometimes the couple found themselves in limbo until they had children. Aunts and grandmothers then rushed to 'ooh', and incorporate the offspring; children should never be lost. By and by, and as statistically predicted, some marriages failed. I speculated on what had drawn those quiet, often reserved people into our families. Was it our effusiveness that drew them and finally repelled them?

Our extended family is a rich resource all willingly sharing their expertise. It is also, as a microcosm of society, a reflection of our imperfect human condition, and as such, many are willing to share their experience with varying degrees of wisdom.

14

Photographs and lies

On bright winter mornings, the sun, lighting up my parents' bedroom with sea views from the corner windows, intensified the contrast between my fourteen-year-old life and what I saw every day in the newspapers.

One day in particular, on page four of the *Daily Dispatch*, a black and white photograph stopped me in my tracks: old women and babies all with the same frozen stare. The women's *doeks* were soaked with rain. A grandmother carried a child on her back and his little face, with a snot-streaked cheek, poked out from a towel covering him. An arm hung limply over the side of the blanket that held him close to the elderly woman. 'Look at this,' I said aloud to whoever was in the offing as I read the morning paper in my parents' bedroom. 'Shocking! This bloody government has dumped a whole lot of people at Chalumna.'

'Isn't that where Rossy's parents have a holiday cottage and Mr Billings goes fishing?' my mother asked.

After hurrying my breakfast, I tore the picture from the paper, folded it into my blazer pocket and raced up the hill to school. If I got there before the bell, I'd be able to talk with Sister Johanna in her kindergarten classroom. She was in charge of our school's Red Cross group. Before school the nuns would have been praying, singing matins and having breakfast. No newspapers in their enclosure. I'd been in there once in the early morning, the east-facing windows and French doors looking over the lawns were bathed in sunlight. Incense wafted from the chapel into the walled atrium where a large square of sky crowned the fishpond set into the terrazzo floor. I imagined fresh rain falling through the opening and those gleaming fish darting about with the pleasure of it. Luckily, Sister Johanna was still setting up the room for the day. I whipped out the picture, 'We have to do something. Can we collect tinned food and blankets?'

'Yes, sure,' she said. 'The Red Cross can be in charge of that'. I rushed to the room where my standard seven classmates were trickling in for the day. When Prime Minister Verwoerd—the grand master of apartheid—was assassinated in the Houses of Parliament in 1966, to my surprise a few of my school friends had joined me in support for the murderer. We had gone around the schoolyard that day a year ago, chanting, 'Saint Tsafendas. Tsafendas. He's going to be a saint now.' My mother had warned us not to say these things as there were some in our school who would report us and we'd 'be in serious trouble. Big enough trouble to go to jail.' My father told us we were mad. 'If there's a conspiracy, they're going to pick up anybody who is not in total mourning for the loss of their hero. You kids had better keep quiet'. One thing my parents both emphasised was that it was neither desirable to murder nor support the murder of people we disagreed with.

My classmates and I worked together to make signs which we put up around the school:

'Winter food and blanket collection this Wednesday. Please help the squatters.'

The nuns supported us wholeheartedly as we were acting out the Christian gospel in a society that we knew was not truly Christian.

As soon as I got home, I rang the regional office of the Red Cross asking if they could help us deliver the collection to the squatters. A flat voice on the other end of the phone said, 'No.'

'Why not?' I asked.

'We have no record of squatters at Chalumna,' the voice continued.

'But there's a photograph on page four of today's *Dispatch*.'

He cut in with, 'We have no record of people there needing help,' and he put the phone down.

I was outraged and assailed my father as soon as he came in from work. 'How can the Red Cross tell lies? He's covering it up. He sounded so dead. He is supposed to be upset when people are in trouble so that he can get help for them.'

My father looked at me for a moment, 'Ring the newspaper and ask for the news editor.'

'I'd like to speak to the photographer who took the picture of the squatters on page four, please.'

'I'll put you through,' the operator said.

But he wasn't in. So I asked the journalist on the other end, 'Can you tell me then, where exactly that photograph of squatters was taken? The Red Cross says there is no such group of people.'

'No, I can't tell you. It is a designated relocation of people. Their village was declared white farmland and they have had to be moved.' By then my father had sidled up to the phone and was encouraging me.

'But where are they? It is cold and we at the Convent have collected food and blankets for them'.

'I can't tell you.'

I replaced the receiver. We trusted the English language newspapers. They were on our side against the government. Now they too were keeping secrets.

I went to school the next morning feeling defeated. Winter. The cold and misery were fighting on the side of the state to win the battle against these people.

With tears burning tracks down my angry face I knocked on Sister Johanna's classroom door to break the news. We stood in front of a mountain of blankets and groceries that occupied half her classroom, 'We'll call Father Magorrian and we can go to Saint Peter Claver's in Duncan Village. There are thousands of people there who are in desperate need.'

After morning prayers, I announced to my classmates that a convoy of six cars driven by six of our mothers would take some of us and our collection over to Duncan Village.

Girls nudged each other, 'It'll be dangerous. Wasn't Sister Aidan murdered there?'

'That was even before we were born,' I countered.

'Do we have permits to go into an African area?'

'We'll have nuns with us on church business. There's no need.'

My father had told me the law and how we could get around it. I was completely confident.

The following week our convoy set off. We had filled all the car boots and taken as many schoolgirl passengers as we could. Sister Johanna was in the front car with my mother driving, while two friends and I sat in the back. I knew Duncan Village but I wanted my school friends to see what I'd long known about. The cars crawled through muddied and pot-holed lanes at snail's pace. Some had brought cameras and broke the law photographing tin shanties, ragged children with sores on all exposed areas, crowds of women clustered around the only tap that served about seventy people in each section.

Father Magorrian welcomed us into the front room of his house next to the church. 'Coloured' and African nuns wearing the same habits as our European teachers served tea and waited on us.

On our return to school after the delivery, we were subdued. We'd seen things we'd argued about in a parody of our parents' pro- and anti-government positions. The nuns handed us literal epithets of Christian love. They told us how grateful we had to be for the privileged lives we lived, and how we were obliged by the Gospels to share our wealth. We listened and felt it was important that we take a stand. Over the weeks that followed, we pooled the contraband photographs and, with the nuns' tacit approval, pasted them up on walls and noticeboards with the tag:

'These are our brothers and sisters. What are we doing to help them?'

15

Murder in our garden

Once again, my father employed Mr Pepper, who ran the church repository selling medals and holy cards, this time to build a replica of the Lourdes shrine at one end of the vine tunnel in our garden. My father had also ordered an eighteen inch white statue of the virgin especially for our shrine. On either side of the grotto they built, lilies bloomed in the fishponds and tall reeds made one think a small search might reveal a baby floating in a basket. Victor, the gardener, was quite a handyman and assisted Mr Pepper. On walks down the garden with Granny, we often chatted with Victor and he eagerly pointed out ripening delicacies to us.

When my mother decided to play a trick on my father around the seemingly barren pecan trees, Victor was a willing accomplice. He climbed the tree for us, planting nuts from Woolworths in the branches and scattering the rest on the ground. The story of my excited father 'harvesting', cracking and eating nuts as he filled a basket was told among visitors and servants alike. The following year both trees bore profusely, as if to shame us.

On a hot Friday afternoon in 1968, when Victor had been with us for four years and I was just fifteen, David, his assistant, came running to the kitchen, calling, 'Madam, Madam, Victor sick.' My mother was out playing bridge, so I followed him to the gardeners' cottage. Victor was standing in the doorway swaying on his feet. As I got closer a projectile vomit of clotted blood sprayed the terrified young girl next to him. Shocked and realising that this had probably been going on for a couple of hours, I raced back to the house and without thinking, dialled the general emergency number, 'Send an ambulance at once,' I ordered. 'A man is haemorrhaging from the mouth, 112 Devereux Avenue, Mr Yazbek's house'.

Fifteen minutes later, seeing the white flashes through the trees as the ambulance came up the driveway, I rushed to direct them to the scene. I was relieved to see the familiar face of Mr Pepper's son, Peter, at the wheel. He followed me through the orchard to where Victor was lying on the ground.

'But he's black,' Peter said to me. He turned and walked away. 'Why didn't you say it was a black?'

I rounded on him furiously, 'Why should I? Isn't his blood the same colour as ours?'

'But it's the law,' he said, walking faster, 'I can't touch him'.

'Wait till I tell my father,' I shouted.

But he smiled and said, 'You'll have to phone for an ambulance for blacks'.

'You can't leave him,' I screamed. 'He'll die.' He started the engine. I was enraged. 'Call yourself a Catholic, you're just a bastard like the rest of them!' and I rushed back to the house, sobbing.

Defeated, I dialled the number for ambulances for blacks. 'A black man is haemorrhaging red blood...'

I took four enamel mugs from the servants' cupboard, put a pile of sugar and a spoon into each, made a strong brew in the green enamel teapot and carried the tray slowly down the garden. Sitting and waiting quietly beside them was all I could do.

'You'll be all right, Victor,' I whispered but he wasn't moving any more. As he lay on his side, blood flowed in a dark stream from the corner of his mouth.

The steaming cups of tea grew cold in the silent waiting. An hour later they came to fetch him.

At five o'clock the hospital rang my father. 'You'll have to get yourself another gardener, sir, this one's kicked the bucket'.

I stormed around the house.

At seven o'clock the family gathered for dinner as usual around the dining room table. I went to the servants' cupboard and took Victor's enamel plate and put it at my place. My mother looked at my father. Solemnly, he began the grace, 'Bless us oh Lord…' I glared straight ahead at the Dutch oil on the wall with its three monks at their refectory table, each with a metal plate and mug. I sat through the meal silently but left the table before dessert. From down the hall, I heard my father, 'We give thee thanks, almighty God... and may the souls of the faithful departed rest in peace.'

I could not see why I should remain at such a table, in such a house, in such a country. My realisation of our powerlessness, despite my father's esteemed position in the town, filled me with a terrible fear. The law had power of life and death over all of us, and that day it had committed a murder in our name in our garden.

MY HEATED SOCIAL conscience was carrying me into the stormy sea of politics. My father was a beacon for me in that area. But I was growing up without any skills around boys, dating and sex. My sisters regarded me sideways. 'No sex appeal. No one would ever want to chaff her.' I looked in the mirror and wandered from room to room looking in everyone else's mirrors to find a trace of something attractive. I had rebelled against my mother's belief and practice of cosmetic grooming and my flat feet were a problem.

The biotechnician at the hospital had built me a pair of polyurethane orthotics to wear inside my Harley Street lace-ups that had to be two sizes too big to accommodate his invention. My feet were planed and gouged by Mr Pamphlett, the chiropodist every month. I couldn't stand up to sing in the choir. After fifteen minutes I would drag my blue feet and sit down on the steps. Miss Chatterton, the physiotherapist, prodded me hard and glared with owl eyes through her thick spectacles, 'You have the ugliest feet I've ever seen. What kind of a girl would tolerate such ugly feet?'

But the nuns were there, always willing to listen and encourage. They had no body problems: they had no bodies.

One day my mother dressed herself very carefully after lunch. She stopped on the top step of the garage stairwell, 'I'll be back later. Look after your brother'.

I was fit to burst. For weeks on end, my mother had been dressing up after lunch and gone out for the afternoon.

'Where are you going? To a boyfriend, I suppose', I shrieked. 'Every afternoon you dress up and go and play bridge or drink tea like a white madam and I have to stay with Paul. Well, I'm not doing it anymore.' She flew back into her bedroom and I followed her.

'You cheeky brat,' she screeched and began to hit me with her hairbrush. I ran up the hill to the nuns and sobbed my dejection to Sister Lina before she rang my father.

My friend Lucia lived close to the school, so I went home via her place.

'Shit Ceel. You look like you've been in a fight.'

'Ja, my mom did it. She's never at home in the afternoons; I just feel like shit.'

'I know what you mean. My ma doesn't hit me any more 'cos my dad made her stop.'

We sat in her shady garden and wondered about our mothers' fury. Lucia's mom was never the same after her little brother drowned in their pool. I didn't know what could make my mother so horrible. I meandered home feeling terribly guilty. I'd cheeked my mother and then I'd told the nuns. The same nuns who held my parents in such high regard as Catholics with wonderful family values. Now I thought I'd broken all that.

That day was one of the few that I remember my father coming in quietly. He looked at me with my swollen red face and carried on getting his beer and newspaper together for the five o'clock read. Nobody ever said another word about that storm but the silence that ensued infected me for years.

16

My kind and conflicted Mother

There were many aspects to my mother that I found confusing as I was growing up. She was kind and she taught us to be kind and generous to the poor and elderly but she was also addicted to shopping for shoes and clothes. I, meanwhile, was uncompromising and felt responsible for the suffering around us. This became our battleground.

Anxiety plagued my mother. She told a cousin recently that a priest suggested that if she was being troubled by a particular thought, she should simply replace it with a comfortable one. My father did his best to encourage her and boost her confidence. In the same way that I have chanted mantras and wandered in eastern spiritual traditions since my university days, she consumed Dale Carnegie.

My mother had difficulties with her Lebanese identity when we were young.

Some of my memory of my mother and her mother are of the fireworks between them. Against my mother's wishes Granny spoke Arabic loudly in public. 'Speak English,' my mother nudged, but she was relentless.

We ate Lebanese food in the kitchen, not because we wanted to protect the furniture or carpets, but in case a client or someone else appeared unexpectedly on the dining room terrace and saw the stuffed eggplant or zucchini we were having for lunch. The cook produced roasts and vegetables that were carried ceremoniously into the dining room but in those early days, we hid away eating the food of our ancestors.

'My darling, it is a rich and proud tradition we come from. Look at Khalil Gibran from the small village of Bsharre. His books are read and sold all over the world. Such genius,' my father tried often and unsuccessfully. My mother's memory of her childhood in Queenstown, where the children at school mocked and teased the '*knoffel mense* (garlic people)' as the townsfolk called them or '*blerrie Grieke* (bloody Greeks)' was part of her shame. I imagine another aspect involved her father and the sanctions he imposed on their mixing with any but his chosen Lebanese in the town.

In 1979, my mother and a cousin, Bobsy Chemaly, produced *A Peep into a Lebanese Kitchen.* All proceeds went to the Rudolf Steiner village near Cape Town where Bobsy's Down syndrome daughter was a long-term resident. The two women appeared shamelessly in the newspapers as Lebanese mothers and cooks, advertising their book. People rang our home with questions about recipes and ingredients. It sold far and wide. My mother's identity was set.

I try to write about my mother and it is food again. In reality, she was so much more of a presence. She tempered my father, who sometimes got carried away. She was the object of my eldest brother's fury whenever he felt thwarted. She taught us about poverty and how we were to say thank you before anything else. We had to respect the women who worked in our home and were not allowed to ask them to do anything. That was her prerogative alone.

In my parents' bed, early in the morning, my father started me reading the newspaper before I began school. It was, however, my mother who read aloud reports of what 'the bladdy government is doing now.'

In the evenings after dinner, she frequently went to the piano and played from the *American Songbook*. My father sang enthusiastically and we learnt about *Roamin in the gloamin* and *She'll be comin' round the mountain*. From this it was a short, confusing step for Sister Cletus to dress Michele and me in *lederhosen* to sing innumerable verses of the *Happy Wanderer* (*Mein Vater wa ein Wandersman)* in hoch Deutsch on the stage at a school concert.

At the piano, Anita and my mother performed *Eine Kleine Nachtmusik* or a Liszt duet. Some mornings, Brother Cuthbert came down from the De

La Salle College with his fiddle and they produced trills and airs till tears flowed for *Danny Boy*.

My mother's piano playing was encouraged by the nuns when she was still at school but she could not take the Licentiate exam to become a teacher as they were moving to East London. As it is, she has generously shared her music for over seventy years. In 1977, Granny Isabel died and my mother did not touch the piano for more than a year: grief robbed her fingers and our ears.

From my father I learnt big values and philosophical debate, always from the Catholic position. At my mother's workbench I experienced her as a kind and caring person. I went with her into the Newhaven Nursing Home where she handed out tea and hand pats to withered crones cowering in steel cots. Her perfumed lace handkerchief fluttered and dabbed each time she put a cookie on a bedside table. We regularly visited Mrs Lines, who'd had both her legs amputated due to diabetes and lived in bed with an African nurse caring for her.

My mother was a beautiful woman and loved clothing, vast quantities of expensive clothing. Boxes of clothes on appro came and went daily to and from The London Drapery or Garlicks. One day in my teens, I was lying on her bed as the afternoon fashion show began. I peeped (strictly forbidden) at the price ticket of a frock and began to berate her loudly.

'That is disgraceful. People are dying of hunger just down the road. That will buy two hundred loaves of bread, three hundred and fifty if it's brown.' I shouted. Coupled with the thimbleful of Swiss embryo cream that cost more than one of those frocks, I felt she needed a reminder.

'You cheeky brat. Shut up now and mind your own business,' she shouted back.

As a teenager, I unrealistically viewed my family, and especially my mother, as having a greater capacity to speak out and change some of the suffering in our midst. It certainly embattled my earlier relationship with her.

In an attempt to cope with her demanding life, she took up yoga in her mid-forties. Vi Moller was her teacher. They wore black leotards and tights, so out of character for my well-dressed mother. In the early mornings she added a few yoga postures to the regular routine she and my father practised together. They did deep breathing, high kicks and joint flexes. When she knelt on the floor and adopted lion pose with the externalised roar, the dog ran from the room and my father announced, 'You are toying with evil spirits and should rather say the rosary'.

My mother sometimes had a fierce temper and we dreaded hearing her say, 'Sara, go and pick me a nice stick from the hibiscus hedge'. I had most likely cheeked her—a frequent sin. When we were all still at home, she confessed to sometimes feeling she'd had too many children. She never looked after young ones, and her grandchildren were acceptable once they could speak, were potty trained and did not require too much physical involvement. She said how much she'd have loved to have entered the convent. Looking at the extent of the household and how she managed five servants, five children, dogs, cats and a husband needing quite a lot of attention, as well as her fundraising and support of local charities, I am not surprised she dreamed of singing hymns and embroidering tablecloths. She spent hours around the dottiest of nuns without demur, but I know she would have died of boredom after a week.

As we grew up, Mother came into prominence in our lives, taking us to the theatre, encouraging music and supporting us around exam time with cups of milky coffee at five in the morning.

I asked my mother what it was like losing her father when she was just thirteen. I could not imagine growing up without my playful, story telling father who only ever slapped me once in my life when I asked for a lift two hundred metres up the road to school.

'When my father died, at least we wouldn't get those hidings anymore,' she confessed. 'We were terrified of my dad.' I left it at that, thinking I knew what she meant. Years later, when I visited South Africa after my father died, I found out a bit more. My mother and aunts and I were sitting in the lounge after lunch on a Sunday. Somnolent conversation was punctuated by the cracking of pumpkin seeds between our teeth. I sauntered out of the room and returned in full belly-dance regalia. The music blared as I shook and wobbled in front of those stunned women. Some smiled, another raised an eyebrow, yet another gaped in utter disbelief. But it was my mother's performance that stole the show. She laughed, screamed and cackled until finally doubled up, she wept a torrent.

Out of breath, I took my aching hips and knees back to my room to change my clothes. I returned to the sitting room as if someone else had just disturbed the peace.

My mother was wiping her eyes when Phyllis said wearily, 'If our father had seen such a thing he would have killed you.'

'Don't say that, Phyllis,' my mother tried to stop her.

'Well that's the truth,' she insisted.

My mother started to giggle. ' I remember how he hit us when we were late home from school because he thought we were looking for boys.'

'That's no laughing matter. My God, it was terrible.' Phyllis said. 'He hit us on our feet until they bled.'

With a strong sense of outrage and compassion, I wonder at my mother, in old age: she'd had painful feet all her life. She spent hours with podiatrists and doctors. She bought shoes by the dozen; when she realised they weren't going to become comfortable she'd buy yet another pair. I remembered then that my grandmother had told us of the time she cut her long hair without my grandfather's permission—he was enraged and wanted to hit her. Better educated and more affluent than my father's family, these children were afraid of their father.

At the age of eighty-six my mother, Bertha, wrote, 'My dad was a man of great integrity, highly principled and most upright, a well-respected businessman. He was generous and aware of others in need. When we were growing up, we were well provided for. A good father, he kept a strict eye on us. He was also a wonderful guardian to most of his brothers and sisters, responsible for their wellbeing and material needs. Because of him, many Lebanese came to Queenstown and from there, they moved to other parts of South Africa.'

My mother's father is now a powerful and benign figure in her memory. But at last, I understood part of the reasons for her anxiety and I felt ashamed for the way, as a teenager, that I had fought with her over her clothing and beauty rituals. They were part of her self-therapy in a world and at a time in which men had not given her due credence. It was my pretty mother's good fortune to marry my father and they were very happy together. Although he was loving and kind, in an old-fashioned Lebanese way, he could be overbearing and controlling, especially around religion. She now asserts her independence from the Catholic Church by attending Bible study groups where she finds great support and comfort. This has attracted criticism from more conservative Catholics.

17

Father Martin Flanagan—wild Irish priests and German nuns

As they'd done for years, my parents attended the seven o'clock Sunday morning mass. My older sisters, allowed to sleep in, went at half past eight. But one particular day I was excused from the morning mass. Though my father regularly warned us, 'Never set your mind on going to evening mass. If something should happen during the day and you can't get there, you lose your last chance. Then you have to tell it in confession.'

At half-past five, I wandered up Devereux Avenue to the church in Chamberlain Road. Clusters of servants back from their weekends at home chatted amiably outside the gates of big houses. I smiled and nodded as I passed them.

There were a few people in church when I arrived. Traces of incense from the morning benediction hung in the stillness. Older women in mantillas kneeled, lips moving, rosary beads held over the pews in front of them. Soft whispering and shuffling paper sounds began to intrude as more people arrived. Teenagers arranged themselves along the back wall so that they could go in and out during the service. I sat in the body of the church, relieved at not being forced to the front by my father.

As the altar boy appeared in the sanctuary ahead of the priest, we all stood up. An unknown priest, more solid and much younger than Father Muckley, followed. His eyes down, praying hands in front of his lips, a fresh devotion in sharp contrast to Father Muckley's mechanical movements. All went as usual, down to the Irish accent—until the sermon.

This man with the slicked black wave on his forehead began, 'If you are not paying your servant a living wage, please don't put that money in the plate. Go home and pay as much of the arrears as you can and increase the wages from now on to a living wage, a just wage. These people are our brothers and sisters. We are not entitled to rob them of their dignity and the very bread they need to feed their families and survive, by underpaying them.'

I heard loud footsteps and scuffling behind me. I turned to see Peter Pepper, the ambulance driver, shoving past people in his pew as he wrestled his way out. A few diehards followed. *Hmm,* I thought, *my father should see them, they're committing a mortal sin.* Attending mass means being fully present until the people's communion and we weren't even halfway there. The sermon continued in that vein and I felt my face grow hot. Straight after mass, I dashed around to the sacristy and asked the altar boy,

'Who is this new priest? Can I speak to him?'

By then of course, he was peering past the boy,

'Hullor, my dear. What can I do for you?' he said in a fresh Irish accent.

'Hello Father, sorry to bother you. That was the first Christian sermon I've ever heard in a Catholic Church. That was wonderful. Have you had dinner yet? I'd like you to come down to meet my family.'

'Shorr my dear, I'd love to.'

I gave him the address and ran all the way home to tell my parents, 'The new parish priest from Mdantsane, Father Martin Flanagan, is coming for a drink and a snack.'

'That's lovely,' my mother said as the doorbell rang.

He came in and sat next to my father as I excitedly related parts of the sermon to all in the sitting room.

'Father is going to change this fossil church and bring it to life.'

'Nor, my dear,' he said shaking his head, 'I dornt think the parishioners of St Partrick's will like all that I have to say. Where I was until now, Keiskammahoek, behind the Amatola Mountains, people are so poor, every one of you here in Vincent is a millionaire'.

'How did you get on with the language, Father? I don't think many there speak English?' my mother asked.

'No. One of the headman's senior wives came after mass and started me off with basic Xhosa until my text books arrived.'

'You are determined,' my father added.

'Well, Joe,' he continued, 'as you can see, half of my index finger is missing.' He held up his right hand. 'To be a priest one had to be perfect in body. After the accident my grandmother went mad with novenas and rosaries, praying for my finger to grow back so that I could be the priest the family intended. To be accepted into the seminary was a privilege. To be sent to Africa was a bonus.'

'Father, let's hope your experiences here don't rob you of your idealism,' my mother interjected.

'According to the novice master, it will take a lot to affect me.' He rose to emphasise what came next. 'The first time I met the master he said "To Africa. Ireland will be too tame for you."' He swung his right leg kicking the air, as if he was being kicked to Africa. His exuberance had us all agog.

'So I have been telling the traditional Red people how Our Blessed Lord died for them on the cross,' and he lifted his right hand, one and a half fingers extended upwards blessing the air. I watched his every move. I'd never met a priest who expressed his feelings so openly before. This one even played golf. But it was his enthusiasm for the job, his love of African people, his disdain for the system and his courage that impressed all of us.

He stood up to leave. 'Please Father, have a little snack with us, no big dinner on a Sunday,' my mother cajoled.

I went to the kitchen to help the cook with toasted sandwiches.

At the table he sat next to me draping his arm over the back of my chair, 'Now wasn't it just great that you had to come to the evening mass?'

'I'd never have met you nor heard a sermon taken directly from the Gospel.' I replied. 'You are the first priest who has the courage to say what we have been waiting to hear from the church in these dark days.'

Later in the week he rang to thank my mother for the meal. 'Is that you dorling?'

'It's Cecile here, Father. How are you?'

'Well, as we all thought, I am no longer welcome in Vincent.'

'What did he say? I bet Peter Pepper was the first to complain.'

'Father Muckley said that as a visitor passing through, I had abused the courtesy he extended by allowing me to say the evening mass. In fact his words were, "You will never stand in my pulpit again. Do you want me to starve and the church to go bankrupt?" I thought he was joking. No my dear, I won't be able to bring those fossils back to life as you put it.'

'That is terrible. How disappointing. We will have to visit you in Mdantsane.'

'Yes, but in the meantime would you like to come with me on Friday? I'm off to Lilyfontein to see Father Ed O'Connor, chaplain to the convent there. We'll have dinner with him.'

I was excited. Lilyfontein was an isolated primary school and convent in the bush, but only an hour from my home—in the middle of Red Xhosa country.

WE SOON TURNED off the Main Transkei Road and bumped along an unmade road until that too disappeared. The *bakkie* swayed and made a terrible noise as it scraped anthills concealed in the tall grass. At one stage he swung too far over to avoid a large rock, and my side of the car connected hard with a thorn tree. The long white thorns glowed like daggers in the twilight next to my window.

'Look here, Father,' I addressed him firmly after a gale of wet-eyed laughter, 'are we going somewhere or is this just an excuse to get lost in Africa with a sixteen-year-old girl in a long skirt?'

'Oh my dear, I didn't mean to worry you. See that light on the hill? That's Ed's house,' and he squeezed my right knee before revving the engine and moving forwards and backwards until we were on our way again.

'Hullor' a tall gangly figure with brown hair, very crooked teeth and a priest's collar waved with both hands from the veranda.

Inside the cottage, a tiny table and two chairs. 'I'll sit on the floor,' I offered.

'No, no you won't,' they protested together. 'I'll sit up here,' and Ed hopped onto the table.

'What will you drink, darlin'?'

'Whisky please, with ice.'

'To be sure,' Ed said, 'someone's been in me cupboard, only half a bottle of brandy here. But since you don't drink Martin, we'll share your coke.' He poured half-and-half coke and brandy into two glasses and handed me one. I lit a cigarette. After a gentle tap on a door that I hadn't noticed before at the other end of the room, a wizened old nun in a black veil came in quietly. In a heavy German accent she told Father, 'Your dinner is ready'.

Ed boomed at her, 'Mother Anna, this is Miss Yazbek.' I quickly pushed my cigarette over to Martin who playfully lifted it up and began to pose.

Mother Anna inclined gently towards me, 'Don't let them do anything naughty to you.'

I smiled, 'I'll be fine, Mother, thank you.'

NUNS AND PRIESTS were always around us and influenced my parents in many ways. From my first school days to my last, nuns held sway over my school life. In the beginning, some of the older sisters were stern and even eccentric. Mostly they were Europeans who came to South Africa before, during and after the Second World War, some wearing the effects, for better or worse, in the classroom.

Sister Johanna, my first teacher was remarkable in so many ways. After her I was with Sister Sixta, who had a horror of germs and twice a day burnt all the soiled tissues in the metal paper basket 'to keep the classroom air clean.'

Sister Clare had taught both my sisters and it was my turn in standard three. She spent most of the day on the floor at the back of the classroom attending to her six canaries. She had clipped their wings and spread layers of newspaper on the floor. Little bowls of water and tiny mounds of seed made our whole room into a birdcage. We had to kneel down next to her on the floor to show her our work or read from our books, first saying 'excuse me' to the bird she was talking to or grooming. Once one of them did a dropping on the page I was reading from in my *Sonneblom Reeks.* 'Flick it off like zis,' she said, middle finger and thumb sending the plop onto the floor. She was not the brightest bead in the rosary, but we knew nothing of her history or past and what she might have experienced during the war.

After Sister Marion refused to teach me piano, I was sent to Sister Cletus to learn singing. I had to stand very close to her and watched her dark moustache expand and contract as she pursed her lips for a long 'hooo', at the end of 'when I'm calling you, whooo, hoo hoo hoo hoo'. The Convent and de la Salle college combined to perform Hiawatha in the new hall. It had a good stage and dressing rooms, thick blue velvet curtains and all the necessities for performance. My sister Michele played Minni Ha Ha Laughing Water and I had to croon across the stage to her.

My lack of skill paled next to the boys' intransigence. They simply would not appear onstage on cue as they were too busy smoking out the back. Tiny Sister Cletus went outside and confronted them,

'Vy are you not cummink ven called? Hurry up.'

Tom, an excellent actor, screamed back at her, 'You're nothing but a bloody little Nazi. Stop bossing us.'

We were scandalized.

After school, he went on to university to study drama but killed himself before graduation. There was talk of the security police putting pressure on him to become an informer.

IN THE CONVENT kitchen garden, Sister Millana, the cook, padded about the pathways between the vegetable beds in her black wellington boots. She'd cut kale and endive and pull turnips and radishes, filling her basket with the makings of the nuns' next meal.

One day I went with my mother to drop off a cake at the kitchen door and Sister Millana came out for a chat. In an excited voice she told my mother how she had had to fire one of the kitchen hands the previous day. Every time she was sent into the pantry, she filled her pockets with whatever she could take home. 'She vos kvietly shtealing,' she said, spitting in all directions from her ill-fitting false teeth.

'But sister, those poor devils don't have enough to eat.'

'Ja, Ja, Mrs Yutzbek, but she vos kvietly shtealing. Ve can't feed zem all. Ve vent sru ze vor and ve hadn't enough to eat. Ve neffer shtole anysing. Anyvay, zis is a vunderful cake. Sank you so much. Ven are you cummink to learn ze sauerkraut?'

My mother was privileged to be allowed into the nuns' kitchen which formed part of their enclosure. The big pot of sauerkraut she brought home had to be stirred every second day over some days. From its nest of blankets in the pantry, next to the wrapped yoghurt pot, the foreign smell overwhelmed the olives and thyme and other comforting aromas with which we grew up. When serving day arrived, 'Poof. What in the hell is that? *Ya dillee anna* (Oh poor me),' my father's exclamations sent the bowl straight back to the kitchen.

One South African nun whose family were market gardeners in the district once accosted my mother and me after school. 'Mrs Yazbek, your husband doesn't like the government. If blacks come to power we will have to share our homes with them,' she spat.

'Yes, Sister Vincent,' my mother said quietly, 'That is what the Gospel says. We are all made in His image and likeness.' I panted next to them, waiting for veils and fur to fly in a cat fight but of course they were two middle-aged matrons, not zealous teenagers.

CHANGES BEGAN TO happen in the church in the 1960s, because of the Second Vatican Council. Mass was said facing the congregation and in English instead of Latin; we could receive communion in our hands instead of on our tongues. Our parents liked the new ways but realised that inside religious orders, there was turbulence. Some of the nuns were anxious and confided in my mother about the new habits that showed their hair and even a little leg. My parents whispered about priests and nuns who were leaving to get married. Hedwig was such a case: a lovely woman whom we felt to be honest and brave.

'Tsk tsk, Reverend Mother, I am so sorry to hear that,' my mother spoke earnestly into the telephone, in an uncharacteristically low tone. 'When did she decide?' After a short pause, 'She'll be such a loss to the school; the girls all love her'. Another break, then, 'Yes, I know she's quiet but she is spirited and strong and they sense that'.

'When would you like me to come up? Yes, half-past four is fine. I'll bring Cecile along and tell her to keep quiet about it. In fact I won't tell her what it's about. We'll come to the front parlour. It'll be a pleasure. Goodbye, Reverend Mother.' As she turned away from the phone she saw me, 'Oh, so you heard all that. I suppose there's no use my pretending.' I remained silent. It always led to further information from the questioner.

'She's leaving as soon as possible. She's such a lovely nun. She was our driver when we went to the motherhouse in Germany last year. A very capable woman.'

'A nun driver,' I giggled, remembering the over-revved Convent Cortina screaming as clouds of blue smoke poured from the exhaust. 'You knew they had smashed their car three times this year and you and Daddy were driven by a nun in Germany?'

'Mother Superior would have ensured we had the best driver. It would have been too embarrassing for overseas guests to be injured in a smash. Anyway, get ready. We'll go to the Convent at four o'clock.'

'What for?'

'Oh just come with me please, we'll see Sister Hedwig as well as Mother Frances.'

'I like Sister Hedwig,' I chattered on. 'She's so normal next to the other nuns.' By that I meant that she had visible breasts, clearly in a bra, and a waistline. We could see her body.

The front parlour was reserved for nuns and priests meeting with lay people on religious business. That afternoon, the door was open. My mother pressed the bell and we went straight in and sat down at the round table. Its finely embroidered cloth of pink and blue sweet peas looked just like the one we'd been given for Christmas. The nuns sat 'at recreation' for an hour after dinner working beautiful silken colours into table linen. My mother had a whole chest full of their efforts as a result of my father doing pro bono legal work for the convent. A bowl of freshly picked red roses and yellow broom spread a light scent. Sister Eustochium, keeper of the door, put her head in from the enclosure, 'Muzza vil be here shortly'.

'How are you, Sister Eustochium?' my mother greeted.

'Ferry vell, Mrs Yutzbek.' She made our name sound German the way she pronounced a "t" in front of the "z".

'You are doing a wonderful job with Barbara, my niece. My brother, Dr Haddad, is very grateful that you are willing to teach her. Poor thing. She is the same age as Cecile here, fifteen. She should be in standard seven.' I watched skinny Sister Eustochium with her dark moustache and stubbly chin fend off my mother's speech. We thought she looked like a scarecrow. It seemed right that she should teach my Down syndrome cousin.

'It is all Gott's vill und I am grateful to do it,' and she left with a bow. When we had tea break at school, we'd see Barbie sitting with Sister Eustochium on a bench under the oak trees. Her nursemaid, usually a young African girl, would sit on the ground nearby in case Barbie became difficult. Occasionally Barbie would start screaming or sit on the ground and refuse to budge. Sometimes one of my other cousins would accompany me and we'd try to help but invariably, she'd be taken home. It seemed important that Barbie learn how to count and recognise colours or, as we'd heard my mother worry, 'What will happen to her when her parents die?'

A loud tap on the door announced Mother Frances' swishing entrance. She was brisk and to the point. Her rosary, which hung from her waist, was still swinging wildly when she began, 'Thank you for coming Bertha.'

'It's a pleasure, Mother, anything I can do to help.'

Three soft taps on the door. 'Come,' Mother ordered.

Sister Hedwig came in looking flushed, nodded and smiled at us. I backed away from the table and stood quietly, close to the corner of the room. I observed my mother look her up and down a few times and then ask quietly, ' What size shoe do you take Sister?'

The nun whispered her way out of the room. I felt so sad. I wondered why they treated her like a servant.

'I will go to town tomorrow morning, Mother, and then I will come and collect her at three o'clock.'

Mother Frances pulled herself upright, 'Oh yes please, after all the girls have gone and the teachers are still in their rooms. It will not do for anyone to be around.'

On the way home, my mother seemed to be wondering aloud to herself, 'She must have brown hair, if her eyebrows are anything to go by, a brown suit with beige shoes and bag. Garlicks. That's where I'll find everything.' We were home and my mother had leapt from the car and gone straight to the kitchen to discuss dinner with the cook before I could find the most suitable question from the long line that queued in my brain. The guest bedroom was already being prepared for Hedwig's transition when I went into the house. The gardener had been sent to cut roses and yellow broom. The night table was covered with a starched embroidered tea cloth like the convent parlour. The venetian blinds were lowered and half-closed.

The next afternoon I went along on the two-minute drive to the convent. My mother swung her car onto the parlour driveway and pulled into the bishop's parking space. We sat and waited with the front passenger door open. Sister Hedwig came out alone. Her face was red and her eyes were puffy behind dark glasses. A nun with sunglasses, I thought, and then I remembered that as a driver she was allowed to have them. She placed her small tote bag on the seat next to me and went to sit in front next to my mother. It was all so quiet but I noticed my mother reach across and squeeze Sister Hedwig's hand as we left the convent grounds. We pulled into our driveway and one of the gardeners appeared to carry the bags but I took the small bag upstairs myself and left it outside the guest room. She took it in with her and shut the door. A few minutes later, Katie, the cook, went in with a tea tray and some freshly brandied fruitcake. Later my mother knocked softly on the door, 'Are you all right? Can I come in?' That evening, as we headed for dinner, the guest room door opened slowly, 'Come on, come Hedwig,' I encouraged and we walked into the dining room together.

'Who is this beautiful young woman having dinner with us tonight?' my father enthused. She went red and looked as if she was going to cry.

He went right up to her, 'You wonderful driver, you look gorgeous,' and he kissed her on both her flaming cheeks.

'All right, darl,' my mother hushed.

'No, darling,' my father persisted. 'You've done a great job, you and Garlicks. Hedwig looks lovely.'

My parents retired early as usual but I sat up with Hedwig in the sitting room. I made coffee. We chatted and our conversation grew quieter yet more personal.

Somehow I felt that she was expressing grave doubts to me about the existence of this Catholic God and all the church laws. It freed me to express my own doubts. I went to make tea.

'Vait, I bring you sumsing,' and she went to her room. She returned with a small paperback. A cringing fellow on the front cover proclaimed the title, *God is for Real, Man.* Handing it to me she said, 'You keep it. You need it. I won't need it anymore.'

'Why not?'

'Because I won't teach religion anymore.'

That set me off questioning her on all the 'mysteries' in the Catholic Church. I droned on and then noticed she was shivering. 'You're cold,' I said and fetched two rugs from the bedroom. We wrapped ourselves up and talked on. I asked strong and difficult questions and she replied quietly and gently. 'Tell me when you'd like to go to bed,' I said.

She chuckled slightly and said, 'I haven't chatted after nine o'clock for the three years that I was in this convent. Three years. Long enough for me'.

She went to bed in the new Garlicks pyjamas—flannelette for our winter, 'as good for a north German summer,' my mother had said.

The next day, my mother took her to the airport and she flew home. For some years we wondered what had become of her. My mother received no replies to her letters. Long after I'd left school, one of the older nuns went home to Europe. Through her we heard whispers that Hedwig had disappeared so thoroughly, she could only have been dead.

Of all those women, Sister Johanna, my first teacher, remained my beacon. In standard five, when Sister Irma insisted I stay back daily for handwriting improvement lessons, I ran to Sister Johanna for consolation. In standard six, stern Sister Judith loaded us up with work and I became quite religious. One day after school, I found Sister Johanna in her classroom and told her I loved her hands and wanted to be a nun like her. Expressing the idea thrilled me. That night I went to my parents' bedroom to say goodnight. My mother was reading the English *Women's Weekly* and my father was dozing. I told them too that I would become a nun one day. My mother put her magazine down, 'Oh' she said. But her knowing smile scared me. I began to question myself, and although I remained prayerful and loved my long rosary, by the time I was fifteen nun-stuff disappeared when I discovered Raynor Bluemel, whose mother owned a dress shop down the road.

Sister Johanna and I still had conversations before and after school. I loved talking with her and soon found that she shared my despair about the situation in the country. Preparing to go home to Switzerland for a holiday, she asked me if I thought my mother would lend her her car so that she could take photographs to show her family where she worked and lived. My mother readily agreed and so, with Sister Johanna behind the wheel and me behind the camera, we set off for the shanty town of Duncan Village. On the way she told me of her early years in South Africa. Our school was her first posting in 1959. Initially, European missionary nuns who went to Africa were never allowed to return home on holidays. The rules had been relaxed now and they could go home every five years. As we entered Duncan Village and drove past the sign warning that only permit holders were allowed inside, I looked across at her robes and billowing veil and felt safe. She accelerated down the muddy alleys between the shacks and I leaned from the car clicking the camera thirty six times. Her deep compassion for the disadvantaged inspired her students as she related the effects of poverty on people all around us, Africans in particular. She had a Red Cross box in her classroom and each week all in the school were encouraged to visit her with groceries for the needy. When anyone did, her room full of five-year-olds were asked to applaud the generosity of the latest donor.

In my final year at school Sister Johanna was the prioress and Sister Lina was the principal. As head girl I constantly protested against Sister Lina's petty rules that we were supposed to enforce. With miniskirts in fashion, we had to line students up to kneel on the floor and holding a ruler, ensure that their school dresses were no more than six inches off the floor. In the end, Sister Johanna had to mediate between us, a difficult task because that fight with Sister Lina was the climax of an ongoing battle we'd had all year in the classroom.

'What are you doing in the corridor?' Sister Johanna asked me one morning during school hours.

'They're having history in there,' I said as if she knew what that meant.

'This is your matric year. Why are you wasting time like this?'

'Sister Lina chose the syllabus and I object to doing yet another year of South African history when we could be studying Europe. I believe that continuing to teach this version of South African history from year to year throughout our schooling is fostering some of the myths that are keeping this government in power.'

'You may be right but aren't you jeopardising your matric results?'

'I'll be fine. I have decided to study South West Africa, the legacy of its former German occupiers and the role South Africa sees itself playing in the further development of the country.' I knew I was still selling out in a way but I couldn't manage anything more at that late stage.

THE CONVENT OLD Girls' annual reunion was held in the school hall. About one hundred women were served lunch and light entertainment followed. My mother and her sister, as old girls of the convent in Queenstown, also attended.

My father, not to be outdone by one hundred women, borrowed a lustrous auburn wig from the hairdresser, and high heels, bra and suspenders from one of my larger aunts. A tall hat with a chiffon swathe and a slinky frock completed his outfit. The make-up was applied generously but no amount of beige powder could reduce the impact of his bushy black eyebrows. But it was the authenticity he insisted on, with the underwear that was interesting. At the chosen time, a drum roll announced that Anita van Tonder had finally arrived off the train from the Transvaal. My father teetered up the hall on the wobbly stilettos and took the stage, pattering in an attempted high-pitched voice with grossly effeminate hand movements. The hall vibrated as the assembled alumni screeched and wailed their delight. The nuns laughed as raucously as the rest. Then he hauled out his banjo ukelele and played so that all could sing along. Having softened them up, he'd announce the latest fund-raising project: a white marble statue of the Sacred Heart from Carrarra, a new surface for the hockey field or a quarter Olympic size swimming pool. He departed waving a large handkerchief with which he frequently dabbed his eyes. Year after year, the same performance caused the same hilarious uproar.

FROM THE LATE 1960s, there had been a shortage of nuns. The convent closed down in the mid-1970s the nuns going their separate ways. Sister Lina went back to Europe and married the fiancé she had left to enter the convent thirty years before. The older women retired, while some of the younger ones went to convents in the north of the country. But Sister Johanna changed her path. She went to work at a school for a thousand deaf African children. Not only did she have to learn Xhosa, but she had to learn sign language in Xhosa as well. She eventually became the principal of that huge boarding school and weathered the terrors of the eighties in South Africa: nocturnal visits from police, pressure from activists and freedom fighters who threatened to abduct the children. She said that the worst was that the children returned to school after the holidays completely traumatised both by police action in the townships and internecine conflicts in the rural areas where they had been staying with family. The war penetrated the worlds of the nuns and deaf children alike.

Not all of the sisters were in agreement with my political leanings. With Sister Johanna, however, I could have a social justice conversation, which helped me to hone my perceptions and ideas into meaningful practice. She was clearly thinking similarly about poverty, homelessness and education. I was deeply inspired when she went to work at St Thomas' School—for so long we white children were the privileged few in the palace while thousands outside had no access to the education we took for granted.

What we share with others in friendship remains with us always. The material structures of our lives change—we become ill, we move countries—but the essence of that relationship sits in our heart memories to sustain and shape the individuals we become. Sister Johanna, with her enormous energy, big smile, warm heart, steely courage to make hard decisions and her voice, always speckled with laughter, has visited my mind through decades of my life. When Auntie Susie was dying in hospital, Sister Johanna, our friendship angel, was visiting her. I will always be grateful for a most compassionate and very dear friend.

18

Olive Schreiner, Cecil Rhodes, politics and police

women of dimbaza and ilinge
you can now provide for yourself
like the women of sada and limehill
you can toil through the week
with the making of beads
to be sold by well-meaning souls
at three rand fifty to seventy-five
the menfolk, too, have their trade
fine carvers of coffins they are
and the left-over beads
could be used to decorate the dead
of the villages of sorrow

women of dimbaza and ilinge
JAMES MATHEWS

'I passed! I'm off to Rhodes!' I whooped to my mother in the kitchen, as I brought the mail in. I'd had a tumultuous final year at school. The fights with Sister Lina, my distress at the unyielding political situation and some of the nuns' apparent racism disillusioned me. I was desperate to study further—social work. My father, however, had law in mind and had already registered me to do a BA LLB. 'As a social worker, you'll be a nursemaid to people with terrible problems and it'll make you cry.' I remembered my aunts telling me how, in the early days of practice, the cases my father dealt with in criminal and family law preyed on his mind and upset him. But I was determined.

The day after I got my results, I went to see him at his town office to have a final discussion about my university courses. When I got there, Mark followed me inside. I greeted him and went straight across to kiss my father. 'Well done, my darling,' he said. 'You'll do us proud here in this office working with Markie and me, three Yazbek lawyers and then who knows when Paulie will join us.'

'Daddy, I really want to do social work, but I'll put both courses together in my first degree.'

'See what I mean, Dad,' my brother interjected, 'she's going to waste her time just like Anita'.

'Well Michele is teaching and Anita's got two children now and I don't think that's a waste of time,' I said.

'Well, don't just come home with a husband. First get your degree,' my father said.

'So Daddy,' I said, taking the conversation back to its original purpose, 'I'll major in Legal Theory and Social Work as a beginning. Then I'll add psychology and sociology.' He agreed. I filled in the forms and we arranged the date when my parents would take me to Grahamstown.

When I arrived home, my mother had already been on the phone to Truworths Boutique in town and ordered a large box of frocks for me. Granny was ready with the pins and tape measure when it arrived and I began to try on: like some, hate some, have some shortened and let some out over the hips. I had to walk this way and that, stand sideways, sit cross-legged, all the while the two women discussed what they were doing. Granny, at eighty, was still a good pinner with a very straight eye. My mother was a ruthless unpicker.

The following weeks were busy and when packing day arrived, Katie rushed to do it. We fought as she scolded, 'Who is going to iron this for you if you crease it like that? You are going to be too busy with studies'.

'Remember, I like the lavender bags in between,' I said.

'Ooh, you and your magic stuff.'

I had been allocated to Olive Schreiner House in St Mary's Hall. Schreiner was a great feminist writer, author in 1883 of *The Story of an African Farm*. Rhodes University in Grahamstown was named after Cecil Rhodes, a thundering imperialist who tried to leave a British boot mark from Cape Town to Cairo. Olive Schreiner eventually had a falling out with Rhodes but both still loom large in African history.

My parents delivered me to university on a late summer Sunday afternoon in 1971. Over afternoon tea on the lawns in front of the dining room, first year students were able to meet. After tea, my father carried the bags into my room, and my mother became anxious and tearful. She helped me to measure my window and bed for the curtains and cover I would make in the first holidays. It was a comfortable room on the ground floor facing west with beautiful sunsets if that first one was any indication.

The bell rang at six for our first meal in the dining room. We streamed through the French doors of a red brick Edwardian building, into a wood-panelled hall. Ten women students sat at each table while a few senior students sat at the high table crowned by the lady warden and her two assistants all in full academic regalia. '*Benedictus, Benedicate*' and we banged and clomped our chairs into position. A stream of white-aproned African women carrying trays poured out of the kitchen and large serving platters of strong-smelling pilchards and beetroot were placed at the end of each table. During the week, it would be flat meat and vegetables. Then the *sissie,* as the African waitresses were called, came back to our table with a plate and gave it to one of the students, Beedle. On it were a tomato, a leaf of lettuce, two crackers and a slab of cheese the size that my mother ordered once a week from the grocer for the whole family. She burst out laughing, 'Cynthia warned me about vegetarian meals.' She turned to high table and waved at her older sister, who waved the lettuce leaf back. Mrs Driver, the hall warden, glared sideways but carried on eating.

After dinner, we sat about the lawns in the late summer twilight. 'Yes, we're vegetarians,' Cynthia had joined us. 'We are theosophists.'

'Is that why you both never stop smiling? You look so happy.'

'Well what's there to be miserable about?' and she put her arm around Coll, her roommate.

I thought about all the terrible things happening in the African township where our *sissies* lived, just up the hill. But I was quiet, dying to know more about the Russian woman they called Madame Blavatsky, the founder of theosophy.

Orientation and initiation by senior students filled the first week, which ended with a picnic at the sea. Mostly I remember drunken first year men vomiting or lying unconscious in the sand. I had only ever seen that among the alcoholics my father brought home to dry out. At the picnic, a smiling second year sidled up to me, 'Hi, my name is Christine. I've come to invite you to a meeting—every Tuesday after dinner in my room. Bible study: we discuss Revelation particularly and why coloured shoes are dangerous.'

My astonishment seemed to draw Christine out even more '…And make-up is not in the scheme.'

I went along that night but soon concluded that my grooming was perceived as vanity, my fashion as immoral and my politics too close to the local leftists. I didn't wait for coffee and cake and was followed out by Jude. Giggling down the corridor as we lit up, 'What ya come in there for?' Jude quizzed, as she puffed rings into the air.

'I could ask you that,' I replied, looking sideways at her Abbey Road jacket and red shoes.

On the first day of lectures, we had to register. By the end of the first month, I was having doubts about social work. The tutorials, loaded with theological students, required discussion and debate and everyone always agreed with everything while I was the only one ever to express views contrary to those held by the tutor. The head of department, Professor Frieda La Grange, was a formidably couturiered grande dame in suits and matching jewellery. She had come to Rhodes from an Afrikaans university in the Transvaal where she had sat on a government board drafting the most stringent anti-drug laws in the world at the time including a mandatory five-years prison term for second offence possession of marijuana. She had repeatedly lectured us on the importance of closed black patent leather shoes and stockings for the women and ties with white shirts for the men.

'Social work is a Christian National profession and we must reflect that in our self presentation.'

Before term ended, the professor, Ma La as we called her, sent for me.

'Miss Yazbek, why are you studying social work?'

After a short meeting, I told her I would apply to change my degree to Arts and left her office.

I felt thwarted by the system. I wanted to be of use in my country. For a few weeks, I was lost and then I became weepy. All my life I had promised to work to alleviate the effects of poverty and discrimination in our society and now I felt the door was closed to me.

DURING ORIENTATION WEEK, I had also signed up with NUSAS, the National Union of South African Students, one of the most defiant anti-apartheid organizations in the country. Founded in the 1920s, its charter was based on the Universal Declaration of Human Rights. Somehow, by the early seventies, NUSAS was not as active on the bigger campuses as it was at Rhodes. I attended regular meetings at which policy was discussed and action planned. Our regional committee had the same divisions as the national executive: NUSED focused on educational matters, NUSWEL on welfare and Aquarius on culture (art and film festivals). I worked for NUSWEL and our brief was to collect funds from students to sponsor schooling and textbooks for the African children of Makanaskop, Tantyie and Fingo Village. Unlike whites, they had to purchase their own textbooks and stationery. Everyone I approached was keen to help, so it was a shock when I had my first encounter with a student from Port Elizabeth, 'I don't agree with education for black people. Who is going to build the roads and mine the gold if they all go to school?'

Before long, I was one of eight members on the regional committee, among them, Karl, a tall muscular Afrikaner from Port Elizabeth. He always wore khakis and passed himself off as a bush lover. I didn't have a lot to say to him, I had the feeling he came from another world—and he did. At the 1996 Truth and Reconciliation hearings he and his brother revealed that they were Special Branch operatives. As a police informer on Rhodes campus, he was not alone. We had been frightened by government sources into believing that on English language campuses, one in ten students was a plant.

GOING AWAY TO university was the greatest excitement for me, especially after I left social work. Sociology and anthropology opened doors into worlds of learning and I discovered the pleasures of a university library. I'd go to the shelves for one or two items and hours later, I'd still be sitting on the floor surrounded by books as I tried to dispatch the lint in my brain. I knew I had mountains to learn.

In my bedroom in residence, we had chain smoking, coffee drinking all night conversations. At dawn, we'd walk into town to buy hot bread from the bakery for an early breakfast before going to bed.

Campus visitors came from all over. Cosmos Desmond was a Catholic priest who fought to expose the 'dumping grounds,' as the government played chess with African communities through the Group Areas Act. His book, *The Discarded People* was immediately banned, and so was he. He fled into exile in Britain.

Oswald Joseph Mtshali, a best-selling poet of the struggle, came to read from his book, *Sounds of a Cowhide Drum.*

Steve Biko said, 'The most potent weapon in the hand of the oppressor is the mind of the oppressed.'* One of the ways the government controlled us was by censoring everything. Without a deliberate effort, it was very difficult to know what they were doing. I felt that whites themselves were oppressed by this enforced ignorance, and the terrible thing was that most didn't realise they were being kept in the dark. In High Street the SPCK (Society for Promoting Christian Knowledge) bookshop secreted banned books for me before their stocks were confiscated.

IT WAS MY first July holiday at home in East London. The winters were mild, no wind or rain, just slightly shorter days. I wore long African style skirts made from fabric I bought at Mr Howell's shop, Vale Stores, down the Main Transkei Road. He sold towels, blankets, and yards of stiff

---

*'White Racism and Black Consciousness' in '*Student Perspectives on South Africa*' 1972, David Philip, Cape Town.

printed cottons as well as the blue and brown German prints, which were made into traditional Xhosa skirts for the women and shirts for the men. I stood in the line with the rest of the customers to be served in Xhosa. They were mostly African domestic workers from our neighbourhood and I overheard plenty of gossip about the wealthy employers, some even relatives of ours.

My mother sometimes even bought unusual kaftan fabrics for me. We had a common interest in dressing up, but widely divergent tastes. My conciliatory parents never criticised my myriad necklaces and bare feet. But my hair—a giant wide Afro bush —was a real focus for my father's angst.

'She's going to jail,' my father said looking at my hair. 'She wants to go to jail.' Turning directly to me, 'You are attracting attention to yourself. They are going to pick you up for questioning. Looks like drugs and politics to them.'

'Too bad,' I said. 'They've got nothing on me, they've known what I think for years.'

'You're playing with fire,' my father said. 'They're ruthless. Tonight, what did you say you're doing?'

'Tomorrow night. I'm going to a play.'

'Your mother says you're taking Katie.' He was referring to our cook to whom I had become very close in the three years she'd been working for us.

'We're going together,' I said. 'It's an African version of *Oedipus* at the Warehouse Theatre.'

'They'll be there, of course. They watch all whites who go to those productions.'

'CEEL, WHAT'RE YOU doing tonight?' My friend Lucia was on the phone. 'I met these two guys at rugby this afternoon. One says he's a friend of my brother Rory. They've invited us for coffee on the beachfront.'

'What are they like?'

'They look all right.'

'Ask Judy,' I suggested, referring to a mutual school friend, 'she lives close to you'.

'No, they mentioned you. They said something about my friend with long skirts and big hair who's at 'varsity with me.'

'Oh, how creepy,' I said. ' Of all those with big hair and long skirts how do you know they meant me?'

'Because one of them added something about "her dad's a lawyer"'.

'Shit, Lucia, I'm not going out with them. They sound funny.'

'Please come. I want to go, but not by myself. I'm sick of being at home. My mother's depressed again and I haven't seen my friends for ages.'

'OK.'

'Good. We'll pick you up at half past seven.'

A gold Ford Capri with a black vinyl top pulled up at the front gate and I squeezed into the small space at the back next to a gangly, acne-scarred face in stove-pipe jeans and leather boots. His too-tight leather jacket looked borrowed from a younger brother. Their heavy Afrikaans accents were unusual to me. Most of the boys I'd been out with were Catholics from the Brothers' College over the road from the convent. There were no Afrikaners there. They all went to their own schools.

I produced my ladies' briar pipe and lit a plug of sweet red amphora. Clouds of blue smoke and the heady smell combined to give the driver a coughing fit and watering eyes. I puffed on, and we raced wordlessly to the beach.

To reach the Pappagallo Coffee Shop at the end of the esplanade, we strolled a boardwalk beside breaking waves lit by a bright moon. The gangly one held back and seemed to be deliberately slowing the pace, while the conversation went nowhere. Lucia and the other were way ahead of us. Next thing he put his arm around my waist. I seethed.

His tone changed, became conspiratorial, 'What are the students protesting about at Rhodes?'

'How do you know about that?' I snapped.

'Seen it in the papers.'

'Gowns to dinner and all that crap—what you're reading is what's happening.'

'There must be more,' he said. 'Others, big bosses behind it.'

'Whatcha talking about? We hate restricted visiting hours and dress regulations.'

'But surely people must be getting instructions from other places like Wits and UCT,' he persisted. 'They're also marching there, you know.'

In my mind's eye, hundreds of black-gowned students were marching in silence. We mourned the loss of academic freedom and the end of democracy in our country. We wanted the hand that eventually became the fist of the government out of our universities. Now I had this punk, arm around my waist, pretending to be naïve and curious, asking me pointed questions. Shit, I thought, I'm close to something evil.

I swung around, calling, 'Lucia, I'm going home now. Come on, it's late.'

'Ah, Ceel, we haven't had coffee yet,' she begged.

'I'm tired.'

The two guys quickened their strangely small steps and I watched them from where I was, leaning breathless against the car door. Looks like they're used to marching bigger steps to bigger bosses, I thought.

'Something wrong, Ceel?' Lucia worried.

'Just cold. Take me home please.'

'I'll warm you,' the gangly one sniggered.

'You'll burn up if you touch me,' I spat.

CE 41285, CE 41285, CE 41285, I repeated the numberplate in my head, all the way home.

I MULLED OVER what they thought I'd been up to. All I could think of was that during second term I had been on a student union excursion to Dimbaza—a dumping ground for Africans forcibly removed from newly declared white areas. Every ninth house shared a toilet and a tap. There was no living inside those corrugated iron shelters. In every row of houses there was an undertaker for a population of children and the elderly. The graveyard was one small mound after another: forty per cent of children died before they turned five . . . It seemed as though to attract the attention of the security police, one had to merely inform oneself of what was happening.

The next day my father sent for me from his office in town. I wondered what he had found out this time. In the autumn vacation, he'd sent for me and ordered me to write a curt letter to a professor who was making advances to me. This man had become drunk one night and had rung me at home. My youngest brother had answered the phone, 'Cecile, it sounds like a drunk professor.' My parents flew out of bed and grabbed the extension phone and listened in.

'Miss Yazbek,' growled the professor down the phone, 'Pray for the dark night of the soul.'

'You don't sound well, Professor Kelly. Maybe you should go home to bed.' The racket in the background was probably the Vic pub, where hardcore drinkers, students and faculty alike drowned their sorrows nightly.

'Daddy says to put the phone down,' my brother whispered, pulling my sleeve.

Feet pounded up the hallway to the kitchen, 'Did he touch you?' my mother wailed, screwing up her face. 'Jesus help me, please, Jesus. Did he lay a finger on you?'

I took a step back. 'You should know,' I snarled remembering how she'd chased me with an hibiscus switch when I was seven. 'You should know,' I repeated, 'that nobody puts a finger on me if I don't want them to.'

'Cheeky devil,' my mother hissed. 'That's what happens when you go to university. Read all sorts of books giving you wild ideas. You read too much.'

The next morning, as instructed, I went to my father's office in town. Crowds of shoppers made parking difficult, but I found a space down the street and walked to my father's building with one of the African clerks. Oswald Ben Mazwi, son of a local chief, had worked there for years. As senior messenger, he had supervised the mailing of the registered letter to the drunken professor the previous holiday. 'How is the university, Cecile?' he greeted me warmly.

'Great thanks, Os. How are you?' I asked, aware that his limp had become more pronounced.

'Getting old now.'

I walked alone into my father's private office, and found my brother Mark standing at the window. 'You see, Dad,' he said, 'you should never have let her go to university. She should have stayed at home. She'll just get married and have kids, a complete waste of a university education'.

I was furious but my father got in before me, 'Aah, quiet, you! That's not what we're talking about now.' He turned to me, 'My darling, I checked the registration of that car you went out in; it belongs to the security police'.

My brother flew in with, 'And they told me they'll get you if you don't stop saying things and writing letters to the papers. Aha, you'd better toe the line from now on,' he smirked.

I left the building and walked outside into the sunshine. I noticed the shoppers were mostly black, with a sprinkling of white faces. Fools, I thought to myself. As if a few uneducated white scum can hold power over all of us. They must have known Lucia and I were old friends and tried to get to me through her. A police car with siren wailing raced through the traffic. I felt sick and went home to phone Lucia.

'Tell me the story again of how you met those two pricks.'

'As I told you before, Ceel, there at the game, on the field near my house. I was sitting in the sun. The next thing these two guys strolled up, sat down next to me and started chatting.'

'But Rory, where was he? Did you ask him about them?'

'No, he was away for the weekend.'

'The fucking bastards,' I raved down the phone. 'They're fuzz, Lucia, police, the worst sort. Powers to arrest without warrant and hold in solitary for a hundred-and-eighty days, no lawyers or doctors.'

'That's terrible, Ceel. If they hadn't mentioned Rory, I'd never have agreed to go with them. I'm so sorry. Are you all right?'

'Furious.'

'You'll be fine. Your dad will get you out of anything.'

'I don't think so, Lucia.'

I wandered outside to the courtyard to look for Katie. Katie Harris, a 'coloured' woman who left a violent husband, home and four grown children in the north of the country to come and work for us. She was a relative of Theresa's and that alone gave her the job immediately. Katie had instructed me in the ways of the world. Judging by her frequent daytime yawning, her nocturnal adventures were quite demanding. From the day she arrived, she took charge of everything and ran our home efficiently and strictly, just like an old-fashioned housekeeper.

'Hey, Ceel, come and look at my dress for tonight. I haven't worn it since nightclubbing in Jo'burg.'

She held up the long black-and-gold halter-neck dress, 'Wow, Kates, that's so glamorous.'

She went coy. 'What are you wearing? Do you want me to iron anything for you?'

'No thanks. Skirt number five and shoes. The floors in the warehouse have got sharp splinters.'

'You'll look gorgeous,' she enthused. 'You must wear the skintight gold top. If that Indian guy from the fruit shop is there, what's his name, Ramshree, he'll be after you again.'

'Ja, I know Ramshree's divine, but sex across the colour line as well as everything else! Don't say that in this house Kates, I'm in enough shit with the folks. My father says my hair looks like politics and drugs.'

'Ag, don't let them spoil your life for you. You're young and sexy… look how that priest comes here to take you for drives.'

'Exactly, a priest having a mid-life crisis. Kate, I had an old dronkie professor after me at varsity last time. Now it's greasy fuckin' security police…'

'Yeah, but you must keep looking good because you'll find someone really nice soon. I know. You'll be fantastic, if you don't muck it up. I taught you well.' She narrowed her eyes seductively.

'Muck it up how?'

'By being too cheeky or fussy, or getting preg. There's nothing better', she said caressing the posy of purple bruises on her neck, 'than a man who is crazy for you. He'll do anything as long as you stay hot'.

'Now preg—that can be a problem.'

'No, never mind. I went to family planning and they gave me a thing that fits inside over my womb, just like a bottle top.' She put her finger inside her cheek and forced it out making a popping sound. 'That's how easy it is. Foolproof. You must get one.'

'Can you imagine old Dr Forest giving me one of those to have fun with?' We screamed with laughter. 'We must leave at seven o'clock. I've got two big cushions. Those railway sleepers are very hard after an hour.'

'Take your seats please,' a tall African man boomed. 'Here in the warehouse of the Covo oil factory, dockside, East London, we are performing a piece written thousands of years ago in ancient Greece.'

Men who were labourers, messengers and in other lowly jobs strutted about the stage in togas and laurel wreaths.

Oedipus, Jocasta, Creon, Tiresias spoke the ancient lines. When Oedipus screamed, '*Isau bona nyok!*' loosely translated as 'You'll see your arse!' Kate and I laughed raucously. The use of such a phrase in a dignified performance was unexpected and it was something that polite women would not have understood.

Going home, the engine of my mother's Fiat roared through town and we beat the two guys who raced us at every set of lights.

The next day, my father rang the hairdresser. I managed to keep only some of my frizz and took the rest home in a bag to my mother for her rose garden.

ALL TERM I had had long conversations with Cynthia as she patiently taught a few of us what they believed. She told us about spiritual exploration and our obligation to learn and discover. She covered reincarnation, a mortal sin for Catholics to even contemplate, and why, as theosophists, they were vegetarians. Those two sisters brought us all close to their profound joy and exhilaration at being alive. At the end of term, when their parents had come to collect them for the vacation, we noticed that they did not look well off but they hugged and kissed one another enthusiastically. They lived on a citrus farm near the Addo Elephant Park and spoke of hearing mud-bathing elephants trumpeting after rain. No one in our college lived quite as close to wild Africa, except for one Rhodesian girl who came from a tobacco farm.

At the beginning of fourth term, Cynthia announced that she'd be taking her first parachute jump the coming Saturday. It dawned a beautifully clear spring day. After morning tea, I strolled down the quiet end of the main street. At about a quarter to twelve, I heard the mosquito whine of a small plane somewhere high in the ether—Cynthia must be getting ready. She was not at lunch of course and we lazed about the lawns waiting for her to come bounding up the path. At half past three Mrs Driver came onto the tea lawn with a red face and a hanky to her nose. Neither of Cynthia's parachutes had opened. Some time later Beedle, her sister, was driving a long flat stretch in the Orange Free State. She had a tyre blow out and was killed instantly. We remembered what she had said after Cynthia died: 'She'd finished her work and it was time for her to go. Our parents are happy with that.'

MARTIN FLANAGAN, THE Irish priest whom I had invited home from mass to meet my parents a few years before, remained a good friend. Our conversation was fuelled by shared political, social and religious views and he educated me further about the issues in our society. He often said that until he encountered my family, he hadn't met any white Catholics who agreed with his views. I relayed what I learnt from him and this provoked even more discussion around our dinner table. My father, who took his religion very seriously, was moved and inspired by what was coming from the priest.

In 1972, my second year, Martin came to visit me at university. He conducted an evening I organised with the Catholic Student Society. By then a parish priest at Mdantsane, the massive township near East London, he spoke about the challenges of life for Africans living in dormitory townships and the difficulties people faced in the rural areas where he'd previously worked. We discussed the Poverty Datum Line, Mean Effective Levels (what people needed to earn to survive) and Starvation levels. The burgeoning population of poverty stricken amidst the economic boom in South Africa in the early seventies was shocking to us.

It was at this time, with encouragement from all of us, that my father went back into politics. He had originally stood in 1950 on a multi-racial ticket in the last mixed living area, North End in East London, but lost. This time, he stood as a candidate for the opposition Progressive Party, of which Helen Suzman was the longest standing opposition MP. Martin was a vocal supporter and Donald Woods, as editor of the *Daily Dispatch*, expressed support for my father politically in the columns of his newspaper. He was elected with an enormous majority and became deputy mayor.

Later in the university year, we white Catholic students from Rhodes hired a bus and went to meet our African peers at Fort Hare University near Alice, about two hours drive south. Fort Hare was a great educational institution founded by Scottish missionaries in 1916. It educated people like Nelson Mandela, Oliver Tambo, and much later, Steve Biko. A sophisticated environment, it was a Mecca for African intellectuals. We were not welcome. The students stoned our bus and hissed and jeered us off the campus. We took refuge in the priest's house, drinking tea made with leaves he had been recycling for weeks. This Irish missionary priest chose to live in a way that approximated the lives of those he lived and worked amongst.

SOMETIMES MY PARENTS' dining room resounded with the laughter, song and stories of three or four of those wild Irishmen who felt at home among us. They sang mournful songs of homesickness, one of the Brothers played a fiddle, and then they picked out stories from the heart of tragedy in their daily encounters. One night at the table, Martin was telling of an amply-bosomed mother of ten who was robbed of her week's wages on the way home. A large woman, three *tsotsis* (thugs) approached her from left, right and front. The one in front brandished a sharpened bicycle spoke and bellowed, 'Open the dairy, Mama'. She was forced to dive in and retrieve the knotted handkerchief that contained a week's rent and food money. The priests roared adolescent laughter at the story of breasts where all sustenance was stored; but he had helped her with food and rent.

One evening, Martin got serious with me, 'Come with me to Ireland. You can meet my family; they'll love you. Then,' and he laughed loudly, 'I'll take you to the west coast where a friend of mine,' he began to whisper, 'will marry us secretly.'

I sat amazed and then I laughed. 'Oh Martin, you're having a mid-life priest crisis. I'm nineteen. I don't even know how old you are. Forty?'

In the end, it was Martin who married me to my husband and when my son was born he told everyone that Stephen was his child. 'After all if I hadn't married them, there'd have been no child.'

Martin's teasing was an outlet for the tremendous pressure of his work and the increasing stresses posed by the attention of the security police. He had begged and borrowed typewriters and office equipment and organised two nuns to teach secretarial practice at night in his garage. 'We must get these women out of domestic slavery and into offices.' Inevitably there were midnight and dawn raids by the security police. They uncovered his school and charged him with running an unlicensed educational institution.

He protested, 'I am not the licensee. That is the Bishop in Port Elizabeth.' Relentlessly, they contacted the bishop who referred them to the Cardinal in Cape Town who said, 'It's the Pope, the Pope in Rome.' So they left him and his secretarial school alone, briefly. One day he came home to a burglary that was more like a demolition. Everything was smashed.

Our friendship had grown and broadened to include other politically active people. Donald Woods, the editor of the *Daily Dispatch*, lived up the road from our house and we'd been friends for a while. Martin cemented that friendship. We had house masses and dinners and loud evenings with Donald, a wonderful raconteur, at the piano. He came to Rhodes a few times, to address us in the Great Hall. On one of those trips he gave me a lift home to East London for the weekend. As a classical music buff, the central console of his car was piled with tapes. On the road, on a dark night, cigarette in hand, weaving at some speed through the bends of the Fish River Pass, Donald nonchalantly searched for a Bach or a cello piece or something else he fancied, while I decided that next time I'd take the bus.

LIVING IN AN all woman residence with strict rules about men not stepping beyond the foyer was irksome and often laughable. One night, about ten, I was puffing away on my pipe when I heard high heels clopping up and down outside my door. 'Oh, it's you, Mrs Clarke.'

'Yes. Good evening. What are you smoking?'

'Sweet red amphora, smells like grass doesn't it?'

'I am looking for a man.'

'You won't find any here—just Jimi Hendrix on the wall.'

She tsked and clopped off. I tiptoed a little way behind her and her posse—two first years and the head student. Apparently one of the Bible students had gone to the loo while Christine was giving her little lecture. She'd burst back into the meeting: 'I saw a man outside the bathroom,' one of them told me.

'Ooh,' breathed the collective anxiety. 'What'd he look like?'

'Long long hair, lots of beads, smoky smell, but he ducked around the corner when he heard me.'

Angels of virtue spun out in all directions to find the intruder. Seniors came down from the top floor, chuckling, but rules were rules and he had to be found, expelled and punished. Eventually they had to call the lady warden. The group stopped outside Jude's room. Again Mrs Clarke, like a white rabbit with her white hair, inclined her head toward the door and sniffed. She knocked loudly. There was no reply. 'Is there anyone in there?'

Two voices breathily, 'Yes, we're here.'

Mrs Clark drew herself up tall and asked, as if to the whole college, 'Well, are you copulating in there?' The door opened slowly and veiled in clouds of smoke, he faced Mrs Clarke in green underpants. 'Get dressed at once, young man. You will be reported and you will both be disciplined.' And that is what happened. No one mentioned the dope. Jude was suspended for letting him in; he got one week for coming in and 'walking around hoping a woman would let him in to share a smoke,' he told the student court. Eventually I decided to move out, into digs in town. I shared a house with a pair of American zoology students and their howling baby. 'Why can't you stay in college with the other girls?' my mother protested. 'Is this move for sexual purposes?'

DURING JULY HOLIDAYS in second year, as a practicum for anthropology, I did a small project in the Industrial Estate in East London, for the Institute of Race Relations. My brief was to gather information on how much the lowest paid worker earned (usually on a weekly basis) in each business, and the frequency of staff turnover in those positions. Initially, I was received politely as many of the proprietors knew my father. But when the nature of my visit was revealed, I was dished half-truths and frequently shown the door.

THEN CAME A bearded stranger—in my second year law class in 1973, a fellow East Londoner, Dirk, an Afrikaner who had crossed the divide and zigzagged between English and Afrikaans schools and universities, now settled at Rhodes. He was an unusual person and his attention was flattering, busy as I was with political matters.

'You'd better get away from me,' I warned him. 'I am going to emigrate. I can't stay in this country.'

Either he didn't mind, or he didn't understand, and he pursued me even more enthusiastically. I had grown up among people who had migrated, but his family were settled Afrikaners with an attachment to the land that was completely foreign to me. There being no medical schools in South Africa before 1920, doctors had to train overseas usually at Trinity College in Dublin or Edinburgh and some went to the United States. His father, a real gentleman, had studied at Trinity in Dublin in the early twentieth century, arriving there at the time of 'the troubles,' when statues and buildings were being blown up. His mother, however, was of provincial country stock.

Dirk did not grow up in a household that was particularly aware of the wider ramifications of apartheid, although he himself was disillusioned with Afrikaner ways. Before he met me, he'd left the Dutch Reformed church and replaced it with Catholicism. While social activism was in my bones from earliest childhood and ongoing experience he was somewhat interested but not really committed to political action. He was eccentric, as friends who shared university digs with him teased. He'd sit up all night drinking red wine and reading Ovid in Latin or, on a whim, dash off on an eight-hundred-kilometre trip to Cape Town. We played on and off campus life and became close friends with common leisure pursuits.

In my third year, as Catholic students, a fellow student Walter Rontsch and I represented Rhodes at an international Jesuit conference on Liberation Theology, held in Europe. We met and mixed with people from all over the world and I especially remember the Filipinos and the Latin Americans who would be returning home to interrogation and even prison. Inspired and encouraged, I had seen a vast world that was all new to me as I peeped out from behind the *boerewors* curtain– Indians and Sri Lankans, anti-Vietnam activists from the United States who wept in the arms of their South-East Asian 'enemies'. A pair of Lebanese, a priest and his cousin, pursued me, offering a home in a mountain village with a car, so that I could 'run around while their sister cooked and cleaned' for me. They assumed that a 'Lebanese wife' from Africa would bring great wealth into their lives.

On the plane home, I sat with an Indian family, on their first visit back to South Africa after many years exiled in England. When we landed in Johannesburg, I looked around to thank them for their company on the flight but of course, I was back 'home' and they had to use a 'non-white' entry point.

On 19 October 1973, the government banned NUSAS and SASO, a black student organization from the University of the North whose most famous leader was Barney Pityana. We wore black armbands to mourn the loss of freedom of speech. Many political detainees died in custody or disappeared. I didn't think I'd be useful in prison or under a banning order. NUSAS was disbanded and I was no longer a member of the Catholic Student Society. Perhaps fear won. Not capable of joining the *real* struggle, I saw myself as an individual with a commitment to 'conscientizing' whites dulled by a lack of information about what was really going on.

Even as I write this, I realise that as privileged students our paltry contribution to the struggle would be as nothing next to the great 1976 protests by African schoolchildren when many were killed. In fact, that was the final stage of the liberation war within the country, a people's movement that culminated in 1990 with the release of Nelson Mandela.

A FEW MONTHS into 1974, Dirk and I became seriously involved. We were both in final year. When we became engaged, my eldest brother Mark asked my father 'how desirable it would be to have an Afrikaner in the family'. I was shocked at such a racist remark. No one said anything more on the topic. Then Dirk's aunt questioned the depth of my whiteness. As a couple, we felt we were beyond all of that. We both wanted to live away from our families and decided that we'd marry at the end of 1974 and settle in Cape Town. My mother relished organising a big fat Lebanese wedding with hundreds of cousins and friends, after which we sped off to our new home in Cape Town.

19

Life and loss in Cape Town

. . .But somehow we survive
severance, deprivation, loss.

Patrols uncoil along the asphalt dark
hissing their menace to our lives,

most cruel, all our land is scarred with terror,
rendered unlovely and unlovable;
sundered are we and all our passionate surrender

but somehow tenderness survives.

EXCERPT FROM *SOMEHOW WE SURVIVE*
DENNIS BRUTUS

Before long, I became pregnant. My first son was born anencephalic and died. I was just twenty-two and devastated—instead of life, I gave birth to death. The hospital matron told me to forget about it. My mother arrived in Cape Town with her Italian friend and stayed in a fancy hotel near our home. In order to 'get over it', I was taken out to dinner. Postnatal abdomen and swollen breasts held me in the truth of what had happened, despite all attempts at denial.

Once again, I was on the fringes. All three of us sisters had been pregnant at the same time. Michele's daughter was born in September, my son died in November and Anita's daughter was born in February. In

East London for Christmas, over tea after mass, I opened my mouth to describe the quaint private hospital I had been in. Anita was still hugely pregnant. Someone pounced, 'We don't want to hear about that. Thank you. It is all over.'

I was stunned at being treated as though I had done something wrong. In fact one of my cousins said to me later when I was pregnant again, 'Make sure you look after your bundle this time.'

Looking back, I see the resemblance to the child I was, the one who carried tragic courtyard stories to the people inside the house. Only this time, as one of them, I brought my own pain and imperfection into the heart of my family.

My doctors sent me to Professor Peter Beighton, head of the Department of Human Genetics at the University of Cape Town Medical School. I was to have a genetic counselling session. I sat there with nothing to say or ask. I was still in shock. Somewhere along the way, I picked up that since this had happened to me, I had a one-in-twenty chance of having another child with chromosomal damage. This meant that if I became pregnant again, I would have to have amniocentesis and other antenatal diagnostics. I was not sure that I could have children after that, and if I did, whether they'd be healthy. When they did eventually come, I received them as if at any moment I could lose them. For better or for worse, I was always aware of the fleeting nature of life, and the brief time of mother and child. As it was, twenty-five years later, after a number of serious illnesses, I had genetic testing in Australia. It was established that I am a carrier of, and suffer from Familial Mediterranean Fever, an auto-immune disorder that is commonly found in Middle Eastern populations. It was possibly the cause of my first child's fatal disability.

In 1975 I became pregnant again and was sent back up to Groote Schuur Hospital. I can never forget climbing the stairs; as I reached the top, a woman in a pink coat, sitting behind a wooden desk bellowed at me, 'Take off your *broeks* and empty your bladder.'

I walked up to her, 'I have an appointment with Professor Beighton'.

'Take off your *broeks* and empty your bladder,' she repeated loudly.

So I walked through the bathroom without stopping, and she directed me to a long wooden bench lining the corridor. Doors opened and shut and people went in and out. Then I noticed a row of about five women, elbows on their knees passing a *zol* up and down. I squashed myself into the corner of that bench and opened my book—Isaac Bashevis Singer, *A Crown of Feathers.* Every time I peeped sideways, at least one of them was looking at me. I was in the queue for the sexually transmitted diseases clinic and these women worked the docks.

Suddenly a door opened again and a man quietly suggested I follow him. Amniocentesis was painful. I had no anaesthesia. I had to go back three times over a period of weeks and then came the phone calls. A doctor rang me every few days, over a period of time, firstly to tell me that my child had two legs and two arms. The next call was to confirm it did not have Down syndrome. Then a call saying it had two functioning kidneys. The last call told me it was a boy. I like to think we've come a long way since then.

My shocking experience left me with two realisations. Firstly, a profound understanding of what it must be like for all those young women who gave their babies up for adoption and were told to forget about them. As well, it has increased my indignation on behalf of the women whose babies were taken from them, as happened in Australia, because it was thought their race precluded them from being good enough mothers. No child can be disappeared from its mother—the body knows and remembers, the heart longs and the psyche is riven. Since my own bereavement, my heart has carried me to places of loving and loss; to mothers and babies, to mothers in grief, to children unmothered and, naturally, to my relationship with my own mother and all the mothers around me in my childhood.

My eyes were opened then to my Aunt Eileen and her daughter, our cousin Barbie, my age to a month. That she had Down syndrome never interfered with our playtime as children. But in retrospect, Auntie Eileen was not fully part of the mother's circle on Saturday afternoons. She was given a hard time by her mother-in-law, my Granny Isabel, which added to the pain she felt because of her child's difference from all of the other grandchildren. To this day, I recognise the look that some women wear—and I know they have experienced deep pain in their motherhood.

Women can be cruel and competitive: the myth of having perfect children is like the myth of a perfect past—we all want it and no one has it.

IT WAS AT this time that, in pursuit of a healthy lifestyle, I gave up smoking! I was just twenty-two but had puffed or smoked for probably seventeen of those years. I think I became hooked when my nursemaid Rosie left just before I began school and the short-fused Sara took charge of me and gave me puffs on her cigarette. Many of the adults in my world, except for my mother who had given up smoking when she was pregnant with me, offered puffs. Smoking was part of life. In fact my mother's obstetrician recommended cigarettes to her for her 'nerves' when she was pregnant with my older siblings. Even Granny Isabel, a real chain-smoker, left burning temptation in ashtrays all over the place. I succumbed frequently. Her packs of fifty Westminster 85 came from Uncle Mickey's shop. Now and again, we'd hear Granny searching for a newly opened packet that was long gone into the courtyard with me. Perhaps that was why Sara and Katrina indulged me, because I always shared my spoils with them. When I asked my mother if she knew that I smoked in the courtyard when I was small, she said, 'The courtyard was the courtyard. We didn't want to know too much of what went on there. But I would never have allowed you to smoke.' In any case, I was never in fear of her finding out.

When Bobsy Chemaly came back from a trip to Switzerland in the late 1960s, she laughingly told us of the school group of twelve year olds, my age then, that they had encountered on Lake Geneva, all of them puffing on little brown cheroots. I took that as an indication that it was not so bad and puffed on happily. My Yazbek aunts turned a blind eye and even gave me packets of cigarettes from the time I was twelve. My mother's brothers and sisters, especially Uncle Albert, the anaesthetist, would never have allowed such a thing as a child smoking. I feel fortunate that I escaped the disastrous effects of a smoking life. It is unimaginable to me now to think that a young child smoked and none of the adults involved saw anything wrong with it.

At the same time, I embraced the vegetarian lifestyle. From my family, I caught flack for going my own way. 'How can you bring up children without our wonderful Lebanese food?' 'Your children will be weak and spindly,' someone shouted.

Tiring of the arguments my father humorously interjected with, 'Why don't you all shut up? Elephants eat only leaves and they're quite strong.'

In Cape Town, we were surrounded by squatter camps experiencing terrible poverty. I had become acquainted with a hunger project called 'Compassion', teaching poor people how to increase protein in their diet using soya beans. But that required a lot of cooking fuel. The *wonderbox* or *wondercushion* was a bag filled with polystyrene beads that insulated a boiling pot and continued the fuelless cooking for some hours. I could not advocate this style of cooking for poor people and then serve a meal in my house, the cost of which could feed a family for a month. As well, I remain horrified at the way we treat animals and the natural environment. The Buddhist belief in the sanctity of all life—all sentient beings—is one I fully accept. I do not espouse the Judeo-Christian idea that we humans are at the top of a pyramid and all beings below us are of lesser value. This belief has enabled us to inflict suffering on so many levels, even on our fellow humans. With a distaste for proselytism, I began a vegetarian cooking school for those who wanted to know and chose to learn. There were always queues of students.

MY SON WAS born in 1976. A mop of black hair crowned his delicate face. We called him *Bombani* beetle, Auntie Susie's name for a lawn cricket, because of his long thin legs. I clung to him and loved him, carrying him everywhere. Mothering pleasures were accompanied by loads of advice and criticism, which I mostly ignored. My boy was just perfect.

Eventually, when he was eighteen months old, I went back to university. I still had one outstanding credit for my degree. As it was, I enjoyed the psychology course so much that I continued on for another year. The view from the university, on the slopes of Devil's Peak, was of the Cape Flats—a landscape of dormitory accommodation for the workers and displaced of the city. Squatter camps sprouted from the hands of black people who had been 'endorsed out' of the cities and confined to the 'homelands'. They were desperate to be reunited with their families in town. On campus, I saw a horrifying film of police and army destroying the shacks of Modderdam Road squatter camp. Police with whips and dogs hounded people from their shelters onto an embankment from where they were forced to watch as bulldozers levelled everything, down to their smallest personal possessions. We'd seen newspaper articles describing how busloads of women and children from the homelands were being turned back by police. So, one Sunday, we took a drive to the foot of the Du Toits Kloof pass and parked behind a mountain of road building material. With our own eyes we saw the buses being stopped and emptied of women and many young children who were then forced at gunpoint straight onto buses lined up to go back on the fifteen-hour journey they'd just completed. I could not believe the sheer physical brutality that surrounded us.

I volunteered briefly, under the powerful Mrs Robb, at the Black Sash run Athlone Advice Office next to Mowbray Station. The Black Sash was a women's political organization founded in the 1950s. They picketed and held protests against government action, always wearing their sombre black sashes. The Advice Office was a resource centre for disadvantaged victims of apartheid laws. Lawyers donated their services and we drafted affidavits and took statements from people seeking help. One morning, I turned up as usual and the front of the building was occupied by a large group of people from a township near Worcester. They all bore dog bites and *sjambok* welts from police beatings. We set about taking statements as a prelude to legal action against the police minister. I found it all terribly upsetting and felt so cowardly next to what these people were faced with on a regular basis.

IN 1976 TELEVISION came to South Africa. We were not really interested as we knew that it would become just another propaganda machine, same as the radio run by the South African Broadcasting Corporation. Younger people listened to Lourenco Marques radio, there was Radio Bantu with its government line and then the A(English) and the B(Afrikaans). Springbok Radio was a commercial station. All in all, they were pretty dismal, especially after cultural boycotts robbed us of BBC shows like The Goons. The A station played one hour of classical music every day at noon. The government used the media to the utmost and it took us two years to install television at home; after a few 'news' bulletins that were nothing more than interviews with government ministers and spokespeople, we ignored it and hardly ever watched, especially as we were seeing the truth with our own eyes on a daily basis. There was no real international news as the country was isolated by the international community; most white viewers were happily distracted by American soapies.

MEANWHILE, IN EAST London where my father was mayor, the political heat was building. One day, in 1977, Donald Woods rang my father to say he'd like to bring an important local political figure to the mayor's parlour. He arrived with Steve Biko and a press photographer. They drank tea served by the mayor's secretary whose husband, ironically, was in the local branch of the security police. The next morning, a photo appeared in the newspaper of my father and Biko in the mayor's parlour. As Biko was a banned person at the time and not allowed to be in the company of more than one other person at any time, Donald stood around the corner when the photograph was taken. It was also an offence to publish a photograph of a banned person. Soon after that, my father received a call from the head of the security police in the region: he was to be charged with treason, aiding and abetting a banned person to break their banning order, constituting an assembly of more than two people with the photographer in the room. There was a long list of charges. And then Steve Biko was murdered in custody. My father was forgotten in the international furore that followed.

In 1978, during a second term as mayor of East London, my father decided to open the beaches to all races, in direct contravention of central government apartheid law. The best amenities were reserved for whites and the laws were enforced by police with guns, dogs and *sjamboks*. The long tradition of blacks holding Boxing Day picnics on whites-only beaches had been banned by the government. Even after apartheid was introduced, blacks continued to hold the Boxing Day picnic on East London's Eastern Beach in a white area. That year, my father declared that over Christmas, all of the beaches in and around East London would be open to 'all God's people.' Donald Woods printed the announcement in large font in the *Daily Dispatch*. My parents were inundated with abusive phone calls. Dead animals were left outside the front door. Paul instructed my mother that when people swore four-letter words beginning with f or c, she should put the phone down immediately. Until then, she hadn't experienced that kind of obscenity. During that time of abusive calls, the cook, Hettie, a prim and proper Bible-carrying sort answered the phone. My mother heard the retort, '*Vok* you too (Fuck you too),' as she hung up.

'Please Hettie, don't swear at the people. They'll think that all the people in the mayor's house swear.'

My father was flown under escort to Cape Town for an intimidating meeting with Adriaan Vlok, the minister for internal security. He was carpeted and told that because of his actions over the beaches, laws pertaining to local government would have to be changed by an act of parliament...blah blah blah. But by then my father was running out of steam. The political process in South Africa had taken a murderous turn. He operated from a deep personal conviction of right and wrong, justice and equality—simple values—but he was not ruthless enough to meet the government's escalating brutality. . He would no longer be in office when white swimmers on Port Elizabeth beaches were guarded by soldiers with sub-machine guns keeping black swimmers away. He became tired easily and withdrew from politics at the end of that term.

Probably the most painful aspect of that time for my father was the loss of long-term friendships from people who turned against him because of his liberal views. He lost large clients who were also family friends. Some in his beloved St Patrick's church cut him dead before and after mass. The old Irish priest didn't have the mettle to speak out in the situation and counselled my father to beware of arrogance. It was a lonely time but he never wavered.

He once asked me if I thought he was arrogant. 'You are a committed person with a strong belief in what is right. Not many are up there with you but it doesn't mean you are wrong or have to stop. Only understand the smallness of some people's experience.' Ian Lipworth, who now lives in Sydney, worked closely with my father in opposition politics in East

London. Ian says, 'There was not a racist bone in his body. He was a good person, my very close friend.'

Not long after Biko's murder, and after trying to force an investigation into those circumstances, Donald Woods was banned. He and his family were subjected to shootings and harassment, right there in our neighbourhood. But when his young daughter, Mary, received a poisoned T-shirt in the mail, he had had enough. On New Year's eve in 1978, we were having a loud dinner with Irish priests at my parents' home in East London. Martin Flanagan was sitting next to me and kept on nudging and pinching me saying, 'Tomorrow, we are going to wake up to a different life. Newspapers around the world will be full of East London.' In fact, he raised his glass of lemon squash, 'To the biggest and greatest news that we will hear tomorrow.'

'What? Please tell me', I begged, my usual curiosity at fever pitch. But he wouldn't say a word. The next day at twelve o'clock it was on the news. Donald and Wendy Woods and their six children had fled the country. My mother started to cry. My father clenched his jaw. We all felt so alone. One of our heroes, a courageous beacon in our small town and in those dark times, had gone. We drove past their house later in the day. The street, although it all looked the same, felt abandoned. But we had no right to ask him to stay banned and silenced as he was, his family at the mercy of powerful lunatics. They went to Britain via Lesotho and Botswana assisted by, among others, some of the 'wild Irish priests' who supped so often at my parents' home.

AT ABOUT THIS time my father received a letter from a prominent East London lawyer—one of those whose firm had rejected, on racial grounds, his application for a legal position in 1937. My father showed me the linen page written in royal blue ink:

> Congratulations on your great work as Mayor. We had no idea of the substance of the man we closed our doors to. How wrong we were so many years ago. We thank you for your civic-minded commitment and service to all the people of East London.

'This, my darling,' my father said as I stared at that page, 'is a measure of the greatness of a person that he can turn around and say he was wrong even after such a long time.' He wiped his eyes.

In 1980, I became pregnant again and decided to have my baby at home. As my due date approached, my excitement was tinged with irritation and annoyance at the security police who parked themselves outside our house for three days. Every time I returned from a stint at the advice office, my phone would ring, up to twenty times, and there'd be no one at the other end. I knew there was a tap on the phone—the listener once gave himself away by trying to engage in a conversation about my cousin Michael when I rang inquiries to get his phone number in Zimbabwe. Mail was intercepted; letters from overseas were slit at the top and taped back. It seemed foolish then, and even more so now. If only I had done something heroic to justify the attention. I wasn't afraid, but realised that my children had not chosen to be born into my activism. Eventually, the police left the street—my husband, in legal practice by then, had roared at them one night in Afrikaans and sent for the regular squad, complaining that there were loiterers about.

My daughter was born at home with my GP at hand. I had wanted to have a home birth, especially after the unnecessary intervention when my son was born. My parents and family were worried and I was advised to 'leave the process to the experts.' It increased my resolve: I was the resident expert of my body. In my last three months, the only midwife licensed to deliver white babies at home was suddenly called overseas to an ill father. So my UK-trained GP offered to help. As a mother with a certain risk profile, I gave him a written disclaimer. I wanted to be sure that a badly damaged baby would not be revived, or put through loops of torment in the name of medical help. At the time, a newborn in the USA underwent a heart transplant at Loma Linda medical centre. I had nightmares about my first child and what a system that allowed such procedures might have done to him.

My daughter was born quickly and easily; years of yoga and healthy eating played a part. Our friendship began at that moment. She was a peaceful baby who accompanied me everywhere until she went to school.

Amidst the tensions of the time, this experience was the most powerful and personally intimate event in my whole life.

Just before my daughter was born, a younger woman, Mona Armstrong, came to help me. She was to remain as a help afterwards. She came to work quietly and full of love, caring for me and my new baby. After some months, she told me about her home in a tin shanty on the Cape Flats. In the morning, her daughter, six months older than mine, would wake with rat bites on her face. I was outraged and managed through a friend of a friend and so on, to secure public housing for her and her husband and their four children.

At home with young children, my love of cooking grew and I would visit Malay shops in the Bo-Kaap to buy Indian spices. The vegetable man who came every week, Mr Fataar, used to say that as he turned his truck into our street, he could smell garlic and coriander; 'must be *Hajjis* living there,' he laughed. Indeed my cooking had expanded to feed some of the younger students doing important work about which I never asked any questions. Pots of soup were delivered to verandas where people had to stay indoors for weeks and months. All I can say I ever did in the revolution was, knowingly and unknowingly, feed people whose courage I admired. One of them was my cousin Michael. He lived in a large share-house in Observatory and all ten or twelve students would come to dinner. The twenty-five-man pot was just enough and they took the leftovers home. Intelligent and aware, they were committed to regime change and I feared for them. One day Michael confided that he could no longer defer his military call up and he was leaving South Africa as a draft dodger; he faced a four-year prison term if he stayed or returned. It would have to be a clandestine departure, through back roads and via Botswana into Zimbabwe—the regular border posts were checking military call up lists. He and a girlfriend and their collie dog set off in a tired kombi van. All I could do for them was cook—enough to get them to Cairo if they took a wrong turn! I was worried for the days I knew they were on the road. Their parents didn't know and when they were told, his father, who'd volunteered in the Second World War, raged at me for 'encouraging' Michael in a shameful act of refusing to 'defend his country'.

LIFE AS A family in Cape Town continued but the socio-political situation was always with me. The Institute of Race Relations opened an artists' cooperative in Rondebosch, a suburb of Cape Town, and I volunteered there for a time. Artists from the townships and squatter camps brought in beadwork, sculpture and paintings for sale. I saw a wealth of talent that would have made artists famous in any other country.

Deciding to have a weekend away, my husband, the children and I took a drive to Matjiesfontein, a restored railway siding and beautiful Victorian hotel. Having tea in the café, I recognized a young man who walked in as Mike, from the student house in Observatory. Aspiring to become a priest, he had joined the seminary at Roma in Lesotho. He was on his way to Cape Town to observe a trial on behalf of the Catholic hierarchy. I felt the eyes of those country people in the cafe on us as Mike sat and whispered that from where he was, the war was hotting up and regime change was not far off. That was good news but I feared that violence by the state would escalate in an attempt to maintain the status quo.

Soon after we returned home, my husband, working as a lawyer, came across an 'in camera' case that was not supposed to be reported. It detailed a trial of South African soldiers charged with a massacre of civilians in northern Ovamboland in South West Africa. The press in Britain reported on it after the Catholic Church had, through the diplomatic corps, expressed grave concern about South African military personnel actions in South West Africa. As time went by, our suspicions were usually confirmed and things were frequently even worse than we'd imagined they might be.

With so much information, I increasingly felt as though I didn't fit in with the 'Southern Suburbs' mums at the preschool. An incident with my sister crystallised it for me.

I felt close to the philosophy and ideals of the Catholic Welfare Bureau, as it was called, and was doing some community work to support them. The redistribution of resources was all very well, but I also had a commitment to disseminating information. I wanted the comfortable white people I lived among to know what was happening in our town and beyond. So, once a week, with the support of the preschool teachers, I put a box at the school door announcing a focus. For example, one week, we collected tins of infant formula for mothers at Crossroads squatter camp; or shoes for the children in Cradock in the Karoo, who had to walk barefoot to school, on frozen ground in the winter. It was a natural continuation of the collections we mounted when I was at the convent. What I didn't realise at the time was that I was trying to rattle a very powerful mindset. I noticed that many whites lived a blinkered life. When I went into the bakery on Sunday morning to buy hot rolls, the number of beggars outside took away my appetite. I was not special or particularly kind: I felt a strong affinity with people generally. One of the ways some managed to live affluently among very poor people, as they did then and continue to do now, is by shutting off their identification with certain categories of people or races. This is a fundamental tenet of racism. As a child who had been loved and nurtured so thoroughly by my African nursemaid Rosie and the other servants, and then my Lebanese grandmother, my awareness of and identification with all of these shades of being never left me.

My sister pulled me aside one day, 'Why are you doing this? You are making yourself unpopular. People don't want to know.'

I knew that, but her tacit agreement with the sentiment hurt me. I realised I didn't belong. I could not live there and give my children an awareness of the broad spectrum of life if I had to participate in the denial of the suffering of most of the people we lived amongst. Our privileged circumstances arose directly from our exclusive access to resources such as health care, education and jobs.

From 1975 to 1986—when we eventually left—South Africa experienced some of the strongest and most widespread protests against the system. Poverty grew. People detained under draconian laws were dying in custody, while continuing disenfranchisement fuelled the fight. Mostly I felt an overwhelming responsibility to help but I did not feel able or committed to becoming a serious fighter. I was not at home in white middle class society. The location of so many dreadfully poor people within our comfortable midst tore at my attempts to live a 'normal life'. In our narrowing world, I asked myself the question, what else were we losing out on knowing about ourselves and about world events blacked out in the media? The whole situation weighed more heavily than ever; I wanted out.

The emigration conversation now came fully to the surface. It appears my origins and growing up close to my transplanted Lebanese grandmother contributed to make migration a real possibility for me. My husband began to look at job applications in Australia. We chose Australia because Canada had recently tightened its requirements; the United States looked too complex to even attempt, and I wanted to remain in the southern hemisphere.

20

Saying goodbye—the texture of the past.

Nay, not without a wound in the spirit shall I leave this city.

The Prophet
Kahlil Gibran

The migration process is a gigantic paperchase with an even bigger emotional overlay than getting married.

In 1985, when Amelia was four and Stephen was eight, we decided to take a drive around South Africa and search for signs of hope amidst the gloom. We left Cape Town to cross the Karoo and visit my husband's family on their farm. He had spent many holidays there as a boy and loved the countryside—I couldn't imagine him leaving this place forever. It was a doubt I'd had since we'd met; eventually it would be confirmed, as homesickness would overwhelm him and take him back permanently.

We set off from Cape Town at three o'clock in the morning hoping to reach the farm before dark that night. The journey of at least nine hours took us to the eastern edge of the Karoo. The children loved those farm holidays: cousin Judy taking care to cook what would delight them and her husband Tom ensuring they were entertained on the farm, borrowed ponies from the neighbours. Their hospitality to us was generous and accommodating. They owned a giant sheep farm, but falling wool prices had forced them to diversify, so Tom had acquired a large and lucrative flock of angora goats to meet the growing demand for mohair.

The road over Du Toits Kloof pass, a thirty-kilometre hike up one of the highest mountain ranges of the Western Cape, snakes its way along the ridge and descends to Worcester on the plains. The next mountain pass, Meiringspoort, is a narrow, winding road through towering mountains that obscure the sky. On both sides the red rocky slopes go ever upwards. These cuttings brought to mind gruesome Afrikaans folk tales of headless horsemen and wild-eyed, rabid draught oxen, terrified by something only they could see. The savage and horrifying mythology of this countryside evoked the difficulties of travel in such harsh terrain in earlier times.

We reached De Doorns at first light. Beautiful orchards and vines were laid out in perfect rows guarded by the mountains that stood between them and Cape Town. Afrikaners had farmed these plains for two-hundred-and-fifty years, local people providing all the labour. They were still not earning much more than they had one-hundred-and-fifty years before, though they were no longer slaves. As part of their six rand monthly wage, they were given food rations and a quantity of alcohol, the latter leading to alcoholism and social problems in all age groups. The beauty of this scenery was tainted by the poverty and violence that stalked the community.

Grand Cape Dutch homesteads were maintained by teams of people sweeping, scrubbing and polishing all day long. Shimmering waves of heat and light carried the glint of the brass fittings and the glare of the white walls across the fields. Gardens around the homestead belonged to the farmer's wife. She had her own staff to cultivate shrubs and flowers. Vegetable gardens and poultry runs were at the back, near the kitchen, and the dairy was a little way off. Excess fresh produce and the products of the kitchens were sold in stalls at the farm gate: fresh and dried fruits, jams, preserves, cakes, bread and flowers—in short, all one needed, if one had the money, for a banquet by the side of the road. We usually bought fresh fruit and vegetables along the way to take to Judy for her pantry, which was stocked with preserves.

As we approached Laingsburg, some of its history went through my mind. African people had lived for a long time on the banks of the river when the central government arbitrarily proclaimed their homes to be in a 'white' area. So the Africans were moved to the higher ground behind the hill, and the whites settled along the riverbanks. Some years later, in 1981, a flash flood in the middle of the night swept away whites, their houses, school, hospital and old-age home. Many were drowned. At first light, people rushed from their shanties behind the hill to search for bodies and help the stricken to find something of their possessions. Photographs in the newspapers showed the destruction. The most moving, however, were the pictures of poverty-stricken people showering loving care on those who had displaced them. In particular, I remembered the photograph of an ancient nursing-home patient in her tattered, muddy nightdress being cradled in the arms of a weeping African woman.

We passed through Colesberg. The gardens were looking pretty—woodland flowers and spring bulbs growing beneath blossoming fruit trees, planted by pockets of nostalgic English people who lived on the edge of semi-desert country. The low hills around the town gave way and the road became straighter. There were fewer stalls and barely any evidence of cultivation. On all sides, as far as the eye could see, the plains of the Karoo proper spread like a brown lake, a great thirsty swathe where the sun baked the earth hard and fifty-year floods came and washed everything away. The dry land remembered water in the *dongas* and caverns of erosion. Wind toured across and sculpted the rock over millennia, creating flat-topped table mountains. The dun colour was hardly mitigated by the khaki of the scrubby vegetation.

In the car, sleepy children surfaced asking groggily, 'Where are we? Are we there yet?'

'Not quite, darling', I replied and offered them treats from the basket. On the flat wide road, my husband played fast and loose, the needle hovering around one-hundred-and-seventy kilometres an hour, while I kept a look out for speed traps. My husband averred that we should 'get the hell out of here as soon as possible', away from the monotony and his fear of too much introspection on those flats.

'Remember the spring lambs you fed with a baby's bottle last time?' I asked the children. 'Ooh, yes, I hope there are more babies to look after', Stephen said, 'I loved picking them up and taking them to the fowl run to go to bed.'

'They pooped on you,' Amelia giggled, 'and they ate Auntie Judy's flowers'.

'And she called them terrorist', Stephen added.

'What a strange name for a lamb', I chipped in. As yet, the children were not aware of the possibility of being attacked on the farm by insurgents in the growing struggle. We were all too familiar with the threat. An enormous floodlight and alarm system had been fitted to the roof of the farmhouse, and thick bars had been welded over the outside of all the windows. We never mentioned it, and it wasn't discussed. Judy and Tom spoke of 'terrorists' and we called them 'freedom fighters'. The coming change would separate us and highlight our different attitudes, but our affection would remain.

Something was glinting ahead, about eight kilometres down the road on the right hand side and I warned my husband to slow down. 'Do you think it's a speed trap?' he said, hitting the brakes.

I raised the binoculars, 'Can't make out, better stick to eighty till we've passed it.'

Just ahead on our left, beside the road, I noticed a derelict, flat-roofed farmworker's cottage with a figure standing in front of it. The woman had one hand in the air, held straight up like someone drowning. My husband stopped the car and reversed a little to where she stood. There were no other buildings in sight, this was truly the middle of nowhere. The midday glare baked the scene into the most solid piece of misery I'd ever seen. Most of the roof still hung over the ragged walls that had chunks missing. The yard was fenced in with chicken wire. Holes in the ground were all that remained of what had once grown or been planted there. The old woman, her hand still raised, had one milky eye. The other stared mutely. Five little children stood in a row next to her; the eldest could have been ten but was no bigger than a five-year-old. Their reddish hair, huge bellies and stick limbs told the familiar story of malnutrition, even starvation and kwashiorkor. The dog was a skeleton in a haircoat, its spine curved like one of the hillocks in the distance, its tail so far between its legs, it could only creep along. Desolation hung in the still air. I found I could not breathe in that fatal atmosphere. My mind filled with questions. Where were the younger people? Where was the nearest water source? Where was the farmhouse? What were they eating? When did they last eat?

'*Molo Mama*—do you want some food?' I addressed her in Xhosa. The blank stare remained. Maybe she's deaf, but even the children didn't respond. 'Do you speak Sotho?' I battled.

'Or Afrikaans?' I ventured.

'*Ja missus, dankie missus* (Yes missus, thank you missus). Has madam got a little food, madam? The children are crying madam.' She formed her hands into a bowl and raised them up to the fence. I dived back into the car. 'Here is a little fruit.'

'*Dankie missus.*'

'Bread.'

'*Dankie missus.*'

I handed packets over the fence, fruit, sweets anything I could lay my hands on, one bottle of water. By then she and I were both weeping. She passed the food on to the children who still did not move a muscle in their faces.

Folding her hands to her chest in an attitude of prayer she bowed over and over, saying '*Dankie missus*' in the language of the farmer. I wondered when last she'd seen her home or any other adults.

We got back into the car and my face froze into the mute expression of those veld children. My husband didn't say a word either. Our children had often seen us hand things out of the car so they asked no questions. We drove on slowly past the glinting object: a shiny new windmill delivering crystal-clear bore water to the sheep trough. The rest of the way we were silent and even the familiar sight of the farm gates made less impression than usual.

Judy was waiting for us on the veranda and our heavy hearts relaxed slowly over cups of tea and family conversation. Soon Judy had the babies' bottles out and the children followed her to the pen where they helped with feeding the lambs. My husband and I wandered down the hill over the dried riverbed to the dairy. There was only one man, Klaas, working there now.

'Where are the others?' I asked him.

He paused, then, '*Dorp, missus.* (Town missus)'

'What are they doing there?'

'Learning *missus.*' I mused for a moment and suddenly he pointed towards Lesotho and the mountains, 'Away *missus.*'

I nodded. I'd already heard from one of the kitchen maids that dairy-Pietie's brother had been shot in the townships in an incident involving police action. After the army helicopters buzzed the townships, the youngsters decided it was no longer safe to stay and they'd secretly gone '*Oor*, (other side).' Judy and Tom would surely have known where their workers had gone.

Behind the dairy, ancient gnarled quince hedges and flowering ornamental blossom trees were all that remained of the original farm garden. Neglect hung over the remembered beauty of the surroundings, hostility tangible in a new moroseness. We wandered back up to the house in the thrall of a fiery Karoo sunset. 'She's painting the sky for you tonight,' Tom said with melancholy in his voice.

In the next days, we ran errands into town for Judy, a sixty-kilometre round trip. There were always hitchhikers beside the road and we filled the car, giving lifts to and from the farm. The white citizens of the dorp looked askance at us sitting in our car with all those farm children. It was not done to put Africans in the car. They could only be carried in the back of a *bakkie*.

In the afternoons we sat on the veranda listening to the sounds of a wide plains farm. Cattle lowed morning and evening around milking time, while sheep bleated in the distance. Crows cawed as they swooped down to the river, probably a dead hare to feast on. The sounds carried so clearly in that stillness. The uniquely African sound I loved most of all was that of people speaking Xhosa to each other across valleys and miles of landscape. It filled the air from cliff to cliff with a sound dimension now lost to the telephone.

The afternoon before we were due to leave, Judy put on a special tea and at four o'clock we assembled on the veranda. I had the feeling that this would be the last farm holiday there with the children and that we were enjoying the last Karoo sunset we'd see for some years. The cook had wheeled the trolley through from the dining room. Judy poured the tea and the children offered the cakes and biscuits around. In a break in the conversation, we suddenly heard Klaas, who was repairing the top of the windmill in the lower garden, calling to a mate some miles away. The conversation was punctuated by raucous laughter, which bounced around the soundscape. Suddenly Judy walked to the edge of the veranda and shrieked at him, 'I wish you would fall off that windmill onto your black mouth so that you can never speak again.' I clapped my hand to my mouth and felt winded. The children both turned to me as my finger sealed my lips. Klaas quietly climbed down from his eyrie and walked, holding his head and back very straight, across the lawn in front of us and all the way down the path to the stone cottage he shared with the other farm workers. As I looked away my eyes were caught by the iron bars welded over the sitting-room windows. Tom said very softly, 'Judy, why did you do that?' But Judy looked as though she herself didn't know what had suddenly possessed her. We tried to continue the conversation until I took the children inside on the pretext of packing for our departure. Stephen opened his mouth to ask, 'Wh..' and I stopped him. 'We can't talk here. We'll have the whole day in the car tomorrow to talk.' It was painful thinking about all of their kindness and hospitality and how mutually fond we were of each other, and then how suddenly angry words had erupted and broken the atmosphere.

Before dinner, we wandered for the last time down the hill to the dairy. The cook was lying in a gully beside the path, a bottle in a brown wrapper protruded from the front of her uniform. The teenagers were gyrating in front of their ghetto blaster, which played pop music at top volume. Clearly a party was in the making. We went back to the house from where we heard bicycle bells ringing and greetings being called as workers from neighbouring farms were arriving for a night of revelry. We retired soon after our meal but couldn't sleep as the drums were pounded and thumped until sunrise.

I felt as though I had wandered very far from the heart of my Lebanese family into the Karoo, a place of scenic splendour and human horror, a symbol for the whole country.

From there we entered the Orange Free State and visited the high mountains of Golden Gate. Radio reception was very poor but early one morning, we heard that a bomb had gone off in the quadrangle of the East London City Hall where the mayor had just left a cocktail party he'd hosted for some Royal Navy officers. Two days later, we went to Pietermaritzburg to see more cousins who filled us in with the news that my parents had had a narrow escape—the bomb went off five minutes after they'd left the function. We left Pietermaritzburg in a solemn mood and slowly drove back to East London.

As usual my parents were nonchalant about 'these times:' 'No one is going to make us stop living,' they said. My mother then told me of Auntie Halia Mukheibir who had maintained regular contact with our family. (She had been on the ship to South Africa with my Granny Isabel.) When we were children, she sailed gracefully into our lives every winter. Now, as the last living member of that first generation of Lebanese migrants and in old age, she had suddenly lost the power of speech and was in the Mater Dei private hospital. Apparently, her home had been burgled and the neighbours had found her wandering in the garden quite confused. I was very keen to see her and say goodbye, so we set off to visit her.

We walked through lush gardens under tall trees and into the frail care centre that was once the maternity section where we had all been born. Auntie Halia was in a long room painted hospital green. Thick wire mesh on the ceiling-high windows hid the view. A row of old women sat against the wall in tired vinyl chairs. Nursing aides were going down the line with nail scissors, hairbrush and face flannel. Every time the nurse tried to take her hand, one of the old women screeched, 'No, don't! I'll tell Mother Beatrice.' Her noisy protest cut into the silence of that hapless group making me feel agitated. My mother pointed Auntie Halia out to me. She sat, like a little sparrow, on a chair near the door. I nearly missed her. Her once glossy black hair was a mottled grey, matted and chopped off; her skin, no longer smooth, was deeply lined. Only the familiar moles remained. She was dressed in nursing-home style with a pink floral housecoat; a worn beige cardigan hung badly across her bony shoulders while her bare legs ended in pink cotton slippers. My heart seized at the sight of her. I turned to my mother but she had taken herself across the room to a full-length mirror and was picking at her meticulously coiffed hair.

I pulled a chair over and sat close: 'Hello, Auntie. Maybe you don't remember me. I'm Cecile, Bertha's daughter. See Bertha over there? She's my mother. I think you know her, Auntie.' I spoke slowly and watched as tears began to trickle down her face.

'Such a long time since I saw you, more than twenty years, Auntie, but I haven't forgotten you.'

I took her hand and she held on tightly: 'Oh, it is so good to see you again. I recall your winter holidays in the Normandy Hotel on the beach-front. Your son Davey brought you in June and you stayed till winter was over in Barkly East. He'd sit in the lounge and wait to drive you to visit us. ' She shuddered momentarily.

'You'd come to our home to visit my Granny Isabel. She was your dear friend, my Granny Isabel, Bertha's mother.' I pointed at my mother, who was still in her mirror world. Auntie inclined her head to me and her face relaxed. I too felt warmed by the memories of my grandmother. 'You wore your beautiful fur coat and I'd hang it in the hallway. Then you'd both go to the sunroom and I'd bring you a tray with tea and cake. I used to listen to all the things you talked about, the children and the grand-children.' I remembered the sounds of their Arabic conversation and how I had devoured the language. My grandmother and her age mates all spoke only Arabic. My parents, however, were careful only to speak it in the privacy of our home. Here in the nursing home, no one would speak Arabic to Auntie. It made me feel as if I was in a foreign country and my approaches to her felt stilted. I wondered whether the absence of Arabic, her first language, didn't have something to do with her muteness, but there was no one to ask.

'Granny talked a lot about her sons the doctors, you know Albert and Henry.' (Auntie's husband had paid for their education when Granny's husband died suddenly.) 'I think Albert visits you here when he comes to work. You talked with your hands and your diamond earrings and rings sparkled across the room.' She looked down at her bare left hand curled on her lap. 'Granny was so happy when you came. She said you were always kind to her.' My reminiscing was watered by the trickle of her tears that fell like a veil covering her whole face. I felt my own eyes brim. 'My heart will always be close to yours because we remember other times and places, very far from here. Thank you for the joy you brought us.'

We continued our trip home to Cape Town with heightened senses, constantly aware that it might be a very long time before we saw something or met with someone again. For me the grandeur of the landscape remained eclipsed by poverty and hatred. I felt the impossibility of trying to reconcile all of the contradictions in my life in South Africa. I wanted to leave. In fact, emigration was well under way in our minds. We told no one of our plans and arrived back in Cape Town to begin the hard work.

My husband was a lawyer with other marketable skills. He approached publishers as well as legal and accounting firms, mostly in Sydney. The replies were encouraging. Even the outright refusals were polite. Most wished him success in his efforts—a contrast to the more robust South African style to which we were accustomed. With half a dozen interviews under his belt, we decided it was time to tell our parents. We knew of many who had left, but we usually heard afterwards. They faced strong censure from those who remained. Our efforts were kept a secret from the rest of our family and friends.

We spent Christmas in East London. My father looked thin; he'd just had his spleen removed. He came back from town one day to announce that the doctors had given him five years. I was furious—how dare they play God. Later I saw it as my father's desperate attempt to keep us there.

In late January, 1986, my husband left for Australia. Neither of us had ever been there. We had a couple of friends in Melbourne, but all the interviews were in Sydney. I didn't mail the application he sent to Cairns. I had met a woman in the preschool who came from there. I thought she was brassy. A father at the preschool came from Manly and he was very encouraging. Other than that, Australia and its peoples was a great unknown. Someone in the Catholic Welfare Bureau described it pejoratively as the 'biggest middle-class country on earth'.

The BBC had managed to defeat South Africa's attempts to jam their broadcasts and I listened in to big events not reported in our local press, in particular a huge funeral in Alexandra township near Johannesburg, attended by the whole diplomatic corps. It was all shown on television in Australia where my husband saw it and it increased his resolve to emigrate.

When he had been in Sydney for five days, I woke at two in the morning, dreaming I heard him call me loudly. I saw him dancing in a square in the middle of a city; he wore his raincoat and was waving papers above his head shouting a number. Five hours later, I answered the phone. 'Accept it, the salary is good.' I began.

' What are you talking about?' he was aghast.

'It was raining, wasn't it? Where were you dancing?'

He explained that he'd received an offer of employment and we'd be there in three months.

The next day, I accepted a cheque from a friend who bought our house for her parents. After all the letters and payments, we began the medical checks and consular interviews. Friends gathered to drink tea constantly. Once more the security police reared their ugly heads to harass me on the phone. 'When are you leaving? What is the name of the ship that is taking your container? When is that leaving?' I 'dunno-ed' everything. I had no idea what they wanted and felt irritated. Then we had to have a police clearance check, fingerprints and interview. The officer at the station was very keen to know all the people we knew in Australia.

'No one,' I maintained.

'Come on, I don't believe you.'

'You tell me what you know about Australia,' I offered.

'I was a Rotary exchange student there in the 1970s. It's quite a *lekker* (nice) place, but too full of communists.'

WE LEFT CAPE Town by train in May 1986. Stephen had attended the Grove Primary School in Claremont; he was nine. Amelia was five and had been in preschool. It was when the children said goodbye to their friends that I felt really sad. At their age they would lose them, while we adults had the wherewithal to maintain our contacts.

◀ Orient Beach, East London, South Africa 1944. Granny Isabel in a fur coat with Mark Yazbek and Donne Haddad, the first two of a torrent of grandchildren.

▼ A Hobo Ball 1956, much like the one at Trennerys on the Wild Coast when Bob, as the paralytic Wee Willie Winkie, was carried to bed by his wife and a few waiters. **L to R**: Joe, Bertha, Bob and Sheila Abrey (probably Katberg)

▲ East London, South Africa 1953. Bertha carries Cecile (aged 6 weeks) in a fashion show modeling christening gowns.

▶ Christmas Eve 1953. Bertha and her four children **L to R**: Mark (10), Michele (3), Cecile (7 months), Anita (8)

▲ Christmas 1957. A posse of cousins at Albert and Eileen Haddad's home. **L to R**: Joffe Saker, Anita Yazbek standing in front of him. Mickey Haddad holding Jennifer, his wife Moine, Henry Haddad holding Renee, Granny Isabel, Margaret Sorour with a pair of her 14 children, Donne holding Barbara, Joe Yazbek. Sitting: Phyllis Saker with John, Cecile, Beverley Saker, Michele Yazbek, John under Dessie Haddad's wing.

▲ East London, South Africa 1957. Great Aunt Eugenie, Colin Hiles, Phyllis Saker, Joe, Anita, Bertha, Margaret, (Auntie Ginny's daughter). **In front,** Cecile with Askim and Michele

▲ Sacred Heart Convent, Albany Street, East London, South Africa 1959. Sr Johanna and the Sub A class. Cecile seated 2nd row, 3rd from right; Judy,2nd row 4th from left; Linda, 4th row 3rd from left; Rossy 3rd row 1st on right

▲ East London, South Africa 1957. Bertha and Joe glide the night away at the Windsor Bowl.

▲ September 1958, Antonville, Devereux Avenue. Michele, Paul and Cecile. Mrs de Witt's house is across the road.

▼ Michele and Anita off to school in town, Cecile in pyjamas, with Daddy's big black chev, 1958

▶ The old Redhouse Hotel which became the nuns' enclosure of Sacred Heart Convent, East London, South Africa 1959

▲ Ouma Florie's grave, Cambridge cemetery, East London, South Africa

▲ A Transkei hut with children, goats and chickens

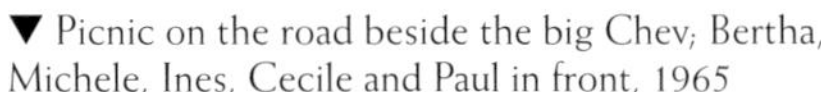

▼ Picnic on the road beside the big Chev; Bertha, Michele, Ines, Cecile and Paul in front, 1965

▲ Askim and Auntie Susie in fond embrace in Antonville back garden, Christmas 1961

▲ Joe Yazbek dressed as his alter ego, Anita van Tonder, at the annual Dominican Convent Old Girls' Reunion, East London, 1963

▲ Joe Yazbek and Cecile cut their birthday cake, 28 May 1969

▲ Cecile and rock paintings between Jamestown and Aliwal North, Cape Province, South Africa, 1982

▲ Olive Schreiner House, Rhodes University, Grahamstown, South Africa 1971. Photo taken in front of St Mary's Hall: Cecile 2nd row 2nd from right

◀ Taize, France, 1973. At the World Youth Congress; CLC, Filipino delegate, Johannes from Germany and Cecile.

▲ East London, South Africa, 6 April 1977. Steve Biko, leader of the Black Consciousness Movement had tea with Councillor Joe Yazbek in the Mayor's Parlour. At that time, Biko was under a banning order which meant he was not allowed to take part in meetings of more than two people (including himself), was not allowed to address gatherings and was not allowed to be quoted. He was on trial in East London charged with defeating the ends of justice. (Photograph courtesy East London *Daily Dispatch*)

▲ Country view over Paarl in the Cape Province, Stephen (7), Amelia (3), 1983

◀ Bertha at the piano, Joe on his ukelele playing their way through life; their constant companionship was the accompaniment to my childhood, filling and enriching all of our memories. 1989

▶ Joe and Bertha at the end of his term on the East London City Council, 1985

▼ Citizenship ceremony, Hornsby Shire Council, New South Wales, Australia, 1989

▶ A Sunday in January 1959. **L to R:** Michele, Anita, Bertha with Paul (11 months), Joe (off to bowls), Mark. **In front,** Cecile and Askim.

The night before we left Cape Town, we slept badly, woken at midnight by a bomb going off in a toilet at Rondebosch railway station, rattling the windows in our friend's house. The next day, a farewell group came to the main Cape Town railway station and stood in a puddle of tears and rain. We were going to East London. As the train pulled out, my equanimity was plundered by a mixture of pain and excitement for the new phase of life that we were embarking on. My thoughts rambled from the little garden I'd planted around our cottage in Claremont that had been our home for ten years—it had turned into a lush forest on a quarter acre block. The new owners said they bought it for the garden. I wondered if there would be trees where we ended up. We used to walk the children along the canal in the next street while the south-easter whooshed through the gum trees. I knew nothing of the forests surrounding Sydney.

The train chugged slowly through the mountain passes in an easterly direction. Amelia leaned against me in a reverie while Stephen sobbed loudly, 'I wish I was too young to know what is happening.' In fact many years later, he told me that during our first year in Australia, he cried into his pillow at night, longing for his friends. On the train, once we turned the lights out, I noticed my husband sipping from a small bottle and he became increasingly drowsy. The train rounded bends in and out of moonlight. We'd soon be with my parents for the hardest farewell of all.

We stayed in East London for a few days. My father and I celebrated our last birthday together at a stilted family dinner in the Dolphin Hotel. My eldest brother, Mark, shouted, 'You are like rats deserting a sinking ship. You have destroyed the family.' A sullen silence ensued, but he continued his diatribe for years, writing vituperative letters to me after we'd arrived in Australia. In our last days in East London, a few dropped in to say goodbye. My mother's brother let out all the anger he'd stored when his son Michael fled military conscription to live in Zimbabwe.

In those weeks before we left, some felt that they had to let us know of their disapproval. My husband's brother said, 'What you are doing is wrong. You are making a terrible mistake.' The obstetrician who'd delivered my son had said bluntly, 'You're leaving because you're racist. You hate black people so you're going to Australia where everyone is white.'

I leapt off the examining couch, 'Who the hell do you think you're talking to? You know nothing about me beyond the parts you poke at in this room.'

I hoped for more from my siblings, but one of my sisters coolly said to me, 'Well, it's your decision and your choice. You'd better be happy.'

My mother said, 'If Paul emigrates, I will kill myself.'

THE COMFORT AND support we received was not from our families, but from vivacious Sister Johanna who brought her bubbling laughter and twinkling eyes to our front door. Having left her family in Switzerland more than twenty years before to work as a missionary in Africa, she knew the path we were on and had experienced the anxiety and pain with her family when she'd announced her choice. Turning to my mother she said, 'This is your most capable child. She is a survivor and she will thrive away from all this suffering here.' With that blessing, she raced back to the waiting car. I stood in awe, deeply grateful to her.

AT THE AIRPORT, my father wept as I'd never seen before. I hugged and held him. 'Daddy, I'll always be around. I'll phone. We can chat. I'll be back to visit you before you know it. Better still, you can come and see for yourself.' From the tarmac at the bottom of the gangway into the plane, I looked back. Through the windows of the departure terminal, I saw my parents standing close together. My father was anguished. His body twitched with sobs he had had to arrest.

We climbed the stairs and took our seats. The preparation hubbub, overhead lockers slamming, last minute adjustments forced me back into my head where Daddy's bitter throwaway line hung like lead. 'I suppose that when I die, you won't even bother to come back for my funeral—you'll just throw a wreath into the water and hope it reaches my grave in time.' At the time, I had countered strongly with, 'How can you say such a horrible thing. I am not running away from YOU.' But through no fault of my own, his words were prophetic.

I wondered why my brother and sisters left my parents alone at this time. They seemed unaware that they needed support at the airport, a time of wrenching separation. Strange that, as a result of their feelings towards me, they hurt my parents, on whose behalf they said they felt aggrieved.

Because of sanctions, Qantas had no direct air links with South Africa. We had to fly to Harare to get the Qantas flight. We stayed with my hospitable cousin Michael, who'd fled conscription a few years before. (He would be able to return to South Africa, under an amnesty in1991.)

At Victoria Falls, we farewelled Africa with drums, singing and dancing. Qantas from Harare to Sydney, and the cabin crew were friendly. One young man in particular was most attentive and seemed to want to talk. Eventually he leant over, the nature of his question belying his reticence, 'What right do you think you have to leave the mess behind in South Africa, after you have benefited from the system?'

My husband was taken aback but I replied immediately, 'Our children did not choose to be born there, nor to suffer the consequences of having politically active parents.'

21

A home in Australia

It was not what France gave you, but what it did not take away from you that was important.

GERTRUDE STEIN, IN PARIS IN 1940, THE YEAR FRANCE FELL TO THE NAZIS

I fell in love with Australia. When the plane landed and I saw the sky through the open door, I felt I'd come home. On the New South Wales north coast, New Agers might say I must have lived in Australia in a past life. To fall in love with one's new country is a blessing.

Continuing our migration as a holiday, we spent ten days in Cremorne while we looked for a house to rent. The first agent we spoke with immediately suggested St Ives. 'You'll be very happy there among plenty of other South Africans.' Little did we realise coming from the same country was not enough to generate friendship, especially when that country was so divided. The South Africans over the road came to say hello. They'd been here for a couple of years. We wanted to update them on the struggle but their mystified faces revealed how far apart we were. Another who'd arrived recently from South Africa lamented her maid's ingratitude when she left her with a hundred rand bonus: 'She's never even written to thank us.'

When we first arrived, we knew no one. In the end, the connections we made with fellow South Africans were based more on our shared reasons for leaving than the mere fact of our being South African.

We chose a large house with a beautiful garden where my parents could visit comfortably. It was set in a neighbourhood full of magnificent trees, a pleasure to walk in. The children went to the Catholic primary school nearby, where the community lived up to its reputation for welcoming newcomers.

I worked in the school canteen and the library and made long and wonderful friendships with some of the parents. When Amelia began school in 1986, a group of mothers became friends and we continued to meet for the next dozen years. Shella was from Pakistan, Barbara was a German from Venezuela, Leonore was from Ireland and I was from South Africa. Later, we were joined by Marietta who had been in Sydney for many years from Sri Lanka. When Leonore's husband died suddenly, leaving her with three children, we were shocked and fearful. Her colleagues at the hospital rallied round to help with funeral and other expenses. Certainly a tribute to the person she is, but as well, a measure of the society we migrants find ourselves in.

Another friend Eileen became as much a close friend as a social mentor to my migrant self. I met her soon after arriving when a friend of mine rented her garden flat. In her nineties, she has lived through a chunk of Australia's history and over the years has filled me in with eyewitness detail.

These relationships made in the first few months after arrival become as those from childhood. Unlike my grandparents' experience in South Africa, we spoke a common language, although in the beginning, I could not understand what many were saying. The first few sessions in the canteen were embarrassing. When the bread man brought a delivery, he asked me, in a strong Australian accent to give him the empty trays. I didn't understand him and one of the other helpers had to explain. Bream fish was 'brim', mayor was 'mair' and a car hooter became a 'horn'. Stephen explained the latter to me after I'd been to the garage asking the technician to come outside and look at my hooter (breast) that made an awful noise when pressed. A ruddy complexioned gent, he examined the car and turned to me, 'You must be missing all them muscular black blokes in Africa.' I couldn't believe my ears.

Sometimes, as migrants, our children become the parents to lead us into the new society and educate us in its ways. On weekend bushwalks, armed with natural history sources, educating ourselves and our children, we developed a love and attachment to Australia's peoples, native bush and open spaces, and a deep appreciation for safety in even the wildest reaches.

The Australian way of communicating, I soon learned, has a reserve about it. South Africans have a reputation for speaking their minds and being overly proactive which has made some very successful. But apartheid poisoned many white South Africans with a sense of entitlement, something we can be aware of and attempt to moderate. In Australia I found an invisible class system based on accent, geographic location or suburb in Sydney; the criteria differed from those in South Africa, where occupation was a class indicator that, along with colour, had been the most obvious sign on which all of life was predicated.

South African theatre in the seventies and eighties was mostly stomach churning protest work with confronting themes and performances. In my early Australian days, Aboriginal theatre with themes of dispossession and marginalisation held meaning for me in the universality of the suffering portrayed. Despite these differences, I still felt very much at home in the wider society and revelled in finding literature that had been banned in South Africa in Sydney's second hand bookshops.

As a communicator, I maintained a regular correspondence with my family. We sent photographs and descriptive letters. My parents visited us in the first year. I think they thought they were coming to take us back home. That changed when they saw how settled I was and how well the society functioned. In fact, they went back to South Africa fully convinced of the wisdom of our decision. After we'd been in Australia two years, we became citizens.

Our home and family environment were stimulating and at times challenging. Intellectually, it was a rich environment but after five years, my husband became increasingly unhappy. He was working in the city in professional practice and teaching at the universities. Where migration gave me life and fresh air, the opposite was true for him. He felt he'd lost his identity. His inner world fell into chaos, ruined by the absence of any familiar externals to sustain him. He plunged into grief and experienced this new world merely as a place of loss of the things that affirmed who he was. In our first year here, he used to say that on Saturdays he felt most at home when he mowed the lawn. The smell of freshly cut grass was the only thing that was the same as in South Africa. Once during a particularly miserable period when he was unwilling to seek professional help, a lawyer 'friend' of his suggested that all he needed was 'confession, a rosary and a bottle of red wine.'

My husband had been a good father to his young children, but his inability to settle in Australia meant it was best for him to return to South Africa and be closer to his family. When he went alone on a holiday visit back to South Africa in 2001, he did not return to Australia. Initially, it was an enormous disruption. Amelia was on exchange at Cornell University in New York State. Stephen was working. I had to sell my home, help Stephen find a flat and book Amelia into International House at Sydney University so that she could complete her degree. The children were both distressed and showed it in different ways but they eventually came to terms with the situation. Stephen is now working as a research analyst and continuing his university studies in Sydney. Amelia is doing her doctorate in English in the United States. They both regard Australia as home, the place where they built happy childhood memories and have grown up.

To migrate with young children is a daring act. Some are forced and some have choice. The consequences of accidents along the way are potentially the same for all. Fear, sadness and loss can strike, but we move with optimism and hope. We learn also that we can trust. That people open their hearts and share their resources so generously with strangers is something that never fails to move me. I believe that among the affluent whites in the South Africa that I left, there was not a culture of helping one another. If someone needed something done, it was too easy to find someone to pay a pittance to do it.

So many things in my personal life changed over the years. Some were a necessary adaptation to new circumstances, some were choices that I made around ways of being in the world lighter, easier, no longer weighed down by the ongoing drama that life in South Africa had become. For me, migration was an enormous liberation. Even though I may have been materially better off in South Africa, it was not an option for me. I wanted to grow and change and that, I am still in the process of doing.

22

Farewell Father

Whenever you pass by the field where you have laid your ancestors look well thereupon, and you shall see yourselves and your children dancing hand in hand.

THE PROPHET
KAHLIL GIBRAN

As a parent, I am aware of our desire to heal the world for our children and to absolve the mistakes of our past through them. Both of my parents, albeit in different ways, suffered as children. The educated, privileged life they made for us was born of my father's poverty and my mother's insularity. Despite the difficulties of their early lives, they both made an enormous contribution to the countless people they met on their path.

Dear Daddy,

Where are you now?

In my mind's eye I see you striding across the beach at six o'clock on a holiday morning, diving into the surf and emerging with great harrumphs from the foamy water . . .

in serious mood behind the huge walnut desk in your office, sorting through the mail and flicking letters toward Oswald for delivery . . .

beside mother at the piano, you pull your five foot five inches up an extra inch and set off enthusiastically, mouth very wide, and when Uncle Bosy was around you both went at

top volume on the road to Mandalay via Jeroooosalem.
In town you slap 'Edgars' on their backs, 'Hello old chap, how are you doing?'
or, 'She's such a galeelie(darling) *that 'Agnes'.*
You puncture a grim moment at Donald Woods' first all race conference at Bulugha playing your ukelele to sing 'Nobody loves me...'

AS MY FATHER got older, he became more serious. His religious conviction and practice grew. He regularly rang all of us children, even when I was in my late thirties and living in Australia, to find out 'What Father said in his sermon at mass today'. I found myself inventing sermons rather than wasting precious moments explaining my religious waywardness and breaking his heart.

When I went away to university, he described to me what could have been an episode of depression when he was a student: 'Strong doubts came over me and I missed mass a few times. I neglected my studies and felt like I was losing my grip. But Father was wonderful in the confessional as I told him I was faltering. The minute I went back to daily mass and communion, I was powerful again.' He then gave me a holy card of St Anthony on which he'd written, 'Keep the faith', to take to university.

HE STILL PLAYED bowls at his club, Exchange, on the beachfront. The egalitarianism of lawn bowls appealed to him after his years on the hockey fields for Border and the Eastern Cape. He spoke fondly of the returned servicemen and working-class players he mixed with. He said they kept him in touch with life and the harsh realities that so many faced on a daily basis.

He would leave home quite early on Saturday afternoons for bowls. My mother would wave to him from the balcony and he'd cruise down the driveway in his latest big flashy Chev or Mercedes. He looked like a caricature in his whites in that black car. When he got to the beachfront, he'd stop at one end and pick up eight or ten street children who crammed themselves into the front and back of the car, and give them a ride up and down the esplanade. Was he remembering being chauffeured around Kroonstad in the Nazareth House orphanage limousine sixty years before?

He was a man who straddled a number of worlds and tried to synthesise them in his life. He was a Catholic in all his actions, judging everything against his religious yardstick. He was a lawyer, shrewd and skilled. He was a Lebanese man—committed to his family and appreciative of the culture from which he grew. He was an extraordinary man who carried extraordinary baggage from his past into the extraordinary South African situation.

I spent a lot of time near him and as I grew up, I did not feel that he treated me any differently because I was a girl. In fact he encouraged me in my academic endeavours. When I changed my course to social work and then later, as I selected from a varied and distinctly non-vocational curriculum, he began to lose patience and wonder out loud if I was ever going to achieve anything.

I cannot say, like Germaine Greer, 'Daddy I hardly knew you.' My father was open and vulnerable and always moved by other people. I could share my deepest distress with him about the political situation in the country. He understood my inability to sleep well while we were surrounded by such poverty and state-produced horror. Looking back, I can say that our communication was mutually honest. I lived away from home from the age of seventeen. Our conversations took place mostly on the phone and he'd sometimes write encouraging and supportive letters. As time wore on and in the months before he died, he finally stopped saying, 'Quickly, this phone call is costing a fortune.'

In 1988, he suffered a major heart attack and was in intensive care for three days before my family told me. At the time he was experiencing excruciating pain in his lower back. His right leg slowly withered until it was a peg leg. He never complained. He poured Lourdes water over his knee and said the rosary as he did so. He swallowed his friend Chris Yiangou's remedies that he brought back from Cyprus, took long walks when able and rested in bed when too weak. But no one—not even his sisters—realised how ill he was. His increasing discomfort took years to be diagnosed as chronic myeloid leukaemia. When he was dying, his doctors realised that he had been unwell for more than twenty years, even serving two terms as mayor and continuing his legal practice.

Two weeks before he died, he rang me on a Saturday afternoon in Sydney. He asked me a few times how I was. 'No really, tell me how you are,' he persisted. The same about my husband his work and performance, both of my children, their behaviour and schoolwork and again, 'Are you sure you're all right?' As I answered his many questions, I knew he would die soon. Finally he said, 'Won't you tell your bladdy mother that I won't die if I go to mass at half past five'. From the other phone she leaped in with: 'Darl, at sunset, the air is unsettled and then there are all those coughing people in the draughty church.'

The next day we left for a week in the snow at Thredbo. When we got home, there was a message on the voicemail from my mother. 'Your father is in hospital. He is fine, I'm just going to have tea with him.' But I knew otherwise. That evening, I prayed and spent the hours before I went to sleep feeling very close to him. In the morning I woke suddenly at five o'clock and sat straight up in bed. The whole world glowed. I swung my legs over the side and floated out into the garden. The trees looked greener than before. The dawn light was shiny-bright but silent.

'Awake! For morning in the bowl of night has flung the stone that puts the stars to flight…' It was as if I walked with my father into the opening lines from his beloved Omar Khayyám's *Rubáiyát* which he often quoted.

I began to water the garden. From that stillness I felt transported some way along the end road with my father. When the phone rang at six o'clock, I knew he had died an hour before and gave me a taste of the peace he experienced as he left us behind.

He died knowing all that I wanted him to hear, but I would love to have supported him more when he was struggling with self-doubt and illness. As it was, his line about my not attending his funeral and throwing a wreath onto the water hoping it reached there, came true. It was not through lack of trying on my part. Someone in the family decided that they couldn't wait the extra day for me to arrive. It was a psychic severance; an anonymous hand wielded the knife. While they held the funeral in South Africa, a small group of us sat in an October sunset on my back lawn where we read poems. My cousin Paul, who had converted to Judaism said *Kaddish* and Ian Lipworth spoke about my father, his friend, the political man.

I wrote this piece and faxed it to my cousin, Dr Ivor Yazbek, who read it at the service.

Daddy

When Anita said to me, 'Cecile, he is gone.' I said, 'Yes, but where?' and I searched for you in all the corners of my house and my garden. When I stopped looking I found you.

I found you in my eyes, where I saw the world as you taught me to see it;
I found you in my hands where I felt the imprint of your hands as you had so often held mine;
In my ears I heard your jokes—and your pain;
In my heart, I found the love you shared with me for all people. This love you shared with us was full of forgiveness for all. You came to this love through your desire for a better life, a life of truth and justice for all. If I have learnt one thing from you, Daddy, it is the gift you had for building bridges between people.
May we all remember you and honour you by at least once in our lives, laying ourselves down 'like a bridge over troubled water'.
My heart is heavy as I am not with you all, but my spirit is light as it soars across the ocean to touch you and share a moment.

IN ANOTHER WAY, something from my life was present as my father was dying. The nurse who looked after him in those last hours introduced herself to my mother, 'You can't forget us, Mrs Yazbek. I am Gladys Khuselo, daughter of Rosie, Cecile's old nursemaid, from before she went to school.'

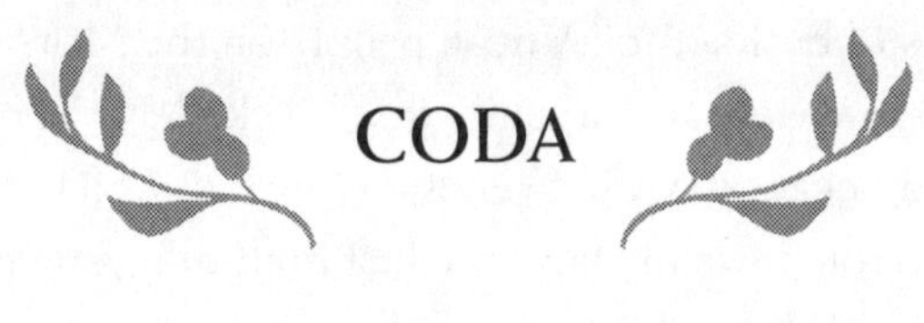

CODA

The Blessing of My Ancestors

We are the seeds of the tenacious plant, and it is in our ripeness and our fullness of heart that we are given to the wind and scattered.

THE PROPHET
KAHLIL GIBRAN

In 1992, I was in and out of hospital and seriously ill. One afternoon at home, in a delirium, I saw my two grandmothers and my great-grandmother in the corner of my bedroom ceiling. The fact that they looked identical to a photograph of them at my parents' wedding didn't faze me. They seemed to be calling out addressing me firmly, 'You can't come to us yet. Go back, go back. You have children who need you. We all suffered sickness, alone, in a new country. You will be all right.'

As I began to get well, I assembled a selection of the old family photographs from the early twentieth century and put them on a table in the living room. In the evenings I would sit close to them and visitors would ask me the stories of those pictures.

Toward the end of the year, while falling asleep on a hot summer night, I heard a truck grinding up the Pacific Highway. I opened a bleary eye to see where I was then tried to go back to sleep. But the truck must have been overloaded or at any rate, struggling up the hill. As I tried to block it out, pictures of busloads of African people on the Main Transkei Road filled my head so vividly and urgently that I picked up the notebook next to my bed and began to write. Scenes and memories filled the page and tears started to roll down my face; the first draft of my memoir was being born. By the time I'd written ten pages, I was weeping, the ice in my chest melting as I allowed myself, finally, years after migrating, to remember with pleasure and nostalgia, parts of my life which had felt too strange for this place at the time of my arrival. As I described and analysed them, I realised how apartheid and racism had intruded on my childhood and, in part, made me the adult I am. Like all children, I had seen things that were carved into my memory. The extent of my experience among the servants in the courtyard belonged to me. The adults inside the house weren't interested in my child view of a world they thought they understood; a world in which Katrina and Rosie fed us pastes of love and hate from the ambivalence of their situation. The Lebanese child who walked gardens with Granny and the African child who incessantly asked, '*Ntoni* (What)'? wandered restlessly together in early morning hours. I came face to face with my Lebanese origins and personal history as a child in Africa.

The food writer, Claudia Roden, describes the Lebanese family as the cloak that warms but also suffocates. This sense of family gives us the capacity to form deep and lasting friendships. Lebanese people I have known love to share their food, passing tastes over the fence wherever they are, South Africa, Australia or anywhere. Although the sound of Arabic accents, people's looks and the food are familiar to me, I am still something of a foreigner in Sydney's Lebanese world. My accent locates me somewhere in the disparate group of ex-South Africans whom I sometimes encounter at concerts, where African music always stirs our hearts and provokes reminiscence.

When my life changed and I moved to Bangalow, in northern New South Wales, I was nervous of settling in an apparently socially homogeneous environment. I look and speak differently. When people asked where I came from with more than a simple curiosity, I retreated further into my foreignness. No matter how educated or likable, we can be treated as outsiders when we move among those who share a history that is not our own. However, as a result of growing up among so many different languages and people I feel able to make connections in diverse situations. My adult children tell me now that when they were very young, I used words and songs from so many languages, that they had no idea what was Arabic, what was Afrikaans, Xhosa or German; so similar to my own childhood except that the languages I heard, were all spoken by the people who owned them.

As a migrant in Australia, I found few similarities with the lives of my ancestors as migrants in South Africa. My admiration for them grew as I came face to face with the obstacles they'd surmounted. Remembering my grandmother in the gardens of my childhood, I cultivate and plant in this place for my children, born in the old country, grown up here, at home in this multi-hued landscape.

Between 1839 and 1876, the Ottoman Empire, which for hundreds of years had displayed excellence in art, architecture, banking and law entered a reorganisation or *Tanzimat*, fuelled by nationalist forces. The capital, Constantinople, contained treasured historic buildings from its time as part of the Roman and then the Byzantine empires. Among them, Hagia Sofia and the Topkapi Palace gave its inhabitants a sense of personal history. It was a city of East and West expressed in the culture and music which blended Byzantine, Arabic and Persian styles. Muslims recognizing Jesus as a prophet, were fully accepting of the Catholic and Orthodox Christians in their midst. The Ottoman Empire posed a serious challenge to the rising power of Western Europe and, while the French were more aligned with the Russians, the British forged links with the Ottomans that would secure them power in the Middle East when the five-hundred-year-old empire was dissolved after the First World War.

As part of the Ottoman Empire, Greater Syria was composed of what is today Lebanon, Syria, Jordan and Israel. Until the end of the First World War, Lebanon was under direct Ottoman rule through two powerful feudal Druze families, the Maans and the Shihabs. The Druze, found mostly in Syria and Lebanon, are a religious group that emerged in the eleventh century as an offshoot of Ismailya Islam. Although they regard themselves as having an Islamic association, they are not recognised as Muslims by all other branches of Islam. In Lebanon, there was unrest between the Christians and the Druze, the latter calling on the Egyptian ruler, Muhammad Ali, to support them against the Christians. In 1840, British and Ottoman troops landed in Beirut and expelled Ali. Various solutions—even partition of Lebanon between Christian and Druze were tried but all failed and in 1860, the Druze massacred ten thousand Christians in their villages. The rulers then restricted Christians to certain villages in the mountains of Lebanon but thus confined, the Christians were unable to make a living for themselves and began to emigrate to Africa, North and South America and East Asia. At the same time, Christian missionaries began to pour into Lebanon and set up schools and universities. The American University of Beirut was established in 1866, and in 1875 the French founded St Joseph's University.

My father's family—the Yazbeks

It was into such a tumultuous environment and time that my great-grandfather Tamar Yazbek was born in Beirut in 1840. After training as a language teacher, he became a tutor in Arabic and English to the Ottoman rulers of his country. He had a special lesson room in the palatial governor's home in Beirut. He was married and had two sons, Wadia(Willie) and Najeeb. But after his first wife died, a new wife, Emily Azerach, a thirteen year old Turkish girl was brought to Beirut to marry the widowed Tamar who was thirty years her senior. At the same time as the conflicts raged in the countryside, Emily and Tamar lived a good life in Ottoman Beirut.

In 1888, my paternal grandmother (Farida) Florie, Tamar and Emily's first child, was born. They would have seven more children, Ilyez(Alex), Eugenie(Ginny), Youssef(Joe), Marie(Mary), Beshara(Charlie), Phillip and Michael, all of whom would share Emily's love for singing and opera.

In the meantime, in 1889, Willie and Najeeb, Tamar's two eldest sons from his first marriage left Lebanon and followed other Lebanese to live in Bloemfontein, South Africa. They wrote to the family at home of great opportunity—diamonds, gold and ostrich feathers. Lithuanian Jews were making a successful business with ostrich farming and were exporting plumes to the Moulin Rouge in Paris. Tamar himself saw fashionable Beirut matrons decked in expensive feathers.

In 1907, the whole family, Tamar, Emily and all of the children migrated to South Africa. They began life in Fort Beaufort, close to some Lebanese traders and ostrich feather farmers. It was a small, dusty village that had been settled by the British in the early nineteenth century as a military town. The fort had been built as part of the defences against the Xhosa in the frontier wars. Feeling isolated, they soon moved to Kroonstad on the Wilger River in the Orange Free State. There was a supportive community of other Lebanese families, among them the Antonies and Adamis. Most of the local people were Afrikaners and quite hospitable to the newcomers, an attitude that contrasted with that of the English, who looked down on the 'foreigners'. Perhaps the Afrikaners, with their scars from the Boer War, were sympathetic to anyone who was not English.

The children Marie(Mary), Beshara(Charlie), Phillip and Michael continued at the local school among the Afrikaners and a few English-speakers and Jews. Meanwhile Tamar built a name for himself in business not only among his compatriots but among the local people as well. The fact that his brother, Father Peter (Khourie Boutros), was a Maronite Catholic priest made them very much at home in the church. Religion was a familiar food among all the other unknowns. Plaster saints filled their home shrines and they loved their rosaries. 'Hail Mary…' they prayed, calling mother across oceans and skies full of stars.

In 1918, Tamar died of kidney failure, a complication of Bright's Disease; Emily was not yet fifty and she had eight children, the eldest already married but Michael, the baby of the family, was just six years old. She lived as a widow for almost fifty years and died in 1965, aged ninety-six. There were tributes to her in the local Kroonstad and Bloemfontein newspapers. My mother said, 'One of the lights went out in the Orange Free State when Granny died.' She was their connection to the past, to a homeland they'd never seen. Her absence left them with a lifelong quest to find it.

YAZBEK IS A NAME found in Turkey, Syria and other parts of the Middle East. It may be that they were all part of a migration from Uzbekistan on the Silk Road, when the state was breaking down in the sixteenth century. The original Yazbeks of Beirut were goldsmiths and gold merchants living in the goldworkers' quarter of the city, their trade consistent with the great gold working tradition of Uzbekistan. Our branch of the family originated in 1760, when our ancestor, a man Sayegh, had five sons whom he named Yazbek, Nemer, Nader, Taref and Deeb. We are descended from the son he named Yazbek. So we might have been called Yazbek Sayegh. All of the Yazbeks in South Africa were cousins, descendants of that first Beiruti couple, Tamar and Emily, who migrated early in the twentieth century.

Yazbek family, Kroonstad, South Africa, circa 1914. **Front L to R**: Victoria (2),Victor (4), Elaine (3), Philip (5), Michael (3); **Middle**: Farida (Florie) Antoun (Anthony), Tamar (Patriarch), Emily (Matriarch). Becharre (Charlie), Eugenie (Ginny), Marie (Mary). **Back**: Naguib, Wadiah (Willie),Yousof (Joe), Ilyez (Alex). Naguib and Willie were Tamar's sons from his first wife who died. He then married the much younger Emily Azerach from Constantinople.

FLORIE, THE ELDEST child of Tamar and Emily was married in an arrangement in 1907 to her first cousin, Antoun, son of Tamar's brother, Father Peter (Khourie Boutros). Antoun's mother was a Khaleefie and Antoun and Florie, my grandparents, were both aged nineteen when they were married in Beirut. They left for South Africa with Tamar and Emily and all the family in 1907.

They had five children Victor, Elaine, Victoria, my father Joseph and Susie(Hazeezie) who was the youngest. In 1923, Antoun like his uncle, died of kidney failure after only sixteen years of marriage. Disaster struck

Beirut, 1907. Antoun Yazbek marries his first cousin Farida (Florie)Yazbek. (My paternal grandparents)

Kroonstad, South Africa, 1922. Antoun Yazbek their father has died. Possibly an orphanage photograph. **Front**, Susie the youngest. **Middle**, Joe and Victoria. **Back**, Elaine and Victor

the family. The eldest Elaine, at twelve, had to leave school and go and work in the shop with her mother, Florie. Because Florie was too poor to care for all of the children, the three youngest, my father and his two sisters, Victoria and Susie had to go into Nazareth House orphanage where they lived for the next seven years. Florie worked all day in the shop but began to suffer with heart and kidney failure too. They moved to East London where she died in 1950 at the age of sixty-two.

My father, Joseph Anthony Yazbek, was born in 1915. He was a bright-eyed baby who was silent until he was four years old. After hoping for a scholarship to study medicine, in 1932 he won a place in law at the University College of the Orange Free State in Bloemfontein where they were taught in both English and Afrikaans. In 1937, he graduated BA

Bloemfontein, South Africa, 1937. University College of the Orange Free State. Joseph Anthony Yazbek, BA LLB

LLB. He had been helped by the Lebanese community and worked at menial jobs, stringing tennis racquets in the days when animal gut was used. The gallery of photographs in our downstairs playroom when we were children, bore testimony to my father's vivacity and determination during his five-year university course. He was in the drama society, debating, playing hockey, tennis, rowing, boxing, strumming his banjo ukelele at every opportunity. His BA major was geology: 'By jove, she was a beauty and I just wanted to look at her all the time,' he enthused fifty years later over his geology lecturer! But after graduation life threw up a challenge. Florie, his mother, was in congestive cardiac failure and needed to live at sea level. He could have stayed in Bloemfontein under the patronage of Toefic Khalil, the lawyer to whom he'd been articled, but decided to care for his mother first.

In 1937 Hitler's emissaries toured smaller towns in South Africa lecturing the population on the dangers of Syrians in their midst, dark Arab people who would dilute the Aryan purity of the Afrikaner unless they were stopped. Other Lebanese families, the Sakers and Shamleys who lived in Graaff Reinet told of hearing a 'bladdy mad Nazi' public speaker in the town square.

While Durban or Port Elizabeth were bigger coastal cities, with possibly more opportunity, the social environment was mostly English-speaking and the atmosphere at that time was not as friendly toward Lebanese migrants. So my father, his mother and his youngest sister Susie went to live in East London where other Lebanese families like the Allams, Michaels and Sanans were well established by the 1930s.

IN SUCH A climate of prejudice, my father went around to the various law firms in East London looking for a position as a professional assistant. He was hounded out of office after office, abused as a dago or Arab by the

Kroonstad, South Africa, 1935. Yazbek family. L to R: Victoria, Elaine, Victor, Florie (Faridie) seated, Susie and Joe

most illustrious lawyers in town. '*Rakhmit bayee* (I swear on my father)', he told his family, 'that Englishman called me an Arab and refused to even consider employing me'. Deeply hurt, he borrowed five pounds from his brother Victor and hired a shabby room in a decrepit building on a corner of the main road, Oxford Street to set up practice. He hired an African paralegal assistant, Darlington, to work for him.

My father made contact with other Lebanese professionals; a lawyer in Butterworth, Transkei, Simon Mahoud was one person as committed to antiracism.

They met and decided that the only way to fight prejudice against the Lebanese community was to facilitate the education of the next generation to get people away from 'informal commercial ventures', such as illicit diamond buying, or dealing in unlicensed liquor and cigarettes. Groups of Lebanese in the Transvaal, a northern province, were destroying the good name of the community by involving themselves in these nefarious commercial activities. As well, the government was threatening to reclassify Lebanese as Asians, which meant non-white, thereby disbarring the Lebanese, like Asians, from owning fixed property or trading in white areas. In addition, they would no longer be allowed to vote. So this group of lawyers formed the Lebanonian Association with a commitment to fostering a desire for university education among youth. Those who could, lent money, others spoke publicly about education and encouraged parents who might not have been educated, to assist their children as much as possible. In short they became mentors and sponsors to other Lebanese children as if they were their own.

WHEN THE SECOND World War broke out in 1939, encouraged by the then Prime Minister Jan Smuts, the English citizens of Natal and the Eastern Cape rushed to enlist. My mother's brothers too went off voluntarily to be stationed in Egypt. Albert, the eldest and a doctor was a captain in the medical corps. Mickey, the middle brother, also took rank and was a tank navigator in the desert. Joffe Saker, later to marry my mother's elder sister Phyllis, also fought in Egypt. Many South African Lebanese, Africans, 'coloureds' and Jews joined the war effort. An Afrikaner faction imbued with a Boer War legacy of hatred of the English, sided with Hitler and formed a pro-Hitler and Nazi organisation, the *Ossewa Brandwag*. They were interned in camps with Germans and Italians who were regarded as enemy aliens. John Vorster, the prime minister who succeeded Hendrik Verwoerd as prime minister in the sixties was one of those interned.

My father felt left out. He wanted to be one of 'the men', a local person and no longer a foreigner. So he joined the queue for the 'medical'. He was rejected because of poor eyesight. He went to Port Elizabeth where he thought he might pass, as no one knew him there. He was rejected yet again. Disheartened, he went back to East London wondering where he belonged in the world. He felt that his pronounced Semitic features, large nose and 'olive' skin, as well as his devout Catholicism weren't helping him to integrate into the society. In later years we would joke about our looks, my father saying of his nose, 'It is a desert nose and will always give trouble in town.'

Back in East London, he put his head down and worked at his practice. He lived at home with his mother and younger sister. The latter, my Aunt Susie, told of my father coming home from the office and weeping at some of the cases he had to deal with. 'He had such a soft heart, he wanted to help everybody.'

Soldiers going away to war make wills. As more and more men were leaving East London and districts, lawyers too, they went to my father to draw up their wills. By the time the war was over and the men were coming back, they came to see him, as he had their documents. His practice ballooned. His affable nature and expertise combined to make him the busiest professional for miles. He moved premises, expanding until he eventually bought a three-storey building in the centre of town to house his business.

My mother's family—Granny Isabel and the Haddads

My mother's father, Alexander or Skander Haddad, was born in Beit Meri, a small village near Beirut, in 1870. His father was a Greek Cypriot, possibly a former monk and icon painter from one of the Orthodox monasteries. Alexander was the middle son in a family of five girls and four boys. Schooled by British and Canadian teachers, they all spoke good English. He trained as a teacher of English, Arabic and French, but soon realised, confined as the Christians were to certain mountain villages, that there was little opportunity for him in the Middle East. Alexander had heard stories of wealth and a comfortable life from other Lebanese in West and South Africa. George Mukheibir, also from Beit Meri had set up a successful hawking business in the Barkly East district of South Africa. Hawking was the way many of those new migrants, such as Lebanese and Lithuanian Jews, started earning a living in semi-rural areas where farmers travelled to town only occasionally. In Afrikaans, a hawker was called a *smous* and when their carts threw up dust on the farm roads, the familiar cry went up, '*Hier kom die smous* –Here comes the hawker.'

At the age of twenty-five, Alexander left Lebanon for South Africa in 1895 and began hawking suit lengths and household goods to the prosperous sheep farmers in the Queenstown district. Within three years, he was successful enough in 1898 to buy a house and shop at number 88 Cathcart Road the main street, and began trading in earnest. Haddad Brothers imported European fine china, fabrics and laces. Month by month, the general store expanded until it was stocking hardware and farm implements for the local farmers, as well as Lebanese groceries for the community that lived in the surrounding villages.

In 1909 Alexander, aged thirty nine and very successful, went back to Lebanon to fetch his wife, Isabel, daughter of George and Rosa Ghiz; she had been promised some time before. As was customary for girls, she didn't have schooling beyond the three R's. He carried a substantial dowry bag of diamonds, rubies, emeralds, sapphires and gold nuggets to present to his wife's family. He sailed up the east coast of Africa and changed ships at Port Said for a smaller boat going to Beirut. On arrival, he went straight to the goldsmith's quarter where he had some of the gems set. The one-carat diamond was set as an engagement ring in platinum in French style by a Russian goldworker. The two-carat diamond was set into a pendant and given as a wedding gift.

Beirut, 1909. Isabel Ghiz marries Alexander (Skander) Haddad. (My maternal grandparents)

A view of Haddad house, Beit Merie, Beirut

Isabel, my mother's mother, is the only grandparent I really knew. She mothered me in my early years in the best grandmotherly way. She was born in 1894 to a comfortable family of silkworm farmers living in Beit Merie, Beirut. The ground floor of their three-storey house was devoted to silkworms. They had electricity, a plumbed handbasin and a maid to fill baths and arrange hair for the women of the house.

In 1910, Isabel was just fifteen and pregnant, when Alexander announced that they had to go back to South Africa to secure his business affairs. Isabel and her family were shocked and resisted the move. When he promised that they would return after one year, she relented and they set sail. She left behind two sisters, Mary and Linda, and a brother, Fareed. Not one of her family members was at the quay as they refused to be complicit in what they saw as the abduction of their daughter and sister. On the ship, she and Alexander met up with other Lebanese migrants. Their tenuous connections sustained them and by the end of the voyage they felt as though they were close family. Sailing through the Suez Canal and down the east coast of Africa, stopping at wild and wonderful ports such as Alexandria, Port Said and Djibouti, they had no idea of where they were headed or what demands would be made of them. The men had mostly been in Africa for some time and told stories of big homes, large gardens and teams of servants, in order to comfort these young girls. As Christian Lebanese the women spoke French and Arabic but only the men spoke English.

This is how I imagine it may have been on the ship…

Isabel and Haseebie (Ross's wife) nudged Halia (George's wife) who in turn nudged Samira (Samir's wife and first cousin) and the four of them collapsed in a heap of giggles on the deck. Those Ingleesie (English) gentlemen with their blonde hair and red faces were too funny when they lost their game of deck quoits, particularly when they played against the swarthy fortune-seekers. Suddenly Skander appeared next to Isabel and gave her a look. He told her that they were on their way to a place full of such blond people who were to be respected because they were first to tame that wilderness and were excellent customers in their businesses. Samir was open in his scolding of Samira, and George told Halia plainly that although they were on the ship travelling together to the same destination, they should know that their new home would not be like Lebanon. Their interactions with non-Lebanese, when they first arrived, would always be only because of business.

The men went to change and puff their cheroots in the smoking lounge while a pall of apprehension settled on the women. They began to fear, as never before, the truth in the warnings of family and friends: 'You will be alone, alone as you have never been before; you will get lost and be lost to us.'

But as the ship sailed on, Isabel consoled herself and the others when she voiced Skander's promise, 'Only six months, make some money, sell the business and go back home.'

Samir and Samira were not to know of the tragedies life had in store for them as a result of their consanguineous marriage. Alone as Lebanese, in Fort Beaufort, a village in the interior, they were to have five children, three boys and two girls. At age eighteen, within two years of each other, their brilliant sons had gone off to university and each in turn suffered major psychiatric breakdowns with cognitive impairment and consequent mental retarda-

tion. Three grown men wearing long shorts, knee-high socks and twill jackets, became little boys of seven or eight who spent their days swinging bats and balls. As they aged, they spent more time living in the psychiatric hospital and coming out on day release. Only their sisters would be normal.

In Africa, far from family and home, with no community to support them, Samir and Samira tried to cope with their children.

The Catholic Church had established a clinic in the town and Sister Beata was the nurse in charge. Over many years, she did what she could to help the family. On one of our drives through the town we called on her and she said to my mother, 'If only Samira's parents had known when they arranged a marriage between their daughter and her first cousin, how it would affect their children. At least the girls are all right. The broken-hearted parents, Samir and Samira, are always in church. But then wouldn't you be, if you had such a load? What a pity that people married their cousins. It was not allowed in Germany. I hope they don't do it anymore. Nobody can predict the consequences but it often brings a life of suffering to the whole family.'

ON ONE OF our many walks in the garden, Granny Isabel answered my question as to who promised her when she was so young:

Well, as Auntie Mary, my older sister, was already married it was my turn. Linda was younger, she stayed home winding silk from the cocoons. Your Grandpa's family spoke with my parents while he was still in Africa. He came back to fetch me. We travelled thousands of horrible miles from home and from civilization. At Port Said we saw Arab children barefoot and begging, we threw money into the sea and they dived in to get it. We were afraid so we never got off the ship until we reached Beira in Mozambique. There, we had to climb into a basket and were lowered into a small boat to be rowed ashore. Then we took the train and somewhere we even had to go in a covered ox wagon. I cried when I got to Queenstown. There were no street lamps, no electricity, no proper plumbing, and I was surrounded by black people. The maid in the house helped me, but I had to show my way of doing the washing to the woman who came for that every Tuesday. At least Haseebie was also in Queenstown. The people

> around me were so different. When the postman came after lunch and I went to the box to collect the mail, some of them would be standing there to watch me as they knew what time I went out. I wore my beautiful Paris gowns. Looking back, I am not surprised they stared at me.

I picture my grandmother, a young exotic beauty, doing something as mundane and human as searching longingly through the letters for an envelope with familiar writing on it. Granny Isabel was a strong woman but I am sure that her sense of foreignness and displacement must have deprived her of a communal life—so much a part of the Lebanese psyche.

Haddad family, Queenstown, South Africa, 1917. **Behind L to R:** Albert, Alexander, his brother George (died in the Great Flu), Isabel and Michael (Mickey) **Front:** Lily (called Lulu, died shortly after of scarlet fever), Phyllis, (Bertha and Henry yet to be born)

'I was only there a few months and Albert was born,' she continued.

> Mrs Jordaan, the Afrikaner midwife who lived in Joubert Street came to deliver him. An Englishman, Dr Howes, was our doctor and she called him if there was a problem. Mostly though, she delivered all of my seven

> babies on her own. Later when I had too many children, I asked Dr Howes to help me and he did, otherwise I would have had ten children. When I was pregnant with Henry the youngest, I begged him but he said he had helped me three times already so he couldn't do it again. I tried everything. I had hot baths, I jumped off chairs, I sat on steaming pots but he was determined to be born. Look at him now: he is an angel, my darling, a few years old when your Grandpa died.
>
> Eventually the lights came to Queenstown. We started with one in the hallway and then put them in one by one. I was almost sorry then because your Grandpa played cards all night and then he came to bed to worry me. He had a terrible temper. If he lost at cards or *Taoulie,* he'd tip the table over and throw everything out, shout, bang his fists.

Tragedy struck when Alexander's brother, George, died in the Great Flu of 1918-1919. In the same year, beautiful Lily, Isabel's daughter, affectionately known as Lulu, died of scarlet fever. She was just three years old. Isabel was stricken and it was years before she could even mention her name.

Granny Isabel continued in answer to my question of what life was like:

> Our house was large and grand. Your Grandpa brought beautiful Turkish copper braziers for the cold Queenstown winter, Persian carpets with silk and gold thread and a few French pieces. The garden was full of all our vegetables, *koosa* (zucchini), *buttenjen* (eggplant), *flayflie* (capsicum). To remind us of home, we built a *birrkie* (pond) under the grapevine in which we chilled watermelon and grapes in those long hot summers. Hidden away at the back, your Grandpa had a still in which he made *arak* (aniseed liqueur). Occasionally he gave the policeman a bottle and there was never any trouble.

In October 1933, when my mother, Bertha, was thirteen, Alexander fell down dead from a massive heart attack. Doctor Thomas in Queenstown told my grandmother, 'Your husband died of too much good food with no exercise.'

A tremendous upheaval followed. Albert was in medical school at the University of Cape Town. In Isabel's words:

> Albert continued his medical studies with the financial help of the Mukheibirs in Barkly East. When Henry's turn came to go to medical school, they helped us again. Mickey left school just before the matric exams to run the shop but he was too young and inexperienced. Slowly we had to sell everything to survive. The black people in the location bought our furniture and carpets because the *Ingleesies* did not like our stuff. Most of my jewellery was sold later.

Granny told one of my cousins that she was sorry when Alexander died but she never really loved him; her main loss was of material security. He didn't keep her company or partner her in a modern way and she was afraid of being a woman on her own with a family. When I asked Granny if she had thought of remarrying after Alexander died, she said Lebanese women didn't often do that. She followed my question with a little story:

Bertha (18), Queenstown, South Africa, 1938

> When your Grandpa was dead nearly a year, Mansour Chemaly came to take me for a drive in his new car. He had gold splits in his front teeth. His pitch-black moustache was like Clark Gable and he was quite well off. Adele Sorour, who was not married, came along and we set off on the road to Indwe. I sat in the front of the car and Adele sat on the back seat but she felt left out. Mansour was saying things to me, kept on looking at me and smiling. Adele was poking her head into the front. I had Henry on my lap.

Isabel's looks were her trump card but Adele was not married so they vied for his favours. Suddenly Adele said, 'What about Albert, Phyllis, Mickey

East London City Hall, 1940. Bertha and her mother Isabel at a war fundraiser, South Africa

and Bertha? They would have loved to come for a drive as well. Henry is her youngest, Mansour. Isabel here, poor thing has five children.' The rivalry between the two women erupted and Mansour lost control of the car and they had a crash. No one was hurt but he never took either of them out again and the two women remained best friends.

Granny Isabel continued, 'In 1938 your mom, Auntie Phyllis and I went to live in East London. We had nothing left in Queenstown. We took a flat near the beach in Buckingham Court. Then the war came and my boys went to fight in Egypt.'

My mother said of that time, 'The most outstanding thing I remember is that your grandmother never complained, never talked about money although we had lost everything.'

MY MOTHER BERTHA Haddad had been born in Queenstown in 1920, the fourth child of Isabel and Alexander. Her brothers and sisters were Albert, (Lily, who died aged three) Phyllis, Mickey, and Henry. All of the children attended the Dominican convent primary school. The boys went on to Queens' College while my mother and her sister Phyllis remained with the nuns. My mother was a talented musician but when the family moved to East London, she worked as a shop assistant at Ackermans. In 1940, after a secre-

East London, South Africa, 1940. The business failed so in 1937 they left Queenstown and went to live in Buckingham Court Flats in East London. **L to R:** Bertha, Albert (Captain in the Medical Corps stationed in Egypt), Isabel, Phyllis. **Front:** Henry (15) in De La Salle College uniform

tarial course at the Tech, she went to work for my father as his secretary. She also entered the domain of his African assistant, Darlington, who was very possessive of my father and resented my mother's intrusion

East London, South Africa, 1940. **L to R:** Florie, Susie, Ha'nie Abdo, Joe (my father), Phyllis and her sister Bertha Haddad (my mother). Perhaps my parents were eyeing each other. Florie had asked Isabel if Phyllis could marry Joe, but he preferred Bertha as 'Phyllis was too feisty!'

East London, South Africa, December 1942. Joe Yazbek marries Bertha Haddad. **L to R:** Francis Chemaly, Susie Yazbek, Taat Sabbagha, Phyllis Haddad

into their world. He heckled and picked on her for typing errors. In fact he even took copies of her typing in to 'show the boss her mistakes'. At first, my mother felt intimidated by Darlington, but my diplomatic father smoothed things in the office and ensured that they both felt they had equal access to his approval and attention. After office hours, however,

At Joe and Bertha's wedding, December 1942. L to R: Isabel Haddad, Emily Yazbek and her daughter Florie (Farida)

Joe Yazbek and Bertha Haddad on their wedding day, December 1942

my charming father worked his magic over my mother until their families agreed. It was not a formally arranged marriage. In the ways of the new world, the prospective partners had some choice; while my grandmother Florie had asked for Phyllis to marry her son, my father preferred Bertha the younger and less feisty of the two.

IN 1942, MY parents, Joseph Anthony Yazbek and Bertha Haddad, were married in the Church of the Immaculate Conception in East London.

1652	The Dutch East India Trading Company establishes a market garden at the Cape with Jan van Riebeeck as Governor, to service ships plying trade between Holland and its colonies in Ceylon and Batavia.
1700	White settlers begin to trek across the country resulting in hostile engagement, murders, wars and land grabs.
1867	Diamond mining begins in South Africa
1886	Gold discovered on the Witwatersrand
1893	Mohandas (Mahatma) Gandhi arrives in South Africa to defend a client.
1910	The South Africa Act takes away all political rights of Africans in three of the country's four states.
1912	The African National Congress is constituted.
1913	The Native Lands Act gives 13% of the country's land to Africans, who make up 80% of the population. Gandhi begins his campaign of non-violent resistance to racial discrimination
1948	Policy of apartheid (separateness) adopted when National Party (NP) takes power.

1950 The Population Registration Act. This law classifies people into three racial groups: White, Coloured (mixed race or Asian), and Native (African/black). The Mixed Marriages act outlaws marriage between races in order to maintain racial purity.

1951 The Group Areas Act designates particular geographical locations for whites, coloureds, blacks and Asians; forced removals and resettlement begins.

1951 The Bantu Homelands Act. Blacks stripped of their South African citizenship and classified as citizens of government-created Independent Homelands e.g Ciskei, Transkei, Kwazulu, Bophutatswana etc.

1952 Abolition of Passes and Coordination of Documents Act. All blacks required to carry an identification document, which became known on the streets as a pass or *dompas*. (*dom*—stupid)

1953 The Preservation of Separate Amenities Act establishes 'separate but not necessarily equal' parks, beaches, post offices, and other public places for whites and non-whites.

Bantu Education Act. The government supervises the education of all blacks in an education system inferior to that for whites. Non-whites cannot attend white universities. The government creates non-white universities.

1956 Torch Commando. All race protests around the country, led by anti-fascist ex-servicemen, against the government's segregationist policies

1960 An anti-pass law protest in Sharpeville ends in a massacre by police: 69 people die and 187 people are wounded. The African National Congress and the Pan-African Congress, are banned. These protests rocked the world community and stirred fear among white South Africans.

Chief Albert Luthuli President General of the African National Congress wins the Nobel Peace Prize.

1961 South Africa declared a republic and leaves the Commonwealth.

1961 *Umkonto We Sizwe,* (The Spear of the Nation), the non-racial military wing of the African National Congress was formed with Nelson Mandela as leader.

1964 Nelson Mandela, head of the African National Congress, is jailed for life in the Rivonia Treason Trial.

1966 Prime Minister Verwoerd fatally stabbed in the Houses of Parliament by Dimitri Tsafendas, who was employed as a steward.

1970s Resistance to apartheid increases. Churches, students and workers increase their organisation of resistance

1976 June 16, school students in Soweto protest against Afrikaans as the language of instruction in schools. Thousands are injured and arrested while 575 people are killed.
Most South Africans remained ignorant of the extent of the violence as TV was only introduced into the country on 6 January 1976 and was too expensive for many people.

1977 September 12, Steve Biko, founder of the Black Consciousness Movement dies after being beaten in police custody.

1978 December 31, Donald Woods and family flee South Africa to live as exiles in Britain. He continued his fight against apartheid eventually dying in London in August 2001.

1980's International economic, sporting and political sanctions against South Africa are intensified.

1990 African National Congress unbanned on 2 February and Nelson Mandela walked free nine days later on 11 February after 27 years in prison.

1991 South Africa President FW de Klerk repeals the rest of the apartheid laws and calls for the drafting of a new constitution.

1994 Elections are held 27 April. This day is now a public holiday Freedom Day. The United Nations sent 2120 international observers to ensure the fairness of the elections. The African National Congress wins power. Nelson Mandela is elected

President and inaugurated on 10 May 1994 – the end of a long road to freedom.

1996 The Truth and Reconciliation Commission, chaired by Archbishop Desmond Tutu begins hearings on crimes committed by the former government agents and forces as well as the liberation movements during the apartheid years.

Acknowledgements

My father often broke into song, recited poetry or supplied a quote at a difficult moment. This was one of his favourites.

> The moving finger writes: and, having writ,
> Moves on: nor all thy Piety nor Wit
> Shall lure it back to cancel half a Line,
> Nor all thy tears wash out a Word of it.

FROM VERSE 50, *THE RUBÁIYÁT OF OMAR KHAYYÁM*
(TRANSLATED BY EDWARD FITZGERALD)

I owe a great debt to Catherine Duncan for all the conversations we had when I doubted that I could find the right words.

Writing groups and courses at the New South Wales Writers' Centre and the Northern Rivers Writers' Centre have been invaluable.

My appreciation to Joyce Kornblatt, *agent provocateur* and facilitator of 'taking tea with one's demons', a skilled mentor who hears with her heart.

My gratitude to Susan Beinart who, understanding my desire to be honest, helped me to remain kind to the difficult characters. Her confidence kept me going when I felt least able. Despite being busy with her own writing, she always finds time to discuss my queries.

Charmaine Silove was my personal migrant counsellor through all the vagaries of this writing task—thank you Dear!

Thank you to Margaret Knowlden who was always ready to help me with the photographs and checking my punctuation.

My family unwittingly peopled my writing—courtyard men and women and their children, cousins everywhere, brothers and sisters especially my mother who so promptly faxed back the answers to my monthly ten questions. She encouraged me to keep writing: 'Remember you are five children and each one of you has your own memory and opinion.'

My daughter, Amelia, despite a demanding academic program, generously shared her time, energy and skill to edit parts of this manuscript.

I thank my many cousins who supplied information to the best of their ability. Ivor Yazbek for his stolid research which gave us a Yazbek family tree, probably the most historically comprehensive there'll ever be; Nelson Restom, for lots of history and photographs; Peter Haddad in New Zealand, always on the end of the phone, whether I was laughing or crying; Evan Petrelis for wonderful conversations.

To all my friends who put up with my coming and going as I disappear to write and dream.

My Grandmother Isabel sat with me then as now—her love enables the voiceless and unspoken.

With grateful thanks to Dennis Brutus for permission to reprint his poem, *Somehow We Survive*

Somehow, we survive
and tenderness, frustrated, does not wither.

Invetigating searchlights rake
our naked and unprotected contours;

over our heads the monolithic decalogiue
of fascist prohibition glowers
and teeters for a catastrophic fall;

boots club the peeling door.

But somehow we survive
severance, deprivation, loss.

> Patrols uncoil along the asphalt dark
> hissing their menace to our lives,
>
> most cruel, all our land is scarred with terror,
> rendered unlovely and unlovable;
> sundered are we and all our passionate surrender
> but somehow tenderness survives.

Doris Lessing, *Time bites: views and reviews*, Fourth Estate, 2004, for the quote from her article on Peter Godwin's *Mukiwa.*

Some parts of this work have been published elsewhere:

Part of 'Life stories in the Courtyard' first appeared in *Bus Stop* 2002, anthology of the Bangalow Writers' Group

'Great Aunt Eugenie's Recipe', Theresa (from: 'Saints and gangsters') and Hedwig (from 'Father Martin Flanagan—Wild Irish priests and German nuns') first appeared in *Body of Work 2, Lost and Found* 2004 . Selected writings from the Northern Rivers Writers' Centre.

Part of Soffiantini from 'Bobby Shafto and other friends' first appeared in the *Daily Dispatch*, East London, South Africa. Wednesday 24 August, 2005.

'Bobby Shafto and other friends' also appeared in *Hot Off the Press,* the 2005 anthology of the Women Writers' Network, Rozelle, NSW.

Rings and Things from 'Bobby Shafto and other friends' appeared in *Now and Then,* the 2006 anthology of the Bangalow Writers' Group.

My Lebanese Past—excerpt from the Coda, appeared in *Kalimat*-March 2006

Isabel—Lebanese Fragments, excerpt from the Coda, appeared in *Kalimat,* September 2006.

Glossary

abakweta (Xhosa)—young Xhosa men at the age of eighteen undergoing initiation. They are subject to a ritual circumcision and a period of seclusion with their age mates. During this time, they make no contact at all with women and may not consume meat, sour milk, liquor or tobacco. At the end of this time, their temporary shelter is burned. Clad in new white blankets, they return to gatherings in their village where older men lecture them on caring for their parents and households. They are then eligible to marry.

babbaganouje (Arabic)—eggplant dip with tahini

bakkie (Afrikaans)—a small pick-up truck

biltong (Afrikaans)—strips of spiced dried meat, like jerky

blaid (Arabic)—the home country

boerewors (Afrikaans)—traditional spicy farm sausage developed by trekkers.

boetie (Afrikaans)—little brother

borma (Arabic)—shredded wheat pastry tube with nuts and syrup

broeks (Afrikaans)—pants

burghul (Arabic)—wheat that has been boiled, dried and then cracked; used in kibbe and tabouleh salad

coloured—a racial classification under apartheid for people of 'mixed' racial parentage

coral tree—*Erythrina caffra*—native to Southern Africa. Bright red/orange flowers followed by pods containing small red beans that we called lucky beans.

derem (Afrikaans)—intestine

doek (Afrikaans)—head-scarf worn by married Xhosa women

donder (Afrikaans)—beat up

donga (Xhosa)—eroded gully originally meaning 'wall'

dominee (Afrikaans)—Dutch Reformed Church minister

dorp (Afrikaans)—country town or village

Egoli (Zulu)—Johannesburg, city of gold

foossed/ foossing (Arabic)—farted/farting

gibit tlet banet (Arabic)—had three girls

goeie middag (Afrikaans)—good afternoon

goyim (Yiddish)—non-Jews

hadeda—local South African name for the hadeda ibis (*Bostrychia hagedash*). A brownish plain-looking bird with a distinctive and loud call especially when taking off and flying—ha-ha-ha-dee-da. They often landed on our lawns at home and we'd watch them from our bedroom windows as they plunged their long pointy beaks into wormcasts.

hajji (Arabic)—a pilgrim; more commonly today for someone who has made the pilgrimage to Mecca—also used by the Moslem Cape Malays; but Christians in the Middle East who make pilgrimage to holy places to be quiet and pray, and return home wearing white, are also called hajji

ja (Afrikaans)—yes

jrin (Arabic)—mortar for pounding meat for kibbe

kaddish (Hebrew)—the prayer a son says for his dead father. Also in Aramaic, Kadish, the song for the dead sung at Maronite funerals.

kaffir boetie (Afrikaans)—insult applied to whites seen to be sympathetic to African people (brother of blacks)

kharra djaj (Arabic)—literally, fowl shit; but used as bullshit

kibbe (Arabic)—spiced wheat and meat or vegetable paste

kishk (Arabic)—burghul mixed with yoghurt, fermented, dried and ground to be made into a soup(*trahanas* in Greek)

knobkerrie (Afrikaans)—a walking stick with a knob at the top: a weapon; in the eastern cape good knobkerries were made from local sneeze-wood trees

koeksusters (Afrikaans)—dough plaits fried and dipped in sugar syrup

kraal (Afrikaans)—village or settlement surrounded by a stockade
kwela (Xhosa)—African pennywhistle music.
lekker (Afrikaans)—nice
laban, labne (Arabic)—yoghurt
land'smener (Yiddish)—compatriots
madalas (Xhosa)—old men/grandfathers
meneer (Afrikaans)—mister
mielies, mieliemeel (Afrikaans)—corn ,ground corn
moerkoffie (Afrikaans)—coffee boiled from coarse grounds
molo/molweni (Xhosa)—hello/hello (plural—greeting more than one)
nee (Afrikaans)—no
nonquase (Xhosa)—one who shouts/gives orders
ntoni? (Xhosa)—what?
ousie (Afrikaans)—an African woman
panga (Nguni East African)—machete or a broad bladed knife used in slashing vegetation
pass—all Africans had to carry an identification document—known as a pass because it indicated where they were allowed to be (pass); angrily called a *dompas* (stupid(*dom*) pass in Afrikaans)
rakhmit bayee (Arabic)—I swear on my father
rahbet (Arabic)—nuns
Red People—Traditional Xhosa: *Abantu ababomvu*—literally the smeared people (*amaqaba*—not as polite) who redden their blankets and bodies with ochre; they chose to remain aloof from white culture
rondavel (Afrikaans)—round thatched-roof cottage. See cover illustration.
rowbee (Arabic)—yoghurt starter/culture
samp (possible colonial derivation from Tibetan word *tsampa*)—corn/maize kernels which have been dried and cracked for storage purposes and cooked either as a vegetable or a soup, sometimes with kidney beans. A traditional food of the peoples of the south eastern regions of South Africa.
sangoma (Xhosa)—an African traditional healer who has undergone years of apprenticeship to become a practitioner. Problems will be diagnosed by divination. Sometimes bones are thrown and dreams

are interpreted. In difficult cases, the healer might enter a trance to converse with the shades to find out which ancestors the ailing person has offended. From the diagnosis a remedy is prescribed. The patient may be given a selection of herbs to consume. Sometimes a *sangoma*/healer recommends the slaughter of an animal such as a white goat to appease the ancestors.

sies (Afrikaans)—yuck (impolite)

sissie (Xhosa)—sister, helper

slip slops—thongs

sjambok (Afrikaans)—whip originally made from animal hide

sumac (Arabic)—dried powdered berries of the sumac tree. A souring agent

taal (Afrikaans)—language

taoulie (Arabic)—backgammon

tarboosh (Arabic)—fez

tata (Xhosa)—daddy/father

thombazaan (Xhosa)—girl

tickey—old threepenny piece

tokoloshe (Xhosa)—an evil entity

tsotsi (Zulu/Xhosa)—street thugs

tula (Zulu/Xhosa)—keep quiet/shut-up/hush

twak (Afrikaans)—tobacco

veldskoene (Afrikaans)—shoes made of untanned hide with a suede appearance (originally *velskoene*)

voetsek (Afrikaans)—bugger off

ya immi (Arabic)—term of endearment used by an elder, usually a parent, for a child; the parent puts herself in the child's space—caring/solicitous language lit. 'my mother'—Arabic; in Arabic, shades of meaning and depths in the language, define the relationship between people

yom tov (Hebrew)—happy day/festival

zaater (Arabic)—blend of thyme, sesame seeds and sumac

zol (Afrikaans)—hand-rolled cigarette

Notes on books and sources

I have used Jean Branford's, *Dictionary of South African English*, OUP, 1978, to verify translation and usage of common South African words.

Over the years, I have read many biographies and memoirs—one of my favourite genres. Reading what others have written about their kin, gave me permission to express the results of my own inquiry.

Here are some of my favourite authors and books.

Anything by Breyten Breytenbach; Riaan Malan, *My Traitor's Heart* 1990; Michael Ondaatje, *Running in the Family*, 1982. His story of his extended family in Sri Lanka; Helen Fremont, *After Long Silence*, 1999. Two sisters in the United States painfully excavate their Jewish ancestry; Brian Keenan, *An Evil Cradling*, 1992, Alchemy; Inga Clendinnen, *Tiger's Eye*, 2000. Her celebration of life, present and past, through all the terrors of her serious illness; Dorothy Hewett, *Wild Card*, 1990. Her searing autobiography; George Crane, *Bones of the Master*, 2000. An inner journey through breathtaking country by an American poet; Margaret Craven, *I Heard the Owl Call My Name*, 1967. An old favourite; Doris Lessing, *Under My Skin*, 1994. Her life in Africa until she moved to England; Susan Varga, *Heddy and Me*, 1994. They came from Hungary to Australia in the late 1940's; The quote by Gertrude Stein is in Alice Kaplan's *French Lessons*, 1993. Learning another language and how life and memory expanded as a consequence; Marjorie Shostak, *Nisa. The Life and Words of a !Kung Woman*, 1981; Graham Saayman(ed), *South Africa In Search of a Soul*, 1986/1990. Jungian wanderings around wilderness;

Jacqueline Rose, *States of Fantasy*, 1996, OUP. How our private identity expresses itself in our external actions; Carol Shields, I love all her writing, especially *Unless*. Edward Said, *Out of Place*, 1999. Identity and geography and so much more; Jean Said Makdisi, *Teta, Mother and Me*, 2005. Edward Said's sister's take on the women in their family; *Seasons of Love*, Adriane Wildencamp 1998. An uplifting inner conversation and an outer journey between Australia and Germany; John Hughes, *The idea of home*, 2004. Thoughtful essays on home and identity.

Familial Mediterranean Fever is now a well-documented condition. My information has come from personal experience and doctors in Australia. FMF, as it is known, is a chronic auto-immune disorder like Lupus(SLE). It is a recessive genetic condition, however, in Middle Eastern populations, carriers occur in 1:20 of the general population. Sufferers experience frequent attacks of extreme abdominal pain that, in the absence of good diagnosis, have led to unnecessary surgery for what was thought to be appendicitis. Patients also experience high fevers, sometimes without precipitating infection. Generalised inflammation can attack the major organs. Some years ago, in the United States, it was found that patients treated with daily colchicine, did not develop amyloidosis, which can accompany this condition. Colchicine is now used with good results for many patients. It is important to have an accurate diagnosis as appropriate treatment can alleviate some of the more deleterious effects of the disorder.

Information on first cousin marriage is hard to come by. I supply mere sufferers' anecdotes. It is still happening, but people, aware of the taboos, are reluctant to discuss it. The results of consanguineous marriage are unpredictable. What it can do, though is to give expression to recessive genetic conditions. Aside from other, more obvious congenital defects, children can develop early fatal cancers and leukaemia.

Biographical Note

Cecile Yazbek was born into a Lebanese family in South Africa and studied social sciences at Rhodes University. She was a voluntary community worker in Cape Town and migrated to Sydney in 1986 with her young family. After working as a Volunteer Coordinator and TAFE teacher while running a vegetarian cooking school, she has retired to write, read, garden, and cook.

Some other titles from East Street Publications

All the Way Home – Stories from an African Wildlife Sanctuary
Bookey Peek
Autobiography, travel, wildlife
ISBN: 9781921037191

Beyond Capricorn: How Portuguese Adventurers Secretly Discovered and Mapped Australia and New Zealand 250 Years Before Captain Cook
Peter Trickett
History
ISBN: 9780975114599

Children are People Too – A Parent's Guide to Young Children's Behaviour
Louise Porter
Parenting, self-help
ISBN: 9780975114582

Cool Hunting – A Guide to High Design and Innovation
David Evans
Design, popular culture, gift
ISBN: 9781921037108

Luca Antara – Passages in Search of Australia
Martin Edmond
Memoir, history, travel
ISBN: 9781921037085

The Twelve Little Cakes – A Memoir From Communist Prague
Dominika Dery
Memoir
ISBN: 9781921037092

Through My Eyes – The Autobiography of Lindy Chamberlain-Creighton
Lindy Chamberlain-Creighton
Autobiography
ISBN: 9780975114537

Transgenders and Intersexuals: Everything You Ever Wanted to Know But Couldn't Think of the Question
Lois May
Self-help, medical / ethical resource
ISBN: 9781921037078

Vintage Adelaide – Beautiful Buildings from the Adelaide Square Mile
Peter Fischer and Kay Hannaford Seamark
Australian architecture, heritage
ISBN: 9781921037061

With the Kama Sutra Under My Arm – An Indian Journey
Trisha Bernard
Travel, memoir
ISBN: 9781921037153

East Street Publications
www.eaststreet.com.au